A Baseball Addict's Diary

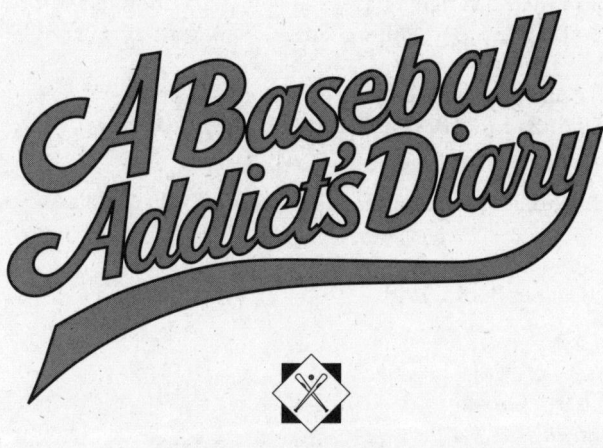

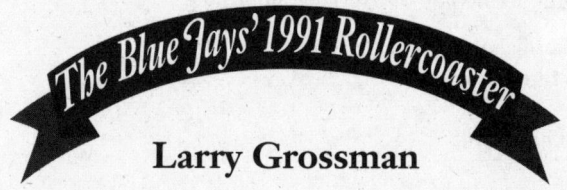

Larry Grossman

Penguin Books

PENGUIN BOOKS
Published by the Penguin Group
Penguin Books Canada Ltd, 10 Alcorn Avenue, Toronto, Ontario,
Canada M4V 3B2
Penguin Books Ltd., 27 Wrights Lane, London W8 5TZ, England
Penguin Books USA Inc., 375 Hudson Street, New York, New York
10014, U.S.A.
Penguin Books Australia Ltd, Ringwood, Victoria, Australia
Penguin Books (NZ) Ltd, 182-190 Wairau Road, Auckland 10,
New Zealand

Penguin Books Ltd, Registered Offices: Harmondsworth, Middlesex,
England

Published in Penguin Books, 1991

10 9 8 7 6 5 4 3 2 1

Copyright © Larry Grossman, 1991
All rights reserved
Quotations from *Bill Mazeroski's Baseball*, 1991 Edition, are
reproduced with permission of Preview Publishing.

Permission to utilize the Blue Jays' logo provided courtesy of
The Toronto Blue Jays Baseball Club.

Manufactured in Canada

Canadian Cataloguing in Publication Data

Grossman, Larry, 1943-
    A baseball addict's diary

ISBN 0-14-016972-5

1. Toronto Blue Jays (Baseball team).   I. Title.

GV875.T6G7   1991   796.357'64'09713541   C91-095456-9

Except in the United States of America, this book is sold subject to the
condition that it shall not, by way of trade or otherwise, be lent, re-sold,
hired out, or otherwise circulated without the publisher's prior consent
in any form of binding or cover other than that in which it is published
and without similar condition including this condition being imposed
on the subsequent purchaser.

*To the fans in Section 13 at Exhibition Stadium —
especially my Melissa, Jamie, and Robbie*

and Carole

Contents

Preface......1
One Flew over the Left-Field Fence......11
White-Hot Start and SkyDome Fans......18
Curse of the Tigers......26
Nolan Ryan: Out of Sight......31
Perfect Alomar, Imperfect SkyDome......34
Jumbo?Tron......43
Nooners and Neophytes......51
Knucklers and Faded Fastballs......58
Jays Ridin' High, Julio Ridin' Low......66
Chemistry and Confidence—and a Little Bit of Luck......78
Managers and Other Masochists......87
Turning-Points and True Grit......97
Strike Zones, Cyclops and Shaker......110
Spooky Sparky in Virgin Territory......121
Beanballs in Tiger Town......133
See You in September......143
I Spent a Week in Cleveland One Night......155
Big Mo and the Triple Play......169
We Left Our Hearts in San Francisco......178
Textbook Baseball, Mookie Magic......189
I Was Never Worried!......200
Outmanaged, Outcoached, Outpitched, Outlucked......204
Strangely Calm......210
Canada's Funniest Home Videos: Cito Uses Timlin in the Tenth......215
Anatomy of a Blow-out......224
There's No Tomorrow—Someone Tell Cito......229
Epilogue and Eulogy......233

Preface

THIS BOOK REALLY STARTED IN JUNE OR JULY OF 1951. We were living on Hillcrest Drive in midtown Toronto. I was seven years old, and my cousin Sheldon was helping me break in my brand new "Phil Rizzuto" glove and teaching me how to throw a lacrosse ball against the front steps so it would bounce back down the front walk, where I could try to field it. I must have thrown more balls against those steps than I would speeches against equally resistant audiences twenty-five or thirty years later.

I was wearing my new Philadelphia Phillies uniform. The Phillies were my favourite team and the defending National League champions, and I was pretending to be shortstop Granny Hamner and dreaming of hitting like Phillies fast centre fielder Richie Ashburn.

In winter, I would take baseball inside with a baseball game that Sheldon taught me to play with an ordinary deck of cards. Each card represented a play, with a red ace being a home run, a red king a triple, any queen a double, any jack a walk, a seven a single, an eight a double play, a four a sacrifice bunt, a ten a sac fly, and two and five giving you strikeouts.

I would copy lineups from all the major-league teams (there were only sixteen teams then) and set up entire seasons and World Series between them. All winter I would learn the players and their batting averages, and all summer I would learn how to play.

I amassed a fabulous baseball card collection, which, if I had it today, would replace my mortgage.

Evenings I would be in my bed, with my Rogers Majestic huge diode-tube radio beside it. It would be tuned to CKEY, and I'd listen to Hal Kelly and Joe Crysdale broadcast the Toronto Maple Leafs against the Montreal Royals. Tommy Lasorda would be pitching for the Royals, a devastating lefty against our own Lynn Lovenguth.

I was young but still knew the sound of the game was weird because it was a road game. Joe and Hal didn't travel to road games. They did them by something called a "wire reconstruction." Someone was apparently transmitting by telegraph, Morse Code or pony express what was happening pitch by pitch. Joe and Hal were experts at describing atmosphere they couldn't see. "Bruno Betzel kicks around the dirt in the first-base coach's box." "Lew Morton steps out of the batter's box and knocks the dirt from out of his cleats." "Hector Rodriguez takes the big lead off first." And so on. None of this was necessarily happening, but they had to kill time between messages from Montreal. Amazingly, when there was a hit, a canned, pre-taped crowd roar was quickly inserted so that the appropriate noise level was reached just as the ball was "going, going, gone."

In 1955, my father took me to see my beloved Philadelphia Phillies play against Willie Mays in the Polo Grounds. Baseball was just coming to TV then, thanks to NBC. I remember sitting in our den in 1956 scoring a World Series game being pitched by a mediocre pitcher named Don Larsen. He, of course, pitched a perfect game.

In 1957, my father took me to New York to see the Yankees and the Milwaukee Braves in the World Series, and through the next few years I would be back to New York to see Sandy Koufax, Johnny Podres and the Boys of Summer play after they left for the coast.

And I was at the last game that Ted Williams played at Tiger Stadium and will never forget having a long foul hit by Williams go off my outstretched right hand.

Through all this, I was a fixture at the old Maple Leaf Stadium. My father was on city council and had a pass to the stadium, and Sheldon and I went down there often.

My interest in baseball never flagged, though my loyalties changed from the Yankees and the Phillies to the Expos and the Jays. I've collected books, cards, stats and pictures. I've been to games in most major-league cities. I was the shortstop and leadoff batter for a B'nai Brith team more than twenty years ago when the league just started, and I returned to it three years ago after leaving politics.

PREFACE ◆

Sheldon and I have been up and down the rollercoaster with the Blue Jays since 1984. It's been an exciting but frustrating team. It's exhibited great baseball and bad fundamentals. It's had great pitchers and Bill Caudills. It's had all sorts of managers, all sorts of personalities, and the wonderful George Bell. Because of our seat location beside the visitors' dugout, we've come to know the opposing teams and lots of their players — their personalities, their habits.

All winter, I count the days till spring training, and then after Labour Day, when I suffer through the pennant drive tension, I count the days till I can be relieved of the pressure, win or lose.

Since I have been a panellist on CBC's "Metro Morning" on sports for three years now, I always make notes after games for use on the program. When I began work on this book in earnest, I started to score each game batter by batter and make copious notes during the game, in particular from June 23 on.

In two hundred–odd pages I can't, of course, summarize 162 games. Nor do most fans want to read details of who did what in every game. Instead, I've tried to pick some of the more interesting games, the ones I remember best, and talk about what made those games special. I've also tried to give a sense of what it's like to watch games in the Dome, and what it's like to listen on radio or watch on TV.

If I have been hard on Cito, Olerud, Manuel and others, it's because I love the game, I love the team and, oh yes, I love to win. In politics, I've won and lost. Trust me — winning is better.

Let me say right off the top that I've been harder on the team than I should be. But they are such a good, classy, consistently superior team that, like a lot of fans, I have come to take the successes for granted and think of the losses as unnecessary, avoidable and somehow personal.

This season ended with the Twins eliminating us four games to one in the ALCS. And you're damn right this loss was unnecessary and avoidable.

The Twins had better hitting. We had better pitching. They used their best, we didn't use ours. Their best pitched, our best were "rested" — "saved" while our struggling pitchers were used often. Same as during the season.

◆ 3 ◆

◆ PREFACE

Cito refused to pinch hit often or early enough all year and continued to refuse to in October. Tom Kelly and the Twins adapted to the short series. Cito was as unmoved as John Olerud.

Unnecessary and avoidable. And yes, I do take it personally.

We have waited a long time for this year. It was ours. Cito took it away from us.

This "addict's" dealer cut him off. Suddenly, but, in retrospect, not unexpectedly.

So this is a journal of a true and long-time "addict." And the views, biases and analyses of this addict are encouraged by, or, sometimes, are notwithstanding, the views of Sheldon. I hope this diary, selective as it is, will help fans remember what a great season it was, full of the tension, fun, successes, failure, sensational plays, bonehead moves and mostly just plain luck that baseball is — whether it's played at the Dome, the Polo Grounds or Christie Pits.

◆ ◆ ◆

My special thanks to many people who allowed this rookie writer to maintain his law practice and his family and other interests while indulging himself in this work of love:

- My kids for their joyful presence always and their (required) interest in baseball.
- My wife Carole for the clippings, computer printouts, foolscap papers and notes she put up with on the dining-room table for weeks and weeks.
- Sheldon for forty-seven years of friendship, political support and baseball.
- Susan for keeping score for me when I went to get diet Cokes (though she insisted on writing crookedly).
- My publishers at Penguin, headed by Cynthia Good and her friendly, helpful, super-bright and responsive team.
- My secretary/assistant — underpaid, overworked, ever pleasant, industrious Nives Montano. Nives, much better liked by clients than am I, typed, retyped, changed, altered and otherwise improved manuscripts by day and by night, all the while ensuring that my law clients were served with continued reliability and efficiency. Without her I wouldn't have met deadlines, would have

lost clients and this labour of love would have turned into a simple chore. If nothing else, she finally learned after two months of typing how to spell "Maldonado."
- Dan Liebman and Mary McDougall Maude for protecting my ego as they massaged my words.
- Frances Hanna, my agent.
- Harold Freeman, my fact checker.
- Gail Longworth and her friends at the *Globe*.
- Tom McMillan and the *Financial Post* and the *Toronto Sun*.
- Siskind.
- Mike Squires (for putting up with me and being a nice guy).
- "Metro Morning."
- My father's widow Betty (she knows for what).
- And, of course, my dear father, who meant so much to me and whom I will miss always.

A Wake-up Call in December

"**W**OULD YOU BELIEVE MCGRIFF AND FERNANDEZ for Carter and Robbie Alomar!" Gary Siskind, one of my law associates, burst into my office on December 5, 1990, and, with these words, ushered in the 1991 Blue Jays baseball season. I was stunned. I was happy to see Fernandez go. An artist with an attitude — or as my kids would say, a "'tude." A joy to watch on the playing field, a picture of sadness and angst on the bench — sitting at one end, talking to no one and acknowledging few. He hadn't been the same since he was smitten by religion several years ago, and since he was badly hurt by a Cecilio Guante beanball a year-and-a-half ago.

Fred McGriff was another story. He was a happy, well-adjusted team player and one of the best hitters in the league in 1990, eighth in batting average, fourth in slugging percentage (an important figure), third in total bases, fifth in walks, second in on-base percentage (also important).

I will miss having Freddy close to where I sit at first base. We'll all miss his smoothness, his long dives to snare a ball hit down the baseline. And most of all, even though I am a fan of National League station-to-station baseball, I'll miss those majestic (yes, an overused word, but the right one here), high, long, quiet home runs he used to hit with his long, slow and ever-so-smooth swing. And even the fans seemed to be quiet, hushed, as they waited to see how high, how far and how long. McGriff's home runs are moments to remember. Snapshots from Toronto baseball history. And the longer he's gone, the longer his SkyDome home runs will seem.

As for the players who are coming to replace these two, the only thing we are sure of is that with the acquisition of Devon White (just days ago) and now Joe Carter and Alomar, our team is moving from long ball to good ball, from strikeout or homer to walk and steal. Alomar is reputed to be a coming — but not quite arrived — superstar. Carter is a proven, put-it-in-the-bank RBI man. But more, the Blue Jays were trading the desultory Fernandez and the quiet McGriff for the rah-rah, smiling, team-first, "love thy teammates" Joe Carter and the unselfish, "just happy to play baseball" Robbie Alomar. This is as big a watershed as any team has ever created.

As we come to opening day, the saddest change is the departure by free agency of our friend George Bell. Love him or hate him, and everybody did one or the other, he was the most visible, the most productive Blue Jay. His blunt, crude and unrefined directness made it impossible for him to hide his emotions. You never heard George go through the insincere rituals of: "whatever the manager wants me to do, I'll do," or, "so long as the team wins, I'm happy to contribute in any way the manager wants me to," or, "I don't hear the fans," or, "this is the greatest group of guys I've ever been with." If George wants to play, and he always does, he'll say so. If he thinks the manager is an idiot, he'll say so. If he thinks his teammates choke, he'll say so. But if George thinks he played badly, made a mistake or didn't produce, he'll say that too. If he thinks the fans are unfair to him, he'll say that and say it colourfully.

George was well liked by many players, hated by some. Loved by Beeston, unloved by Gillick. But he played and mostly he produced. Lots of RBIs, lots of home runs and lots of hits. When he lost power because of a shoulder injury, he was not ashamed or too embarrassed to work on hitting the ball to right field for a single, simply to move runners along or to get on base himself. His bat, if not his presence in the clubhouse, will be missed. His enthusiasm and his style are gone, and we got nothing in exchange.

I love this team. I've loved it since I sat in the snow on opening day, April 7, 1977. I actually thought Jerry Garvin was going to be a star, that Gary Woods could play centre field and that Rick Cerone would become one of the best catchers in baseball. (Unbelievable, but Cerone is still around today.) Though I wished they had one-colour hats, like real teams do, these guys were ours and they were big time. (I also wished their uniforms had "real" numbers, not those funny ones, which remind me of North York nouvelle cuisine.)

I learned baseball — what it was, how to play it, who the players were — from my cousin Sheldon Taerk. He's nine years older than I am, but baseball made us the best of friends — and Sheldon into my brother — from the time I was 5 and he was 14. Through the years he took me almost daily to Maple Leaf Stadium. We would dream — it was only a dream — of the day Toronto would have major-league baseball. When it looked like it would come, we reacted faster than Sheila Copps in a parliamentary slugfest.

I got our seats — first row beside the visitors' dugout — by writing for them the moment I heard the initial murmur that the San Francisco Giants might be moved to Toronto. Though we ended up as an American League expansion team instead of a National League icon, I was delighted to discover I was only the twenty-sixth person to apply for season tickets and the first to ask for the first-base side. And I've lived there since Doug Ault defended first in 1977. And those first years were great.

It's funny, but, when you've got just a hopeless little expansion team, you can see only good. You see the occasional great pitching performance by Tom Underwood, Dave Lemanczyk and, yes, Jerry Garvin, a great catch by Bosetti or Al Woods, and countless young, always-to-be-nameless future stars who would have four-for-four days. And you'd say, "Maybe we can be the Miracle Mets." We'd argue on the way to the parking lot that a couple of our players were just as good as the Yankee stars and didn't strike out as much as Reggie. And so on. We'd never get down on them; it was always upside. We were excited at the potential and at the odd superplay, and any win was juice.

I can't help thinking how much this reminds me of politics. In an election campaign, the long-shot challenger gets a couple of voters at the door saying nice things, or sees a couple of volunteers walking in; and he or she gets an enormous rush of adrenalin and reports to the world that an upset is in the works. At the same time, the incumbent, who will win easily and has hundreds of workers and thousands of followers, gets some heat from disgruntled constituents who won't take his or her lawn signs as they did last time, suddenly panics, gets into a depression, and can think only of an unstoppable erosion and certain loss.

By 1984 Blue Jays addicts had become incumbents, even though we hadn't yet won. Until 1985 I was a political incumbent, never losing, while the Blue Jays were underdogs, never winning. We each found a way to reverse that pattern.

Yes, the Blue Jays became incumbents, and, instead of being excited at the smallest success, we became aggravated by the tiniest failure. In 1978 we could just enjoy an Alvis Woods double off the wall. In 1984 we complained that Moseby didn't stretch his double off the same wall into a triple. We stopped admiring Randy Moffitt's ability to save ball games with no stuff left on his ball at the tail end of his career, and we started to jump all over Duane Ward for his occasional failure with great stuff in the early days of his. It was more fun being an expansion team. Now it was work. But still it was a labour of love, and, over the late eighties, the Blue Jays regularly made sure love hurt.

So from incubation to incumbency, it was sheer joy, and from incumbency to 1990 it had a pattern. Lots of writers picking us for first. Dave Stieb winning ten games quickly and then not being able to win twenty. Barfield maturing into a front-line ball player with a cannon arm but swinging wildly at pitches in the dirt to strike out in key situations. Bell hitting the last home run at Exhibition Stadium and having a career year in 1987, but his bat going quiet in the horrendous last week of the schedule. At times a laid-back club. God, you've got to love them, but they're like your teenage son who spends his days being perfectly happy as a couch potato watching everything from Vanna White to "MuchMusic." Whatever is on is okay by him. You can't stop loving the kid, you'd die for him, but you can't stop being aggravated.

I also learned over years of watching my kids play hockey that I could find a thousand faults in their game even though they were at or near the top of the league in scoring (may I modestly add), while I could find few faults with their teammates' game. Finally I came to realize that maybe it was because I was watching my kids' game more carefully and more critically. I wanted them to win and excel so much I got frustrated by the tiniest of errors (if they were errors).

This team has driven me crazy. It teases me. It comes close all the time: 3–1 on the Royals in the 1985 American League Championship Series; three-and-a-half up with seven games to go in 1987; work hard to win it in 1989 and let Rickey Henderson beat us single-handed in the American League Championship Series.

We've always had the talent but not the spirit or intensity. I really wanted to like Junior Felix. He was fast, he seemed aggressive, but for me he epitomized my frustration. It seemed to me I wanted him to succeed more than he did. (I know that's not true, but it looked that way.) I clearly was more aggravated over losses than was Tony Fernandez. Fernandez seemed as untouched by an Ernie Whitt grand slam (or for that matter, a Fernandez home run) as he was by a strikeout or an error. Fred McGriff? Wonderful — wish we had him. But also too cool by half. George Bell? You knew he cared like hell and would work like hell, but then he would nonchalant an opponent's single to left field into a double.

And the team itself? Corporate to the end. The management kept Moseby in the lineup and batted him leadoff, no less, long after he was up to it. Then they did the same thing to Mookie Wilson two years later and then to Kenny Williams. I think management made the same mistake I did: it fell in love with the players.

So, by December 1990, when Siskind came into my office to announce the big trade, it was a breath of fresh air. The new team would be easier to root for. It would clearly be exciting station-to-station ball, and it sounded like these players would have energy.

The 1990 team reminded me of a good marriage that lasted too long. The fans had got used to certain patterns of very good but not great baseball — of the long ball type — as well as of high hopes and great disappointments. And the players somehow had got used to it too. It was also like a book we had read before, and, while we loved it, we really did not want to read it again.

One Flew over the Left-Field Fence

THE 1991 SEASON IN FACT BEGAN ON DECEMBER 5, 1990, WITH the big trade, but life was reborn and summer officially rung in on Monday, April 8. For me opening day has always been the first day of summer, the day my high school studies became secondary to my allegiance to baseball (in those years, the Toronto Maple Leafs, the New York Yankees and the Philadelphia Phillies). Opening day then was a ride down Bathurst Street to Maple Leaf Stadium. (Where were we when they tore it down, less than ten years before the Blue Jays arrived?) Along with a bunch of others who were supposed to be in school, I got on the bus at Bathurst and Eglinton. At St Clair we caught the streetcar and grabbed the preferred seats before we collected the refugees from Cedarvale and Vaughan Road Collegiate.

The 1991 opening day, of course, was not just another opening day. It was opening day for a new team. Of the nine Blue Jays who took the field, six were new to their position. Olerud not McGriff on first, Alomar not Lee on second, Lee not Fernandez at short, Mookie Wilson not George Bell in left field, Devon White not Mookie Wilson in centre, Joe Carter not Junior Felix in right. Even third-base coach John (Maybe-You-Should, Maybe-You-Shouldn't) McLaren is gone; McLaren, whose poor judgment cost us at least two games in 1990 — a year in which we lost the pennant by two games. He left ignominiously at the end of the season, when the Blue Jays "failed to renew his contract." (The voters "failed to renew *my* contract" in '87.) McLaren will mostly be remembered for his role in the CNN play-of-the-year, where Kenny (Wrong Way) Williams ran to third, back to second, back to third and then, rounding third coming to the plate, knocked down McLaren. Something I'd been trying to do for several years.

What I worry about, of course, is that McLaren was replaced by Rich Hacker, who was fired as third-base coach by the St Louis Cardinals. When the new traffic cop at third is someone who was fired as third-base coach by a team that finished the year in the cellar, twenty-five games out, you'd better call the paramedics.

So here we go. I can hardly remember an opening day with this much excitement since I tumbled off that Bathurst Street streetcar to watch Eddie Blake, Archie Wilson, Sam Jethroe and, finally, Rocky Nelson (after he had killed us for years with other teams in the International League).

One of my recent pre-season rituals is to read the predictions that hit the book stands in March and April. Smith and Street's, and Bill Mazeroski's *Baseball* have now come to rival *Sports Illustrated's Annual Baseball Edition* and *Sport Magazine* and *Inside Sport*. *Sports Illustrated* used to be the best, with several pages devoted to each team. Since it was the first into the field and devoted a lot of space and energy to in-depth analysis, I would keep it on the book shelf near my bed and would refer to it all year. Just like television, *Sports Illustrated* has diluted its content to reach a broader public, and specialty mags like the once-a-year Mazeroski have replaced it.

The Mazeroski mag is the one I like best, and, prior to opening day, it's great to see what it says about the 1991 Blue Jays. It picks us to win easily over the Red Sox, with the Orioles third (wrong), the Tigers fourth (too high), followed by the Brewers (yes), the Yankees (higher) and the Indians (just behind the Quebec Nordiques). It says, among other things: "By making the trades and waving goodbye to Bell, Gillick initiated an overdue overhaul that should dramatically improve the Blue Jays' chemistry on the field and, perhaps more important, in the clubhouse. With a rotation that should be more dependable (if healthy), plus a monster bullpen and vastly improved outfield defense, the Blue Jays remain a sound (if boring) pre-season selection to win the AL East." It ranks the starting pitching — Stieb, Stottlemyre, Key, Wells and Leiter, Boucher or Fraser — as "a capable staff — capable of better."

Of Stieb, it says: "Stieb still has first-rate stuff and has learned to control his temper. When he gets into that hypnotic rhythm, locking batters' bowels with his fabled slider, he can be unhittable." Of Key:

"Once he finds his rhythm, he's in complete command." Of Wells's move to the starting rotation: "a stroke of genius." Of Stottlemyre: "His slider is a quality major league pitch. To become the 18- to 20-game winner scouts have projected, Stottlemyre needs to change speeds better and get ahead in the count more consistently."

Of the relief pitching, after waxing jealously over Henke and Ward, it goes on: "The rich get richer with the signing of free agent Ken Dayley. The 32-year-old lefthander owns one of the nastiest curve balls in the business and has been the top setup man in the NL for the past several years."

Of the catching: "This is where the Jays' next All-Star resides. Pat Borders." Infield: "Lee ... is a natural shortstop with quick hands and feet ... While Lee can hold his own with his predecessor defensively, he isn't anywhere near the offensive player."

Of the outfield: "In Devon White, they have a player many consider the finest defensive centerfielder in the game." Of Carter: "In addition to being a consistent run producer, Carter is a competent outfielder — something Bell wasn't." After speaking highly of Glenallen Hill and Mark Whiten as important and highly rated comers with power, it concludes: "Mookie Wilson ... will see some action in the outfield and at DH ... His weak arm limits him in the field." Of the manager: "Gaston is the proverbial 'players' manager.' He never criticizes a player publicly and lets the players prove they can play. If you can't play for him, you deserve to play for Dick Williams."

◇ The Game

On with game one. Stieb starts off opening day just as Mazeroski said he would. Once he gives up the obligatory Wade Boggs single on the first pitch of the season, Stieb sends down the next six batters quickly and easily until Tony Pena doubles to lead off the third and moves to third base on a sac bunt.

Boggs then walks, as does Jody Reed. Walks kill you; they're the surest indicator you're going to lose a game. I hate them.

Greenwell then singles to right to score one, bringing up Jack Clark. This is Clark's first AL game since his unhappy experience with the Yankees a couple of years ago. Clark is a pain. Throughout his career he has been injured often, but when he's playing he walks or homers. His homers aren't cheapies, either. If McGriff's home runs are long, slow, loping trips, Clark's are Patriot missiles, shooting out of the park before you can blink. And sometimes he comes up there with that mean look on his face, which says he's about to slam a ball into some guy's face in the second deck.

As Clark comes to the plate, I experience that feeling in my stomach, a feeling that will be repeated maybe two or three times in the course of the season: a sense of knowing, just knowing, what's about to happen. It isn't something I have alone. I bet two or three hundred fans in the stands feel the same thing. And, unfortunately, I think Dave Stieb has that same picture in his mind. It'll happen, as I say, two or three more times this year. But this is the first and it's in the first game, in the third inning, and the damned bases are loaded. We just *know* Clark is going to take Stieb over the fence.

Sure enough, after Stieb gets ahead, two strikes on Clark, he tries to sneak a fast one over the plate. And Clark, intense and confident, doesn't tap the ball, doesn't hit the ball; he lambastes the ball into the second deck for a grand slam. Red Sox 5, Blue Jays 1.

Roger Clemens is pitching for Boston, and, as always happens with Clemens, he becomes a new man once his team takes the lead. This game is no exception. Having allowed four hits in the first two innings before the grand slam, he then gets thirteen straight outs, giving up no hits till the seventh.

A loss, due to one pitch. There are going to be lots of these in every baseball season. In fact, in most games, the winning team scores the majority of its runs in one inning. There's a message here

BOXSCORE

Bosox...6
Blue Jays..2

BOSTON	AB	R	H	BI	TORONTO	AB	R	H	BI
Boggs 3b	2	2	1	0	White	4	0	0	0
Reed 2b	3	1	0	0	RAlmr 2b	4	0	0	0
Grnwll rf	4	1	1	1	Gruber 3b	4	0	1	0
JClark dh	3	1	1	4	JCarter lf	4	1	2	1
Burks cf	3	0	1	1	Olerud 1b	3	0	0	0
Brnsky lf	3	0	0	0	Mllniks dh	4	1	2	0
Quintana 1b	4	0	0	0	Myers c	4	0	0	0
Pena c	4	1	1	0	Lee ss	4	0	2	0
Nhring ss	3	0	0	0	MWilson rf	2	0	0	1
Totals	29	6	5	6	Totals	33	2	7	2

Boston   005 000 010 - 6
Toronto   010 000 001 - 2

LOB - Boston 5, Toronto 6. 2B - Burks (1), Pena (1), Lee (1). HR - Clark (1), Carter (1). S - Reed, Naehring. SF - Wilson.

	IP	H	R	ER	BB	SO
Boston						
Clemens (W, 1-0)	8	6	1	1	0	6
Gray	1	1	1	1	1	0
Toronto						
Stieb (L, 0-1)	5	4	5	5	2	2
Acker	2	0	0	0	0	3
Leiter	2/3	1	1	1	2	1
Timlin	1 1/3	0	0	0	2	0

PB - Pena

and it's one Cito should not ignore. When you've got something going in an inning, you're not likely to get it going that good again in that game; so you have to capitalize on it. You have to move the runner; you have to play aggressively and you have to pinch hit when you've got it going. Not when there are two out in the eighth, or two out in the ninth, with none on.

The Red Sox won today in one inning. One punch and it was a ball game. The Blue Jays' team is built around station-to-station baseball. That should result in more single-run innings than normal, but it also means we'll get far fewer big innings than normal. When we have a small rally going, we have to milk it, coax it, coddle and nurse it into a big one. This year, there'll be no "Bell home run, 3 RBIs" signs on the Jumbotron.

◇ Rocketman, Rules and Umps

If Clark was the headline today, Clemens was the story ... and the story was his presence, not his pitching.

The last time we saw Roger Clemens was on TV in the AL Championship Series, when he chose to tell plate umpire Terry Cooney what he thought of Cooney's eyesight, IQ, judgment, physique, and mother. A TV camera was relaying Clemens's message to 50 million people, of whom at least three could read lips. One of these three was baseball commissioner Fay (Frozen in Time) Vincent.

In a league championship series game, Cooney overreacted and tossed Clemens out of the game. This is a bit like giving Wayne Gretzky a game misconduct in the fourth game of the Stanley Cup Playoffs or calling any penalty at all in an overtime hockey playoff game. It just isn't done. This isn't to say that Clemens will be invited to give the sermon at your local Presbyterian church next Sunday. But Cooney is an experienced umpire. He knows that the game is a player's game. He knows we didn't come to the park or turn on the TV to see Terry Cooney. We came to see Clemens. It would have to be a situation blatantly embarrassing to baseball — as opposed to insulting to Cooney — to justify the umpire's tossing out the best pitcher in the game and thereby possibly determining the game's outcome. If Clemens had clearly thrown at Jose Canseco's head (maybe the safest place to hit Canseco, by the way), then the umpire should have tossed him out. But please, not for hurling juvenile locker-room epithets at a mediocre umpire.

In any case, this is relevant today only because, once Clemens opened his mouth and Cooney overreacted and tossed him from the game, Clemens was bound to be suspended. Since the Red Sox played to their level of competence in the AL Championship Series and went out quickly to the Oakland A's, that game was the Red Sox' last of 1990. When the league held its hearings, it suspended Clemens for five games. Of course, when a position player gets suspended for five games, it is serious — five games amount to almost one week out of the twenty-six–week schedule. When a pitcher gets suspended for five games, it's really one game because he would pitch only once during that span. A pitcher will make thirty-five or so starts during the year, and missing one is not much of a punishment.

Clemens committed this offence last October. The hearing was held during the off season, and he got his one-game (five-game) suspension and did nothing. He did nothing until the weekend before opening day. And then he appealed the suspension! Surprise! I guess Roger just couldn't decide through November to February whether nice Mr Cooney was right or not, or whether he wanted to awaken the hibernating Mr Vincent. Finally, just before the Blue Jays' season he decided that in the names of the Virgin Mary and Bobby Richardson (Jesuit ex-Yankee second baseman) he had to appeal.

The appeal having been filed, the suspension was suspended, thus allowing Clemens to pitch against Stieb and thus almost guaranteeing the Red Sox an opening day victory. The Red Sox knew it, the Blue Jays knew it, AL president Bobby Brown knew it.

What they also knew was that after he had got in this start, his appeal would be withdrawn and he would serve his suspension. The whole point of the exercise was to arrange things so that he could pitch against the Blue Jays.

If baseball wants to have meaningful control over the behaviour of its players, it should start with its umpires. The umpire's temper should not determine when a player is to be tossed out of the game. The league should set clear guidelines outlining the circumstances under which a player should be thrown out. The Clemens situation in the AL Championship Series was not such a case. Also, someone should tell the umpires to shut up. Most fans are really tired of seeing umpires respond to players/managers who are irritated over a bad call. You know the player/manager is upset; whether he's right or wrong, he's agitated and it's apparent. The umpire is paid *not* to be agitated. He's paid to be calm, cool, balanced, unemotional and to make the right call. But no, when the umpire's call is challenged, he can't just stand on his decision and say, "I'm sorry Lou, that's the way I saw it." No, he has to take off his mask and go toe to toe, swearing at the already riled player/manager. This exercise only further inflames the player/manager, interrupts the ball game, irritates the fans, extends a one-minute argument into a five-minute argument — and usually gets the player/manager needlessly ejected. Who needs it?

This sort of display undermines the integrity of the umpire and makes fans question his impartiality and balanced judgment. If umpires don't have the tolerance and self-control to handle such a situation, how do we know they have the balance and control to put the argument behind them a moment later, when they're back calling balls and strikes? No dice. The umpires should shut up. In fact, this area may be the only one in which the National Hockey League sets an example for anyone. In every hockey game, a player or coach argues a call. But how often do you see a referee argue back? Never. The referees invariably make the call, skate to the penalty box, tell the officials what the call is and skate away. The referee usually does not even look at the player because if he does, he may have to call a misconduct penalty. No, the referee just wants to make the call and let the game continue. Cooney, take a lesson from Koharski.

◊ Post-Game Notes

Stieb showed how mean a pitcher he can be by hitting Ellis Burks, the first batter after the Clark home run. No brawl. But it's a scene we'll see again. Maybe these Jays are playing for keeps.

I don't miss the Bathurst streetcar. Driving is the better way.

Did I go back to the office after the game? Yes. Jack Clark had already ruined my day and killed my joy.

White-Hot Start and SkyDome Fans

Sunday, April 14, 1991   1:35 PM   Toronto SkyDome
Pre-Game Standings

	W	L	Pct.	GB	Ho.	Strk.	P10	Div.
TORONTO	4	2	.667	-	4-2	L-1	4-2	4-2
Milwaukee	3	2	.600	1/2	0-0	W-1	3-2	1-2
Baltimore	2	2	.500	1	0-2	W-2	2-2	0-0

Final Score: Blue Jays 9, Brewers 0   Attendance: 47,136

BLUE JAYS END THEIR FIRST HOME STAND, leaving us happy and excited. Having gone 2–1 against the Red Sox and then 3–1 against the Brewers (who are our nemesis), they go on the road with five wins and two losses. This is easily the hottest start in Blue Jays history. The Jays' best record after the first ten games of any season is a wonderful six and four. This year they started with their worst spring-training record, winning only nine games (in 1989 they won twenty-one), but at the conclusion of the first home stand we're off to a (Devon) White-hot start.

More than that, there are lots of good signs. In the Brewers' series, David Wells pitched one of his best games ever, a 7–3 win. He pitched a four-hit shutout for seven innings, letting only two hits get out of the infield. This is a funny game. In spring training Wells was terrible, with thirty-nine hits in thirty innings and an earned run average of 5.64, but he was never in trouble against the Brewers. It's clear now the Brewers are going to end at or near the bottom of the league. They have a couple of good pitchers who are always on the disabled list, Teddy Higuera and Chris Bosio, and a whole bunch of bad pitchers who are never on it.

The Brewers are a curious team. They are always boring, notwithstanding guys like Robin Yount, Paul Molitor and, when he's healthy, Jim Gantner. Then there's Gary Sheffield, a talented, immature ball player. When he strikes out he blames his manager, his teammates, his trainer, and, probably, the batboy and even his hairstylist. He's letting his personality stop him from becoming a front-line major-league player. Sheffield needs either Cito Gaston or Dick Williams as a manager (see Mazeroski). He needs a real ego-boosting soft guy who will father him out of his immaturity, or he needs someone who will kick his ass all over the clubhouse unless he behaves. Sheffield is the kind of guy who'll never play up to his potential and will end up being traded before he's thirty, who'll always be a difficult-to-manage backup player instead of a front-line all-star.

◇ The Game

The Jays finish the series against the Brewers with a really encouraging sign. Pitcher Jimmy Key looked like the Key of a few years back, when he was the unheralded best lefty in baseball. The Brewers got only two hits off Key, and no runner got past first base. Key made it look easy. One hundred and seventeen pitches, seventy-three of them strikes. He painted the corners and had the Brewers confused all day.

Not to make too much of this, but the Blue Jays scored nine runs (final score 9–0), mainly based on a six-run second inning, blowing Don August from the mound. If the Brewers are going to keep Don August in their starting rotation, they may end up behind Cleveland.

But the Blue Jays on a Sunday afternoon finished this stand on a roll. Nine runs on thirteen hits. Whiten ends the series with some key hits. Devon White continues to hit like Rod Carew, not like a glove-only centre fielder. At the end of the first week, White has seven RBIs. Last year he had forty-four all season. He sure doesn't look like the .217 batter he was last year, and the fans think he's terrific. We expect a double every time he comes to bat. Alomar, on the other hand, has hardly any hits but has performed smoothly in the field. It seems he has executed a perfect bunt every game. The pitching staff has been irregular but with some good signs. The only problem so far is Pat Borders, who didn't get a hit in the Series.

The Blue Jays head out of town on their first road trip — nine games in Detroit, Milwaukee and Boston.

◇ Etiquette

I accept the fact that those of us who take the game seriously and unjustifiably raise it to something one part religion, one part science and one part art have to share our shrine with transients, celebrants, tourists, beer drinkers, sightseers and B.J. Birdie Fans.

I enjoy the Art Gallery and the Royal Ontario Museum. I go to each of them somewhat less frequently than I go to the SkyDome. And though I do not understand in depth all the art and displays that I see at these institutions, I'm glad they are there, and I'm happy to pay my share of the freight. So at SkyDome, I don't object at all to the "non-fan" spectators.

But just as someone has to tell me what the rules are in an art gallery, I think that the SkyDome visitors have to be given some sense of what is acceptable.

Some rules or suggestions:
1. Unless you are:
    (a) invited by the public address announcer to visit the customer service window on an "urgent personal matter"; (b) in labour

BOXSCORE

Blue Jays..9
Brewers..0

MILWAUKEE	AB	R	H	BI	TORONTO	AB	R	H	BI
Molitor dh	4	0	1	0	White cf	5	2	2	3
Rndlph 2b	3	0	0	0	RAlmr 2b	5	0	1	1
Shffield 3b	4	0	0	0	Gruber 3b	4	2	3	1
Yount cf	3	0	1	0	JCarter dh	4	0	2	0
Hmilton cf	0	0	0	0	Olerud 1b	4	0	0	0
Bchette rf	3	0	0	0	Whiten rf	4	1	2	2
Brock 1b	3	0	0	0	Myers c	4	1	1	0
GVghn lf	3	0	0	0	MLee ss	3	2	1	0
Surhoff c	2	0	0	0	MWilson lf	4	1	1	1
Spiers ss	2	0	0	0					
Sveum ss	1	0	0	0					
Totals	28	0	2	0	Totals	37	9	13	8

Milwaukee   000 000 000 - 0
Toronto   160 000 02x - 9

DP - Toronto 1. LOB - Milwaukee 3, Toronto 8. 2B - White 2 (6), Carter 2 (6), MLee (3). HR - Gruber (1). S - MLee.

	IP	H	R	ER	BB	SO
Milwaukee						
August (L, 0-1)	1	6	6	6	0	2
Machado	3	2	1	1	2	4
Holmes	3	1	0	0	1	6
Plesac	1	4	2	2	0	2
Toronto						
Key (W, 2-0)	9	2	0	0	2	5

August pitched to 5 batters in the 2nd. WP - August, Machado 2.

with pains only thirty seconds apart; (c) chasing your four-year-old, who escaped your clutches a moment ago; (d) trying to rush down to the Blue Jays' dugout to explain to Cito that you pinch hit with two on and none out for Manuel Lee in the eighth inning, NEVER, NEVER, NEVER stand up and work your way along the row during an inning.

2. If (a), (b), (c) or (d) apply and you *must* leave during an inning, do NOT under any circumstances do so just as the pitcher is about to throw the ball.

3. If you catch a ball in the stands off the head, chest, arm or leg of another fan, give that fan the ball.

4. If you feel obliged to bring one, two (or four) beer(s) back to your seat, sip a little bit out of each so that you don't drip suds on others on your way by.

5. If you're sitting down the right-field or left-field line, do not, do not, do not try to catch a ball that Mookie Wilson or Joe Carter or Kelly Gruber or John Olerud (unlikely) is trying to catch. (Note: this rule does not apply if a player on the other team — say Don Mattingly, Carlos Quintana or Wade Boggs — is going after a foul ball in the stands.) Equally, if a ball is hit fair over third or first base and then goes into foul territory in the outfield, let it go. Let it hit the wall and go back onto the playing field, allowing the outfielder to play it to second base so that it is a double, not a "ground rule" double. If you go after one of these balls and succeed in touching it, you may affect the game's outcome — and you're going to get heaved out.

6. Do not propose marriage, a first date, a last date, a child or a divorce by way of an aircraft dragging a message flying over the stadium (unless the roof is closed).

7. When the SkyDome robot who runs the Jumbotron invites all the fans in your section to cheer against all the fans in another section for the right to have the Fan of the Game selected from your section, do not cheer.

8. Do not reserve your loudest cheer of the night for the grounds crew after the fifth inning.

9. When the opposition pitcher is coming out of the game after an excellent or even a mediocre performance, give him a solid round

of applause. You do it when you hear even a poor speaker. You do it out of courtesy.

10. When a new Jays player, whether a call-up or as a result of a trade, makes his first appearance on the field, give him a huge, huge round of applause. It'll make him happy, it'll make him feel welcome and it'll relax him a little bit.
11. When our team has had a big inning, stand up and give them an ovation as they run to take the field.
12. Give the team a standing ovation when it takes the field at the start of every game.
13. Do not applaud a Blue Jays player who hits the ball to second base with one out and a runner on second. Hitting to the right side to move a runner to third is a great idea with none out. With one out, the name of the game is to score the runner.
14. When a Blue Jays player makes a great catch, acknowledge it, and, when an incredible play is made at bat, applaud until the player has to come out to take a curtain call.
15. Don't wave. The wave is passé. The wave is an annoyance. The wave distracts the players and blocks out the game for people who want to sit and watch and keep score.
16. Don't use foul language. Now, I admit we hear it on rare occasions only, but foul language should be saved for your boss, your stockbroker, your ex-spouse, the GST or the ban on Sunday shopping.
17. Try to decide what you actually want before your turn comes at the food outlets.
18. When you're walking down or up the aisle during the game, keep your eye on the playing field, and when the pitcher is about to throw, please bend down so that you're not blocking the people sitting at or near the end of the row. There are usually twenty-five to forty seconds between pitches, so you'll probably have to stop only once or twice, if at all, on your way up.
19. If you're an adult and you catch a foul ball, why not take it up to the back of section 100 and give it to the kids in wheelchairs.
20. Sing "O Canada." In parks south of the border, they belt out "The Star Spangled Banner." I know all the clichés about Canada are true. I was in politics a long time, so trust me. But couldn't we

just kind of start here? Couldn't we all sing the words and sing them loudly?

21. Bring signs. I don't mean the signs that say "Espanola says hi to Buck and TSN." I mean the ones erected in left field that say "Carter Country." Or how about big "Ks" when Candiotti or Guzman is pitching? Put one up after every strikeout.

22. Do not, do not, do not throw anything on the field. This especially applies to the idiotic paper airplanes that most often appear when there's some sort of freebie given out. These missiles risk the eyesight of innocent fans and ball players, and it's only a matter of time till someone gets hit. As strongly as I feel about ejecting fans for interfering with balls in play, I feel twice as strong about turfing out fans who float these dangerous things.

23. Make noise. Cheer our players when they come to bat. Cheer them when they are slumping and when they are hot. When we're winning and when we're losing. Really cheer when they make a hit. Go crazy over a stolen base. Cheer loudly when the Jumbotron shows that Alomar is close to the league lead in stolen bases or that Carter is third or fourth in RBIs and homers. Have fun. Show some appreciation. Make the place noisy. Remember, the Metrodome fans played a real role in taking a mediocre Minnesota Twins team to the World Championship in 1987. We complain about our baseball players seeming too calm and laid back. Look to your right and left in the stands and you'll see the same thing.

24. I love it when fans in Wrigley Field throw back home-run balls hit into the bleachers by opposing teams. That's the kind of fight and spark we want to generate in our players. Why don't our fans do the same? If Jack Clark hits one to the second deck in left field, throw it back!

◇ Post-Game Notes

As we consider the season before us, some thoughts occur. By early August, we'll be finished with the Red Sox — our main competition in the American League East. We've played them this year on April 8, 9 and 10 and face them again on April 22, 23 and 24, then on August 2, 3, 4, 9, 10, 11 and 12. So if they are going to do any damage against us, they've only ten games to go, and we're up 2-1 on them. More importantly, those ten games will be over by August 12, with seven weeks remaining in the season, and it will be really tough for them to catch us in the last forty-seven games if they don't play us head-to-head.

On the other hand, the Blue Jays have to build their lead by September 1, because from September 10 to the end of the season they have twenty-three games against the West. The Blue Jays are what is called the "swing team" — they spend September and the first week in October in the other division. Who is the weirdo who makes up the schedule? Who can't figure a better way to set it up than to pick one team and send it out of its division for the last month of the year? In any case, the Blue Jays must have a lead of five or six games (eight would be better) going into September, because the West is sure to be much, much stronger than the East. I figure the Blue Jays would end up second or third in the West behind Chicago and Oakland (in that order) and the Red Sox just a little further behind, but every other Western team should finish ahead of every other Eastern division team. The sleeper in the West is, I think, Seattle: great pitching staff and a really solid lineup at the other positions, headed by Ken Griffey Jr in centre field. We finish the season in September/October with five games against Seattle, six against Oakland — which is usually in post-season form by then — six against California and six against Minnesota. Nothing easy in there.

◆ ◆ ◆

I like to see the Brewers come to town because Chris Bosio lives at our end of the dugout. He always discusses good restaurants in Toronto and assures us that he makes better pasta than he's ever found in any restaurant in American League cities. Chris throws us some Bazooka bubble gum and chats with us freely about how much he likes the new Blue Jays lineup. Bosio makes you like big-league ball players.

◆ ◆ ◆

Looking at the Blue Jays as they head out on the road trip after their first week in town. The catching? Mediocre. First base? I've always thought Olerud needed a couple of years in the minors, and don't anyone say "sweet swing" to me again. I didn't think his stats last year were that good, and I don't think he's anywhere near major-league level in power or batting average. In the field, forget it. Awkward, ungainly, unsure, slow. A liability at first base. Alomar doesn't yet look settled at second, but it's sure nice to seem him lay down a bunt. Lee, I predict, will be gone by June — with Eddie Zosky replacing him — but I have to admit he's off to a good start with the bat and in the field. So far, he hasn't given anything away to Fernandez with his glove, and, if anything, he seems to field and throw the double-play ball better than Fernandez. Gruber is showing a little bit of power but is not off to the jackrabbit start of last year.

The outfield is a dream, so long as Mookie isn't in there. Carter is hot, having a good time, hitting homers and getting RBIs. White has given a whole new dimension to centre field. With deep fly balls, we are used to seeing Moseby, Bosetti and Wilson turn back, forward, right then left and, at the last moment, lunge and either make an ice cream cone catch or miss the ball entirely. With Devo, he's off with the first stroke of the bat. When the ball arrives he's casually waiting for it. He tends to catch with his glove at chest level and beside him to the left and just tucks it away, with never a cause for concern. In my view, he'll be worth up to ten runs a season to every Blue Jays' pitcher. Whiten in right? He's getting hits with what looks like a strait-jacket swing. It's an awkward swing, but in the field he's a cat. Great arm, great reaction, great baseball sense and great glove. Pitching staff's okay, but with the exception of Key they've not settled down from the world's worst spring training.

All in all, this is exactly the new team that was promised. Exciting, station-to-station, interesting ball. But I think it is interesting only to the true baseball fan. The antics of Bell are gone; so too the huge homers of McGriff and Jorge's RBIs. If the fans are going to stay as interested and find the games as exciting as last year, Gruber is going to have to have another great season, which is unlikely. Looks to me like a bunch of 3–2, 2–1, 1–0 games. It's National League baseball here in Toronto. But does Cito have the baseball skill and the intensity to play National League baseball at this stage? I doubt it, but we'll see.

To a baseball fan who loves National League ball, the first week has been great.

Curse of the Tigers

Wednesday, April 17, 1991			1:35 PM			Tiger Stadium	
Pre-Game Standings							
	W	L	Pct.	GB	Ho.	Strk.	P10	Div.
TORONTO	6	3	.667	-	5-2	L-1	6-3	6-3
Cleveland	4	4	.500	1 1/2	0-1	L-1	4-4	3-1
Baltimore	3	3	.500	1 1/2	0-2	W-1	3-3	1-0
Final Score: Tigers 5, Blue Jays 4							

MIDWEEK AFTERNOON GAMES at home are perfect. Just skip work without a second thought. That's half the fun. Midweek games on the road aren't the same. They're like hidden games because you never think of staying home to listen or, on the odd occasion they're on TV, to watch. Today's game is one of those rarities: it's on TV though it's an afternoon game in Detroit. No chance I can stay home and watch, however; several commitments, including a meeting in Agincourt with a big client.

The Blue Jays are off to a 6–3 start, having split the first two games of a three-game series in Detroit. Since we play seven of our twelve games against Detroit by the end of April, it's very important to get rid of the pesky Tigers, who can't be serious this year. They are a collection of ex-Japanese league, ex-waiver, strikeout kings and cement hands. Nonetheless, they are always a nemesis, and it would be great to keep on the roll by winning two out of three on our first trip to Tiger Stadium.

◇ The Game

This game is no problem as I watch it on the mini-TV I brought to the office while I make some phone calls and prepare for my meeting. Denis Boucher pitches effectively and with a rabbit's foot (an emery board would be better) in his pocket. After giving up a run in the first inning (to tie it 1–1 after Gruber's home run), he works through the Tiger lineup. He loads the bases with two walks, a balk and a hit batsman, but, through seven innings, his team bails him out twice with double plays.

Meanwhile, the Blue Jays put up four runs thanks to Gruber and Carter.

I turn off the game, finish my work and head down the nine floors into the parking lot. I get into my car to find Ward has replaced Boucher and is into the ninth inning protecting the 4–1 lead. I am driving east along St Clair, listening to Tom and Jerry describe the ninth inning, and I suddenly get that bad feeling in my stomach. After the first two batters in the ninth strike out, Mickey Tettleton gets a single. Now, with a three-run lead and two out, a little single shouldn't worry you. But somehow my experience with Duane Ward tells me to worry and I do. A moment later, I am relieved to hear that John Shelby (he couldn't hit when he could hit) hit a two hopper right at Robbie Alomar. The game should be over, but of course, this being Tiger Stadium, it isn't.

Alomar, who I guarantee won't have trouble with two balls like that in his lifetime, misses the ball in what was an error to everyone but the home-town Detroit scorer. Now Sparky Anderson, who plays his team like a violin and who really works ball games, is working hard as always. Tony Phillips, one of the great underrated ball players of all time, is up. He came to Detroit from the Oakland A's and was a real steal for the Tigers. I'd love to have him for the Blue Jays. He's typical of the player Sparky Anderson would look for and somehow find a way of adding twenty points to his batting average. Nonetheless, Sparky decides to pinch hit for Phillips and sends up Lou Whitaker to bat. Whitaker is in the evening, if not the twilight, of his career and has been one of the premier second basemen in the

American League for years. If he has had thirty key hits in his lifetime, I guarantee you twenty-seven of them have been against the Blue Jays.

So Tettleton and Shelby are on base with two out, and, as I come to the stop light at Mount Pleasant and St Clair, I can feel my salmon sandwich from three hours ago starting to rise. I can picture a thousand home runs that Whitaker has hit against us with that tight, short, quick swing of his. And, while I'm picturing it, suddenly Tom Cheek is describing it. Yes, you got that right, a three-run homer with two out in the ninth. Blue Jays 4, Tigers 4. How many times have I seen this game? I can't stand it. My client is not going to greet a happy lawyer when I get there.

Ward gets out of the inning, if you can call it getting out of the inning, at 4–4, and we go to the tenth. But there's no doubt in *my* mind, or *Duane Ward's*, or *Cito's*, or in that of *anyone* wearing a grey and blue uniform in Detroit, about who is going to win this game, and it ain't the guys in grey and blue. Not many blocks later, I listen as an unbelievable but typical Jays-killing Tiger rally takes place. In the tenth, Ward gets his two outs quickly before he does his usual freeze up. Another instant replay of the ground ball to Alomar with two out in the ninth, this time with two out in the tenth, and, again, for the second time this year, Alomar boots it. For the second time, the home-town scorer says it's a base hit.

Now this is the kind of situation Sparky loves. Incaviglia, who hit that error (single), is replaced by Milt Cuyler, who is told by Sparky to steal second. He does, and Pat Borders, thinking it's a September pennant race already, panics and throws the ball into centre field to put Cuyler on third. Still there are two out and we should be all right. Good old Duane Ward, having given up a three-run homer with two out in the ninth, now throws his first pitch to Travis Fryman. It's low and outside — outside the plate, and way outside Pat Borders's glove. Tigers 5, Blue Jays 4.

Blue Jays were one strike away from a victory in the ninth with a three-run lead and lose 5–4 in the tenth. We lose on Borders's error, not to mention Alomar's two errors and somewhat questionable luck and pitching by Ward.

If as in most years the pennant is decided by one or two games, we'll have to remember this one. Is Ward still unable to be the kind of reliable stopper with the belly to close out a game with two out in the ninth (with a three-run lead, no less)? Has Alomar been infected with a case of "Tigeritis"? Did Cito stay too long with Ward? It's too early in the season to say, but this is a game that was in the bag and we let it get away.

◇ Patterns

Ken Dryden, in his outstanding book *The Game*, said in a paragraph or two that each hockey game has its own pattern and that every game is *not* different. It's almost as if you've played this very game before, and you kind of know midway through the first period how this game is going to turn out.

There was something about this game in Detroit that was déjà vu. What Dryden says about hockey is true of baseball. There's an infinite number of games, but a finite number of patterns. The pitcher's duel, the hitting derby, the laugher, the never-out-of-the-game comeback and so on. When you've seen it hundreds if not thousands of times, you just get a "feel" for what's going to happen. There is simply something about Detroit, Lou Whitaker, Duane Ward, the lead, the failure to score with runners on base even when ahead or the way the Detroit players carry themselves. But I just couldn't start to smile even with two out in the ninth.

BOXSCORE

Tigers...5
Blue Jays..4

TORONTO	AB	R	H	BI	DETROIT	AB	R	H	BI
MWilson cf	5	1	1	0	Phillips 2b	2	0	0	0
RAlomar 2b	4	1	0	0	Whitaker ph	1	1	1	3
Gruber 3b	4	1	1	2	Trammell ss	4	1	1	0
JoCarter lf	4	0	2	1	Deer rf	4	0	1	1
Tabler 1b	2	0	1	0	Fielder 1b	4	0	1	0
MWhiten rf	3	0	0	1	Incaviglia lf	5	0	1	0
Borders c	4	0	0	0	Cuyler pr	0	1	0	0
ManLee ss	3	0	0	0	DeLosSnts dh	3	0	0	0
GHill dh	4	1	2	0	Bergman dh	1	0	0	0
					Fryman 3b	4	0	1	0
					Allanson c	3	0	0	0
					Tettleton c	1	1	1	0
					Shelby cf	4	1	2	0
Totals	33	4	7	4	Totals	36	5	9	4

Toronto   103 000 000   0 - 4
Detroit   100 000 003   1 - 5

Two Outs When Winning Run Scored.
E - Borders. DP - Toronto 2, Detroit 2. LOB - Toronto 5, Detroit 8. 2B - Trammell. HR - Gruber (3) (Off Searcy), Whitaker (2) (Off DWard). SB - Cuyler (2). SF - Gruber, M Whiten

	IP	H	R	ER	BB	SO	HR
Toronto							
Boucher	7	4	1	1	3	2	0
D Wrd (L, 0-1)	2 2/3	5	4	3	1	5	1
Detroit							
Searcy	2 2/3	5	4	4	2	2	1
Petry	6 1/3	2	0	0	2	2	0
Hennemn (W, 1-0)	1	0	0	0	0	1	0

BALK - Boucher 2. PB - Borders. HBP - Fielder by Boucher, Trammell by Boucher.
SO - Tor: Man Lee 2, M Whiten 2, Gruber. Det: Deer 2, Bergman, Shelby, De Los Santos, Incaviglia, Fryman.
BB - Tor: Tabler 2, R Alomar, Man Lee. Det: Phillips 2, Deer, Bergman.

And I know I'm not alone. Everyone who has followed the Blue Jays and the Tigers for years gets the feeling that the Blue Jays' wins are "narrow" wins. It's as though the Tigers are supposed to win, and, when we win, it's an accident. Through the rest of the season we're going to see games where we are leading but we feel like we are losing. Games like today's, where we had what appeared to be a safe lead that we just knew wasn't safe. It's the pattern, and Ken Dryden will tell you the players feel the same pattern and that the inevitability of the result too often dictates the result.

But when are we going to break the Tiger Stadium jinx? By the time we get to Detroit in August for our next and last series, they should be out of it and we should be ahead. God willing.

But I'll bet both the pattern and the jinx are still identifiable.

◇ Post-Game Notes

Though I try to avoid listening to games on the radio, this is far from the only one I'll be tuning in to. I find games on the radio to be particularly aggravating. You can't see what's happening, and when the announcer, no matter how skilled, says "there's a ball hit to right field," you can't tell whether it's deep or shallow or into the gap or down the line. Even when he adds the adjective it doesn't tell the story. If it's deep, it could be to the warning track or against the fence or over the fence, and, as the announcer waits to judge it and transmit it to you, the fans invariably beat him to it. You can always tell where the ball is before the announcer tells you because the fans are going to be cheering wildly if the ball is heading over the fence. Since several thousand of them are sitting right near the fence, they can spot it quicker than the announcer (unless McGriff or Fielder have hit it). Same with a strikeout or a walk on a 3-2 pitch. Just think how many times you hear the announcer say "here comes the 3-2 pitch" and the crowd cheers before he says "strike three."

Today, you knew Whitaker's hit was over the fence. You knew it from the bleacher fans in Tiger Stadium, who were cheering long before Tom was crying.

Nolan Ryan: Out of Sight

Wednesday, May 1, 1991			8:35 PM		Arlington Stadium		
Pre-Game Standings							
	W	L	Pct.	GB	Ho.	Strk.	P10	Div.
Boston	11	7	.611	-	6-4	W-3	8-2	5-6
TORONTO	12	9	.571	-	8-3	L-1	6-4	12-8
Milwaukee	10	9	.526	1 1/2	4-5	W-1	5-5	6-7
Final Score: Rangers 3, Blue Jays 0								

THIS IS A GAME I REALLY WANTED TO WATCH. Blue Jays at Texas on CTV, with Nolan Ryan pitching against Jimmy Key. We're in pretty good shape, still bunched at the top, but Detroit and Milwaukee will fade soon, leaving us and the Red Sox to fight it out.

But no matter the season and the standings, Ryan is an event, and, when he's against another good pitcher, like Key, it's going to be a great game.

Won't be able to watch the game, however. I've been hired to speak at a meeting of senior executives of Mutual Life at the Hockley Valley Inn.

◇ The Game

Yes, it was the no-hitter. You will all remember it, especially those of you who were fortunate enough to see it. No book about the season would be complete without it.

◆ A BASEBALL ADDICT'S DIARY

	1	2	3	4	5	6	7	8	9
White	Ks		Ks			Ks			G/O
Alomar	G/O			Ks			Ks		Ks
Gruber	Walk			F/O			Ks		
Carter	P/O			Ks			Walk		
Olerud		Kc			P/O		FL		
Whiten		Kc			F/O			F/O	
Hill		Kc			Ks			Ks	
Myers			F/O			Ks		Ks	
Lee			Ks			F/O			G/O

Ks: strike out, swinging
Kc: called third strike
G/O: ground out
P/O: pop out
F/O: fly out
FL: foul out

BOXSCORE

Rangers..................3
Blue Jays................0

TORONTO   **TEXAS**

	AB	R	H	BI		AB	R	H	BI
White cf	4	0	0	0	Pettis cf	4	1	1	0
Alomar 2b	4	0	0	0	Daugherty lf	4	0	1	0
Gruber 3b	2	0	0	0	Palmeiro 1b	4	1	2	0
Carter lf	2	0	0	0	Sierra rf	4	1	1	2
Olerud 1b	3	0	0	0	Franco 2b	4	0	0	0
Whiten rf	3	0	0	0	Gonzalez dh	3	0	1	0
GHill dh	3	0	0	0	Stanley c	3	0	1	0
Myers c	3	0	0	0	Buechele 3b	4	0	1	0
Lee ss	3	0	0	0	Huson ss	2	0	0	0
Totals	27	0	0	0	**Totals**	32	3	8	2

Toronto   000 000 000 - 0
Texas   003 000 00x - 3

E - Palmeiro, Lee, Myers, Gruber. LOB - Toronto 2, Texas 8. 2B - Gonzalez, Stanley. HR - Sierra (5) (off Key). SB - Pettis (8). CS - Gonzalez. S - Huson.

	IP	H	R	ER	BB	SO	HR
Toronto							
Key (L, 4-1)	6	5	3	3	1	5	1
MacDonald	1	2	0	0	0	2	0
Fraser	1	1	0	0	0	0	0
Texas							
Ryan (W, 3-2)	9	0	0	0	2	16	0

HBP - Gonzalez (by Fraser).
SO - Tor: Gruber, Carter, White 3, Olerud, Whiten, Hill 3, Lee, Alomar 3, Myers 2. Tex: Sierra, Daugherty, Pettis 2, Franco, Huson, Buechele.
BB - Tor: Gruber, Carter. Tex: Stanley.

Let's look at some interesting statistics about Ryan. This was his seventh no-hitter. The most by any pitcher, ever. It was the 209th time he has struck out at least ten in one game and the twenty-sixth time he has struck out fifteen or more. Only three times have Blue Jays pitchers struck out twelve batters in a game.

Ryan now has 5361 career strikeouts. He threw 122 pitches, 83 of them for strikes. His fastest pitch was 96 mph (in the fourth), his *average* was 93 and the last pitch of the game was 93. And, oh yes, he's 44 years old.

A memorable night in baseball. Couldn't happen to a nicer guy or a harder-working guy. In fact, he does it at age 44 only because he's worked hard all his life. Can't understand why lesser lights don't work as hard as he does.

◇ Post-Game Notes

Well, for me, it was like this. I finished my speech just after 10:00, and, as I got in my car, I immediately flipped on Tom and Jerry to hear how we were doing. Now, only Ernie Harwell, the veteran (he's in his seventies and was recently fired, effective the end of the season) announcer for the Detroit Tigers, really knows how to do this. He knows that we don't care about gossip, anecdotes or "in" jokes. All we care about is the score and the game stats. I listen for almost ten minutes, trying to figure out what the score is. All I hear is talk about Nolan having great stuff and "fanning another batter." Finally, at the end of the seventh, they give the totals: Texas three runs on seven hits and one error; Blue Jays no runs on no hits and no errors! I almost swerve off the road. I then calculate how long it will take me to get home — down Highway 10, pick up highways 409 and 401, south on the Allen Expressway and east on Eglinton — and I figure I just might be able to do it by the top of the ninth.

Don't tell my sons, but this time I was prepared to eat the ticket and even the three points. I wanted to see what was certainly Ryan's last and historic no-hitter. Let me be clear. I love baseball and I love Ryan, but I love the Blue Jays more, and I was hoping they would break it off and win the game. It became clear that they weren't going to do either as I pushed the car as hard as it would go.

There I was, just passing Yorkdale, when Robbie Alomar struck out to end the game.

Perfect Alomar, Imperfect SkyDome

Friday May 10, 1991			7:35 PM		Toronto SkyDome		
Pre-Game Standings							
	W	L	Pct.	GB	Ho.	Strk.	P10	Div.
Boston	16	9	.640	-	8-5	W-2	8-2	5-6
Detroit	16	10	.615	1/2	8-5	W-4	8-2	6-6
TORONTO	17	12	.586	1	10-4	W-2	6-4	12-8
Final Score: White Sox 5, Blue Jays 3					Attendance: 50,198		

WELL, WE MAY BE A GAME BACK OF BOSTON and just behind Detroit, but, as I head down and listen to Cito in his usual way say nothing in the pre-game show, I'm liking this team. We have won three of our last four and five of seven, and the team is coming together nicely.

Both Gruber and Henke are out, and yet we've put up good numbers in the last week. This three-game series against the White Sox, who are second in the AL West and who I picked to win the West, will be a good test. In fact this whole month is a dress rehearsal for September. As is the case in September, we play all of May against western teams. After Thursday night's 2–0 win over the Sox, we've got Stieb and Key on Saturday and Sunday, and so, if our fifth starter, Denis Boucher, can do it tonight against Fernandez, we may be on a roll — despite injuries.

◇ The Game

Boucher starts badly when the next big superstar, Frank Thomas, smacks a two-run homer in the top of the first. The Jays scratch back for one and it stays like that. The White Sox play the slowest games in the majors, even when Carlton (Human Rain Delay) Fisk isn't catching. In this tight game, he visits Fernandez more often than John Olerud visits second base in a month. The game drags along, with lots of fans losing interest at 3–2.

Through the game the Blue Jays have no trouble getting base runners, but insist on leaving them. It looks like a sure loss in the bottom of the ninth, with two out and the one and two count on Robbie Alomar. Bobby Thigpen predictably is in to pitch for the White Sox. Thigpen, of course, set the major-league record for saves last year and is without a doubt one of the premier relievers in baseball — in spite of the fact that he doesn't have a big smoker.

Sheldon and I sit some forty rows down from the exit and have a habit of heading up the aisle to watch the end of the game from the top of the row. It saves us an extra ten to twelve minutes' waiting at the end of the game while the stands ahead of us empty.

So we have our rule. When the Blue Jays are winning, we head up the aisle with one out in the ninth and watch the last two outs from beside the Ford parked at level 100 in right field. If it's a tie game, we sit in our seats. If we're losing, we head up with one out in the bottom of the ninth. So today we head up and are standing beside the car with our feet pointing towards the exit, when, with a one and two count, Robbie Alomar, batting left against Thigpen, drives the ball out the park in right field to tie the game.

This is the stuff you only read about in books. It's the stuff you dream about as you stand in right field in your elementary school playground. We already know Alomar can hit. He's feeling comfortable, making sensational plays in the field, and is becoming a vital part of the new blue machine. We didn't know he had power. With this jolt, the stadium suddenly is lit. Not only is Carter leading high-five sessions in the dugout, but we're also having our own out in the right-field stands.

That run sends us to extras. Now, playing extras against the White Sox can make you sorry you didn't bring the sleeping bag.

In fact, by the time this game is over, Stieb and Hough will be warming up for tomorrow afternoon's game. I tell Sheldon I'm returning to our seats. Sheldon stays in the bleachers.

In the eleventh, Chicago scores, and, with one out in the bottom of the eleventh I trek back up and take a seat of thousands now available beside Sheldon in right field. We're really unhappy because we fought back, we got good pitching from Acker and rookie Bob MacDonald (and even Boucher didn't do too badly), and Alomar hit that clutch homer to get us back into it. In any event, I'm back in the bleachers with Sheldon when Alomar comes up with one out in the eleventh, this time batting right-handed with Scott Radinsky pitching for the White Sox. Alomar blasts this baby 400 feet to left field to tie it for the second time in three innings. This is as amazing and as exciting a clutch performance as I have ever seen from a Jay.

This time we persuade Sheldon that he's got to come back to our seats, so we all trek back down.

Needless to say, by the time we get to our seats and settle down again, Sammy Sosa smacked a two-run homer off Fraser in the top of the twelfth. This was too much. As soon as it went out of the park, we once again got up and made our way back to our spot in right field. This time, since Alomar is allowed to bat only once every nine batters, we didn't think we'd come back.

BOXSCORE

White Sox..................................5
Blue Jays...................................3

CHICAGO	AB	R	H	BI	TORONTO	AB	R	H	BI
Raines lf	4	0	2	0	DWhite	5	0	0	0
LJohnson cf	5	1	1	0	RAlomar 2b	4	3	3	2
Thomas dh	4	1	1	2	JCarter lf	5	0	1	0
Fisk c	6	0	4	0	Olerud 1b	5	0	0	1
Karkovice c	0	1	0	0	MWhiten rf	6	0	2	0
Sosa rf	5	1	1	2	Tabler dh	3	0	1	0
Ventura 3b	4	0	1	0	KWillims dh	1	0	0	0
Cora pr	0	0	0	0	Myers c	3	0	1	0
Grebeck 3b	2	0	1	0	Borders ph	1	0	0	0
Snyder 1b	3	0	0	0	MLee ss	4	0	0	0
Pasqua 1b	2	1	0	0	Giannelli 3b	3	0	0	0
Guillen ss	5	0	0	0	RGonzls 3b	0	0	0	0
Fletcher 2b	5	0	1	1	MWilson ph	1	0	0	0
					Sprague 3b	0	0	0	0
Totals	45	5	12	5	Totals	41	3	8	3

Chicago   200 000 000 012 - 5
Toronto   100 000 001 010 - 3

E - JoCarter. DP - Chicago 1. LOB - Chicago 11, Toronto 13. 2B - Myers, Raines. 3B - MWhiten. HR - Thomas (5) (off Boucher), RAlomar 2 (4) (off Thigpen, Radinsky), Sosa (5) (off Fraser). SB - JoCarter (5), DWhite (4). CS - JoCarter 2. S - Sosa, LJohnson.

Chicago	IP	H	R	ER	BB	SO
Fernandez	7	4	1	1	8	5
Palf	1	1	0	0	0	0
Thigpen	2	2	1	1	2	0
Radinsky (W, 2-1)	2	1	1	1	0	0
Toronto						
Boucher	6	6	2	2	2	4
Acker	2 1/3	1	0	0	1	0
MacDonald	1	1	0	0	0	0
Fraser (L, 0-1)	2 2/3	4	3	3	2	1

WP - Acker. HBP - by Thigpen (Jo Carter).

Sure enough, Radinsky gets through this inning without problem in one of those weird paradoxical games that I would call an "uplifting loss." We lost it, but we exhibited spark, spunk, enthusiasm. Alomar showed us he can do it all — field, bunt, run, steal and now homer. He's batting .400 in his last eight games and showed incredible heart and enthusiasm.

◇ SkyDome

Major-league baseball. Somewhere there ought to be an entry in the record books for the two most serious baseball fans holding the two most senior government jobs at the same time: Bill Davis and Larry Grossman, September 1975–January 1985. We talked baseball at first ministers' conferences, at retreats, at cabinet meetings. Even on our then well-publicized trip to New York City to save Ontario's triple-A credit rating in August 1984.

I had flown down the day before to meet with Standard and Poor's, to get to know the people and the issues to be dealt with at an "appeal" the next day at 4:00 P.M. Bill Davis flew down at 2:00 P.M. and my entire opportunity to brief him was a forty-minute ride in from Newark Airport, during which I threw facts, figures, papers, documents and analyses at him. After twenty-five minutes of listening, the Premier took yet another puff on his pipe, turned to me and uttered his very first words of the briefing. "I think the Phillies and the Mets are playing here tonight. What time will our meeting be over?"

How could I not love the man? Nine months previously, he had taken me aside after an off-site cabinet meeting at the Ontario Science Centre (an appropriate place for the conception of the SkyDome) and asked me to become chairman of a three-man stadium corporation with Paul Godfrey and the world's best aide, Ed Stewart, the Premier's deputy minister. (Stewart's only shortcoming, and I mean the *only* one, is that he is a devout Tigers' fan.)

The SkyDome story will be written elsewhere, for different reasons, but this is the appropriate place for the first chairman of what became the SkyDome to make some comments about its birth:

- It never was to be a pure baseball stadium, but rather a facility to house the Toronto Argos as well.
- I argued unsuccessfully that the additional cost of accommodating the Canadian football field — at least $40 million — as opposed to the U.S. football field, which is 40 percent smaller — was unjustified since the CFL couldn't last.
- When the $175 million cost was originally announced, we said quite clearly that this figure did not include a lot of "extras" essential to proper completion of the stadium, and we anticipated that the final bill would be as much as $275 or $300 million.
- I called Trevor Eyton to ask him if he would agree to put together the consortium he had talked about for some time. He assented and acted quickly.
- When negotiations began between the consortium and my Treasury officials, it was a simple, straightforward investment by some public-spirited companies that would get some recognition.
- When we invited bids for the various roofs and structures for the retractible dome, there were lots of interesting and innovative ones submitted, but only four that merited serious consideration.
- At the time I resigned my position for the leadership (round one) in October 1984, we'd narrowed the choice down to three designs. I felt the best was the one designed by Bregman & Hamann. It appeared to be the least costly and the simplest to operate, and it came completely off the stadium, leaving it with a feeling of total openness. With the roof off, it would look, except for the light standards, similar to any open-air stadium. Ten months later, when I'd lost the leadership and we had lost the election, or at least the government, it was still the front runner. Not long thereafter another roof design was selected by the new government, to be built by the company owned by the president of the Liberal Party of Ontario.
- The option of real grass in the stadium was still open when we left office, but it was bound to be a losing one as the price of the stadium went up.

Events soon picked up a lot of momentum. Chuck Magwood, an entrepreneur — no further comment — became president. A baseball/football stadium with a retractible roof suddenly blossomed into a hotel, restaurant, Hard Rock Cafe, athletic club, multi-purpose, multi-use extravaganza with state-of-the-art technology. This is not to suggest the SkyDome is not — as Toronto so desperately wants everything in it to be — a world-class facility. What it isn't is what we began to build, a baseball/football stadium with a fully retractible roof. The stadium will now accommodate anything from Motor-cross to Madonna; from political fund-raising to basketball (I hope). I'm not happy about the fact that our baseball stadium has turned into a multi-use "facility." But I accept it. Kind of like I accept Peterson, Rae and Cito.

But, having made all these concessions to other events, there are a lot more things that can be done to make the baseball experience a more complete one. One gets the feeling that the SkyDome is operated by technicians. They seem to lack a feel for the game and fail to transform the Dome into a real baseball park. For baseball, you need to understand where doubles to left hit the wall, how a ball plays off the padding, the importance of being near the playing field and hearing the sounds, the value of the bullpen, the dugouts and the out-of-town scores and the role a properly done sausage or hot dog with mustard plays in the experience.

So here are some things that I would have liked to have seen happen for baseball at the SkyDome had I been able to stay on as chairman — or had the voters let me stay on as treasurer or my party let me in when the convention counted.

- ◆ The fully retractible (and cheaper) Bregman & Hamann roof would have been selected. The technical committee agreed that it had ranked it technically equivalent to the Rob Robbie/Liberal dome that was selected.
- ◆ Real grass. Here we let the proverbial tail wag the dog. First a decision is taken to build or overbuild the facility by putting in (1) the most expensive roof design; (2) accommodating the CFL; (3) adding $40 million for it; (4) putting in a hotel; and (5) putting in a health club, fancy restaurant and other things totally unrelated to baseball. Having done all this, it then became so expensive a facility that it had to be used 300 nights a year. Once it had to be used 300 nights a year, it meant accommodating a number of

events that would in turn dictate the kind of surface to be installed. The only surface that could accommodate it all was artificial turf.

To say it simply, I would have planned everything in the stadium around real grass, which can be grown and maintained in a retractible dome stadium. Have you ever been on the turf at the SkyDome or any other artificial turf stadium? You'd be surprised to feel how hard it is. In fact, it's harder than the broadloom in your den. It is a thin covering on concrete.

- Bullpens are a vital part of a ball game. They tell the fans what moves the managers are thinking of making and what the options are. The fans should be able to see the bullpens.
- Balls hit high into the air that land fair near the outfield wall almost always bounce over for a ground-rule double. One of the most exciting plays in baseball is a triple because the dimensions in the field and the ability of most outfielders almost always mean a close play at third. But at the SkyDome, we lose the opportunity to see about two dozen of these plays a year because balls bounce over the fence. Soften the turf out there or raise the fences.
- Out-of-town scores. Baseball is a game with a certain pace. The actual time that a ball is in play is limited, and there's lots of time between pitches and innings. Fans love to watch out-of-town scoreboards, especially the scores of the teams close to us in the standings, but also other pennant races and teams with former Blue Jays on them. We can't do this at the SkyDome because we have to keep glancing away from the play, hoping we'll get the Detroit or Boston score. The scoreboard can only accommodate four out-of-town scores. The SkyDome should have been built to allow the classic Comiskey Park, Fenway Park out-of-town scoreboard, which shows every game, inning by inning. It is too late now to do this, but it is not too late to use some of the concrete dividers between the levels to add some additional boards that would at least show the score of each game without rotating it, and the inning and who is pitching. And if we always knew where to look for the Detroit or Boston scores (or whoever the contending teams are next year), it would be even better.
- Using the roof that we have. I would have wanted that roof to be as flexible as possible. During several games this year the roof has been closed because rain threatened in the morning, but, by the

time we got to the game, it was bright and sunny. The SkyDome rule has been that the decision is made at 10:30 A.M. to allow the grounds crew enough time (I don't understand this) to get it open. The additional rationale for this decision is that teams must take batting practice under game conditions, so you can't have batting practice indoors for an outdoors game. Please, save me from this. Players play a half-dozen games a year with no batting practice at all when it's raining prior to game time in open-air stadiums. You mean to tell me that these boys can't have batting practice indoors and then play a game outdoors? Come on.

It takes less than half an hour to open the roof, and it could be opened as soon as the rain, or the threat of rain, passes. We paid a lot of money as taxpayers for the privilege of a roof that opens, and now, for some reason, we are not allowed full access to what we paid for.

This argument equally applies to mid-game circumstances. If it's raining at 1:30 P.M. and clears up at 2:00 P.M., why can't we see the rest of the game outdoors? When I've asked various officials this question the answer is that "league rules prohibit the opening of the roof during a game because this would be unfair to the visiting team." I don't buy that. Why not ask both managers at 2:00 P.M. if they would agree to open the roof and, if they do, simply open it. Has any manager complained when the game started with the roof open but had to be closed in the middle?

◇ Post-Game Notes

Thirty thousand of fifty thousand fans sat through seven uneventful innings and then left for five of the most exciting they would have seen all year. Wait for the fat lady, folks. We always do. Maybe not in our seats, but we wait.

◆ ◆ ◆

A "fan" decided he could field Tim Raines's hit to left field better than Joe Carter. The difference is, if Carter makes the play, Raines might have been out at second. If the fan makes the play, (a) Raines gets second automatically, and (b) the fan gets ejected automatically. For my money, they can't eject such fans far enough. This is the second time in three nights that there's been an incident down the left-field line with fans ejected. Why are you ruining the game for us, folks?

◆ ◆ ◆

McGriff has seven homers while George Bell has eight. The Blue Jays? Carter has four, as does Alomar (now). In fact, the Blue Jays have only nineteen while Bell and McGriff have fifteen themselves. Hmm. And all those runners left on base today. Don't panic, Larry. We said it was going to be different this year, and it is. It's National League, station-to-station ball. Not long ball, but I did enjoy Robbie's tonight.

◆ ◆ ◆

Ozzie Guillen is a ball player who makes you happy. He enjoys the game, the players, the umpires, the fans, the media. He always looks for us and talks with us between winks, laughs and autographs. I tell Ozzie that I haven't been able to buy one of the new great-looking White Sox hats (they returned to their traditional design this year).
 Ozzie: "No problem. What's your hat size?"
 Larry: "7 1/2."
 Ozzie: "One second."
Ozzie disappears into the dugout and returns quickly with a hat. Nice guy. And he can hit too.

◆ ◆ ◆

Everyone is a baseball fan.
 Linda has been our receptionist at Macaulay, Chusid & Friedman for twenty-seven years. She is ebullient, bright, friendly and fun. She has a word, or a few thousand words, for everyone. Her nickname is "Lovely."
 As I left the office talking baseball, Lovely asked me why all the umpires are named "AL." She deduced this from the letters on their caps. Wonder what she thinks the names of all the National League umpires are.

Jumbo?Tron

Friday, May 31, 1991			7:35 PM		Toronto SkyDome		
Pre-Game Standings							
	W	L	Pct.	GB	Ho.	Strk.	P10	Div.
Boston	25	20	.556	-	15-8	L-2	4-6	10-12
TORONTO	26	21	.553	-	15-8	L-1	4-6	12-8
Detroit	23	22	.511	2	14-9	L-2	6-4	7-10
Final Score: Blue Jays 5, Angels 1					Attendance: 50,252		

WE'RE ABOUT TO CLOSE OFF THE FIRST OF TWO MONTHS with the West. The next one will be the terrible month of September. If we can win the pennant as this year's "swing team," it will be a miracle. The West is simply too good. So far it has 167 wins against 149 losses, while the East is playing under .500 at 147 and 165. Boston, three percentage points ahead of us in first place, would be third in the West. We would be fifth, Detroit would be seventh, and New York, Cleveland and Baltimore would all trail Kansas City, which is the last-place team.

So far this month, we have won fourteen and lost twelve. Not too bad, considering we've played twelve home and fourteen away games. Boston's had an easier schedule, and yet for the past couple of weeks each team has been playing .500 ball most of the time. June brings our first trip through the dog pound: six against the Yankees, seven against the Orioles, and seven against the Indians — and we are ready to make a run for it.

For this Friday nighter, it will be Mark Langston against David Wells. Last week in the same match-up in California, Langston beat Wells 6–2, with Wells lasting only two-and-two-thirds innings. But in his five other starts this month, Wells is 5–0, with an earned run average of 0.46.

On the other hand, Langston is 6–1. I like him a lot, and in my pre-season picks selected him to win the Cy Young award.

The Blue Jays have lost four out of their last five, including two out of three to the Angels in Anaheim and two out of three to Oakland back here, Tuesday, Wednesday and Thursday. Tonight's game is a pretty big one.

◇ The Game

Wells gets off to a bad start, giving up a double to Luis Polonia. Luis Sojo sacrifices Polonia to third, and Gary Gaetti hits a sac fly to score him. Station-to-station baseball played by the Angels, who know they may not get too many chances to score off Wells. The Blue Jays' lineup is not going to scare Mark Langston a heck of a lot. Two of the starters, Williams and Sprague, are Syracuse Chiefs. Tabler's batting .230 or so; Glenallen Hill is at .200

But baseball being baseball, the Blue Jays bounce back with three runs in the bottom of the second. Manuel Lee knocks in two runs with a solid single — the key hit. After Sprague walks, Borders singles and Kenny (Wrong Way) Williams embarrasses me by hitting a double off the wall.

Pretty standard stuff through the next four innings. Wells really has trouble only with Polonia, who gets another double. Meanwhile, Langston has trouble only with Manuel Lee, who is on base when Devon White hits his first home run of the year in the bottom of the second to sock it away for us at 5–1.

Wells will finish neatly, walking only one and striking out nine. Wells retires fourteen batters in a row after Parrish leads off the second with a single. But the highlight of the night isn't White's home run or Lee's incredible three-for-three night or Wells's pitching.

It occurs in the fifth inning, when Polonia, a quick, much underrated hitter, lays a perfect drag bunt down towards first base. Alomar roars in from second base, grabs the ball with his bare hand and, as he falls face first onto the ground, tosses the ball to Tabler to get the speedy Polonia. You won't see that play in a decade. Alomar had everyone gasping.

Meanwhile, if that's the highlight, the "almost" highlight is turned in by Ed Sprague. Sprague is merely batting .400 since he was called up to fill in for the injured Kelly Gruber. In the sixth, Sojo bunts down the third-base line. Sprague rushes in, bare-hands the ball and hurls his body forward as he fires the ball to Tabler. I think Sprague ended up doing a full somersault, and I suspect Doug Rader did one too in the Angel dugout when he saw the second of two sure bunt singles converted into outs. If either of those bunts had been successful, the game might have turned out entirely differently. It won't show in the box score, but sensational fielding by Alomar and Sprague may have made the difference.

BOXSCORE

Blue Jays...5
Angels..1

CALIFORNIA	AB	R	H	BI	TORONTO	AB	R	H	BI
Polonia lf	4	1	2	0	White cf	4	1	2	2
Sojo 2b	3	0	0	0	RAlmr 2b	3	0	1	0
Gaetti 3b	4	0	0	1	Carter lf	4	0	0	0
DPrker dh	4	0	1	0	Tabler 1b	4	0	1	0
Wnfield rf	3	0	0	0	Sprgue 3b	3	1	0	0
Felix cf	4	0	1	0	Brders c	4	1	1	0
Parrish c	3	0	1	0	Wilams rf	3	1	1	1
DHill 1b	3	0	0	0	MLee ss	3	1	3	2
Schfield ss	3	0	0	0	GHill dh	3	0	0	0
Totals	31	1	5	1	Totals	31	5	9	5

California   100 000 000 - 1
Toronto   030 000 20x - 5

E - DHill (2), Langston (1). LOB - California 5, Toronto 5. 2B - Polonia 2 (7), Williams (2). HR - White (1). SB - White (8), RAlomar (12). CS - RAlomar (3). S - Sojo.

	IP	H	R	ER	BB	SO
California						
Langston (L, 6-2)	7	8	5	5	3	3
JDRobinson	1	1	0	0	0	1
Toronto						
Wells (W, 6-4)	9	5	1	1	1	9

Lots is happening in the out-of-town games. Mike Gardiner from Sarnia, Ontario, pitched his first game in the majors for the enemy Boston Red Sox against ex–Blue Jay Jose Mesa of the Orioles. Can't tell you much because the Jumbotron didn't tell us too much about the game, and the out-of-town scoreboard kept flipping too quickly. This is one of those nights when the Jumbotron is misused once again, not immediately showing Alomar's great play but, because it ended an inning, going straight to an advertisement instead. They've got to do better. Meanwhile, I'll call it —

◇ The 2/3-tron

The Jumbotron should, in my view, be called the 2/3-tron. Much was made of its being the largest screen of its type in the world, by far the largest in a sports facility. When first we saw it, we were stunned by its size and its obvious potential. It would give phenomenal replays, it would dominate, it would be larger than life and it would add new dimensions to the game.

Only it didn't turn out that way. And here are some of the ways it might be used:

- Use all of it! I call it the 2/3-tron because we never see all of it. Someone, somewhere decided to sell off one-third of it to various advertisers. If they were going to do this, why didn't they save a ton of money by buying a smaller "tron" and selling advertising space immediately adjacent to it? We have seen replays only four or five times on the full screen. They were wonderful. The images were much larger. There was a bigger sense of the game and the field. It really was impressive.

  Come on, folks. We taxpayers paid a lot of money for a full screen, not a two-thirds screen. Sell that advertising space on a separate screen beside, above, below or near the 2/3-tron. I wouldn't even object to replacing between-inning "Bluepers" and "Highlights" and "Fan of the Game" silliness with full-board advertising messages. I don't know how much the SkyDome makes from selling this advertising, but personally I would pay a dollar more for a ticket (and if everyone felt this way, that's $4 million for a season) if that would compensate.

- Get a "stats freak" to run the board. Too often we see stats giving a batter's batting average with runners in scoring position when there are no runners on base. Or giving his stolen base percentage while he's at bat.

  There's so much that could be added to the game and to the knowledge of Toronto fans. Instead of using the 2/3-tron as a big baseball card with a bad picture of the batter and a meaningless statistic beside his face, why can't we have important information — his on-base average, his batting average over the last two weeks, his slugging percentage, his lifetime batting average, his strike-outs/walks ratio, his batting average against left-handed and/or right-handed pitchers, his sacrifice bunts? This kind of information tells the fan what's going through the pitcher's (and the manager's) mind. It would let the fans know that this particular batter is on a hitting streak, or that he strikes out a lot, or that he's a patient batter.

Similarly, it would be great if the batting order of the team at bat were on the screen, giving fans a sense of batters due up.

- We know that some replays can't be shown on the screen. American League rules protect their umpires from the scrutiny that referees, judges, politicians, business people and all other mortals face daily. There's no chance we're going to convince Fay (We're Perfect) Vincent to change that. But why can't we automatically see replays of every other play? Now, the 2/3-tron robot decides maybe eight or ten times a game to show us a replay. Why can't we see all of them? There's a lot of time between batters and pitches to show them to us and, yes, on the entire screen.
- One little portion of the 2/3-tron could be reserved for showing us the bullpen when pitchers are warming up.
- The fans at home get a lot more information than we get. For example, when a player leaves the game with an injury, we're never told what happened. Was he seriously injured? Was he injured at all? Was he taken to the hospital? Was he removed as a precautionary measure? When a pitcher has been taken out of the game, we do see his stats, but the 2/3-tron could tell us more, such as how many pitches he threw. For that matter, the 2/3-tron could tell us how many pitches each pitcher has thrown at the end of every inning. When a pitcher has been taken out of the game, we'd like to know how many of his pitches were strikes.

There are lots more examples. Think of how much Buck Martinez, Tommy Hutton and even Jack Buck and the Americans tell us when you watch the game or listen to Tom and Jerry on radio. That's why so many fans take their transistor radios and listen to the game at the park. Come on. Let's have that information on the tron.

- Often during ball games, there are other important sporting events going on. Why wouldn't someone arrange for clips to be put on the tron?

For that matter, instead of telling us that Jack Clark has just hit another three-run home run or Cecil Fielder another moon shot, or that Nolan Ryan is carrying another no-hitter into the ninth (God willing), how about showing us those highlights between innings? Again, the fans at home get to see a lot of these, and the SkyDome and Dome Productions have the same information and equipment and can provide it to us. Think of how much that would add to the SkyDome experience.

- Out-of-town scores. The Blue Jays are trying hard this year to improve the out-of-town scoreboard. If they don't give in and build sufficient additional space to have permanent information on all out-of-town scores, at least provide these between innings or between at bats using the full Jumbotron. This would allow us to know when to look instead of having to glance continually away from the ball game to try to catch the Red Sox' or Tigers' score.
- The "Bluepers." Fans are "entertained" by showing bloopers between innings. These invariably are tapes of players bumping into each other, misplaying routine ground balls, running into walls or otherwise embarrassing or injuring themselves while trying to earn a living and play all-out baseball. The worst, and the favourite of the operator and of too many fans, is, of course, the baseball hitting the ball player or the umpire in the groin. This is a staple, and some of the very same shots have been put up now for two years. Just in case the fans don't laugh hard enough, someone has edited into the tape a clip of ball players in the dugout laughing hysterically. There's no evidence that these ballplayers were laughing at the ball-in-the-groin incident in question, and, in fact, I would guess they were not. An all-time low has been reached this year, with these baseball-in-the-groin shots "complemented" by a video of Chris Sabo sitting in the Cincinnati dugout doing up his fly with some difficulty. Wouldn't you like to have someone videotape you trying to do up your fly and then show it nightly in front of 50,000 fans? This is demeaning to the players and to the game.

Why not use the same time on the tron to show the *best* plays, not the *worst* plays? To show the most skilled of athletes making the most sensational of plays? Every single night the sports telecasts show at least half-a-dozen and even a dozen superplays. A collage of those would be far more enjoyable, far more appropriate and far classier. I have more faith in Toronto fans than does the 2/3-tron operator. I think they would enjoy highlights much more than lowlights.

The Jumbotron has the potential to be a magnificent tool. It can raise the level of the game and enhance the reputation of Toronto and the SkyDome. Come on. Let's do it right.

◇ Post-Game Notes

I'll always like Mark Langston and always feel sorry for him since the game at Exhibition Stadium a couple of years ago when he took a no-hitter into the ninth, only to lose the no-hitter, the shutout and the game. But I like him because, during that game, instead of becoming solitary, lonely, mysterious, suspicious and moody, he was animated and lively as he came off the mound in the later innings. After his teammates made a couple of good plays behind him, he shook their hands, laughed and thanked them. He looks like a real good teammate to have, and I almost wanted him to get the no-hitter that day ... almost.

◆ ◆ ◆

Meanwhile, Dave Stieb missed his last start because of tendinitis. With injuries to Gruber and Henke, if Stieb truly develops some serious shoulder or tendinitis problems, it will be really serious for us. Tomorrow's game will be important as we see just how well Stieb can do.

Alomar scared the hell out of me when he stole third in the first inning and hurt his hand or finger. If the list were to become Henke, Gruber, Stieb and Alomar, we'd be lucky to end fourth. Why does Alomar take these chances? He's sensational to watch, but the Rickey Henderson, head-first, hands-first slides are far too dangerous. I'd rather have Alomar steal five fewer bases than put his fingers at, near, beside or, God forbid, under the third baseman's spikes.

Here's what worries me. Henke was warming up to come in in the eighth last night, but Gaston decided to let Wells finish. I thought Wells was going decently enough and wouldn't have pulled him either, but Cito's reasoning scares me. He said, "I thought he deserved the chance to complete the game." This is a team game. Who gets the win doesn't matter, as long as the team gets the win. I think LaRussa would take out a pitcher who is throwing a no-hitter if he had walked the bases loaded in the eighth inning. But Cito is too concerned with helping his pitchers get "Ws." If Cito wants the team to play hard, he's got to manage hard.

I'm glad Henke is back, but I must admit that I'd just as soon stick with Ward for the time being. He's hot and throwing great. If we need him tomorrow, let's go with Ward.

◆ ◆ ◆

Sojo and Felix for Devon White? White goes 2–4 with a home run and two RBIs. Sojo and Felix combined go 1–7 with Felix striking out three times. Sojo is batting .218, Felix is batting .265, and White is batting .282 and gobbling everything in the air between the foul lines (or so it seems).

◆ ◆ ◆

The California Angels' dugout — once presided over by Gene Mauch, manager of my beloved Philadelphia Phillies, who blew a seven-game lead in 1964 with eight games to go but who remains one of the great managers — is now presided over by Doug Rader. He will not be presiding over the dugout next year and probably not by the end of this year. He is responsible for Devon White being in Toronto. He couldn't get along with him. He's not patient with rookies, and the tension he emits is evident throughout the dugout.

◆ ◆ ◆

Meanwhile, the Blue Jays still seem unfamiliar with one another. But they're clearly on their way to putting the pieces together. It feels like it's going to be right. No tension. No conflicts. And a bunch of players who seem to be willing to put the team ahead of themselves.

When this chemistry clicks, it could be good.

Nooners and Neophytes

Monday, June 24, 1991			12:35 PM		Toronto SkyDome		
Pre-Game Standings							
	W	L	Pct.	GB	Ho.	Strk.	P10	Div.
TORONTO	38	31	.551	-	21-14	W-4	6-4	22-16
Boston	36	31	.537	1	22-14	L-1	6-4	11-14
Detroit	32	35	.478	5	18-13	L-1	5-5	12-14
Final Score: Blue Jays 4, Indians 3					Attendance: 50,263			

12:12 P.M. THERE'S NOTHING BETTER THAN A NOONER.

The prototypical fan is a Wrigley Field bleacherite, sun-soaked in the afternoon. Wrigley, before it put in those *Bonfire of the Vanities* lights, had only day games for a sport that was, of course, meant to be played in the daytime. Today, and a Monday at that, it's a fan's doubleheader — you get to sit in the sun, enjoy a ball game and, at the same time, feel like you're playing hookey.

So here we go. It's 12:28 P.M. Jimmy Key is going against Nagy. Any baseball historian will tell you that Cleveland may be at the bottom and the Blue Jays at the top, but the odds of sweeping any team, in any league, at any time, are not great. Still, we do have Key going today.

Over the years, the Jays have had trouble with Milwaukee, with the Tigers in key series in Detroit, and with the absolute dogs. We have always seemed to let down against the slum dwellers. We have beaten the Detroit hex lately, but we've now blown two home series against the Orioles and the Yankees — losing four out of six. The dogs still hound us. The Indians have been the exception — we've managed to beat them easily and often.

As we head down the stretch to the All-Star break, it's important to regain our momentum by bouncing back after the two losing series at home.

Today's paper confirms that the Blue Jays are in first place in the win column, but only tied for first in the loss column. As always, the loss column is the one that counts. Our one-game lead comes from having played two more games and won them both, something the Red Sox are eminently capable of doing. Just watch.

◇ The Game

The Blue Jays jump out quickly to a 2–0 lead, which, if Olerud hadn't been batting fifth with his usual .218 batting average, could easily have been 4–0 or 5–0. Key has good stuff, but not great.

Lots of deep fly balls to the warning track. Devon White pulls them in so effortlessly, he makes it *appear* Key is pitching better than he is. In fact, he is being taken deep too often and too early. All is okay until two out in the fifth, when poor Ed Sprague makes yet another error — his second of the game. Talk about streaks. The kid comes up, makes some incredible plays at third and bats .440 for a few weeks. Gruber returns Sprague to the bench, and the kid cools off. He must have made half-a-dozen errors in the last few starts he's had. I haven't checked the stats, but I wouldn't be surprised to find out he's booted 30 percent of all the balls hit to him the past four or five days. Anyway, there are two out in the fifth when he throws away an easy, routine ground ball that should have beaten the runner by ten feet. He one-hops it to Olerud, who doesn't bail out his infielders often enough. Clear error to Sprague, but avoidable by Olerud.

Fast forward to the end of the inning, when, a couple of hits later, it's 3–2. At the end of a half-inning like that, it's vital that the team clinging to a one-run lead come back with a quick run, just to break the momentum. It's the way Oakland always breaks your heart. But the Blue Jays go down quickly in the bottom of the fifth. Sprague, the number-two batter in the inning, takes a called third strike.

Interestingly, as Jimmy Key gets to the Blue Jays' dugout after the half-inning, he throws his glove onto the bench. He is angry, a quality quite out of character for him. Key grabs a towel and heads to the other end of the dugout and into the locker room. Hard to say from this distance what it was, whether it was the kid's error or Cito indicating that he was going to replace him with Ward. Key's strength has always been consistency and control, especially self-control ... none of which he's had today.

Meanwhile, a Cleveland runner tries to stretch a single into a double and is thrown out at second base. The next inning, Mookie Wilson singles and makes it a double on a close play at second. He looked out to us, but the ump called him safe. Not to worry, the ump will give it back later. John McNamara, the hard-bitten and usually unpleasant Cleveland manager, is standing at our end of the dugout and throws his hand in the air. We yell, "he was out, John." But a moment later McNamara turns around and invites us to "—off." Nice touch, John. Helps us understand why your dugout is such a happy place.

Maybe they should have kept Albert Belle and sent you to the minors.

The Blue Jays push a run across later in typical Alomar fashion. White opens the inning with a double, and, with the Indians expecting a sacrifice bunt, Alomar strokes a ground ball to the right side, thus moving White to third.

BOXSCORE

Blue Jays...4
Indians..3

CLEVELAND	AB	R	H	BI	TORONTO	AB	R	H	BI
Huff cf	3	1	0	0	DWhite cf	4	2	2	0
Cole cf	2	0	1	0	RAlomar 2b	4	1	2	0
Browne lf	4	1	3	0	JoCarter rf	2	1	1	1
James rf	4	0	2	2	Mllniks dh	3	0	2	1
SAlomar dh	4	0	0	0	Tabler ph	0	0	0	1
Baerga 3b	4	1	2	0	Olerud 1b	3	0	0	1
Jacoby 1b	4	0	1	0	GMyers c	2	0	0	0
Manto c	3	0	1	1	GHill pr	0	0	0	0
Aldrete ph	1	0	0	0	Borders c	1	0	0	0
Skinner c	0	0	0	0	Sprague 3b	3	0	0	0
Fermin ss	4	0	1	0	RGonzls 3b	1	0	0	0
MLewis 2b	4	0	0	0	MnLee ss	3	0	0	0
					MWilson lf	3	0	2	0
Totals	37	3	11	3	Totals	29	4	9	4

Cleveland   000 021 000 - 3
Toronto   201 000 10x - 4

E - RAlomar, Sprague. DP - Toronto 1. LOB - Cleveland 7, Toronto 7. 2B - Wilson 2, Carter, James, RAlomar, Baerga, White. SB - RAlomar 2 (22). CS - GHill. SF - Carter, Olerud, Tabler.

	IP	H	R	ER	BB	SO
Cleveland						
Nagy (L, 3-8)	8 1/3	9	4	4	3	5
Orosco	2/3	0	0	0	0	0
York	1	0	0	0	0	1
Toronto						
Key	6	9	3	1	0	3
Ward (W, 1-3)	2	1	0	0	0	3
Henke (S, 12)	1	1	0	0	0	0

SO - Cleveland: Huff, SAlomar, Manto, Cole, James, Baerga. Toronto: Myers, Carter, Sprague 2, White, Borders.

For the second time in two days, this takes the bat out of Carter's hands but does get White to third with one out. Carter is going to be walked intentionally. Rance Mulliniks goes out for a pinch hitter, Pat Tabler, who is in the world's worst slump. But Tabler quickly lofts a deep fly ball to left field — a sac fly — which brings White in easily from third. It's all we need.

Ward and Henke follow. It's April in June for Duane Ward. He fools a bunch of batters and switches the momentum back to the Blue Jays.

Henke mops up in the ninth, ending the game by picking off Alex Cole, whom he had allowed to get a single.

◇ Neophytes

Ed Sprague — rookie — has been in the lineup for the past few days. One frustrating thing about this organization. Other teams bring up raw rookies and have great success with them. Chris Sabo (Cincinnati) was one; Mark McGwire (Oakland), another; Gant and Justice of the Braves; Kevin Maas last year for the Yankees.

Sprague batted .400 early and is still batting .311. Today he has fifteen RBIs while John Olerud, who has played much more, has only twenty-three. Olerud still gets played every day, but Sprague is put back on the bench when Kelly Gruber came back unexpectedly from the DL. (Feeling the heat, Kelly?) Sprague did not even pinch hit for almost a week. This guy shows a lot of potential. He's got a hot bat. Why sit him down? Why cool him off? Why not just see how long he can go? Sprague should be at first base.

While Olerud gets every chance in the world, the Blue Jays have Whiten, Hill and Sprague — three young future stars — sitting and sitting and sitting. If they're not going to play them, let them go back and learn how to play the game better (as Sprague already has in the minors).

Sprague shows the importance of getting minor-league experience. Olerud, who has none, is uncertain in the field. When he fields a ground ball and the pitcher is going to first, he almost always hesitates to decide whether he's going to run to first or throw it to the pitcher covering. He's tentative on ground balls and tentative about positioning. He simply looks awkward.

Sprague, on the other hand, always looks confident, controlled and professional, even when he has a bad at bat. Sprague's minor-league hitting stats were not sensational, about .210 in Class A and .240 in AAA, but he seems to have an inner confidence. He was clearly learning the game, growing and maturing. For some reason, the Blue Jays won't give Olerud that chance to grow up in the minors. He's growing up the hard way, and I don't think it's going well at all. It reminds me, so far, of the Toronto Maple Leafs, who used to draft hundreds of defencemen from Belleville. They'd take the Boimstrucks, McGills and Bennings and then throw them in without conditioning, coaching, training or minor-league experience until they had blown all their confidence and had their careers prematurely ended.

I don't think that will happen to Olerud, but neither do I think he will be as big a star as he might otherwise be. He should have had the benefit of life in the minors.

The irony, of course, is that the one who's had that sort of learning experience is *not* being allowed to play and the one who is short of it is being required to play.

The organization believes in planning for tomorrow. A laudable goal. But do it in the farm system, not in the SkyDome.

Cito goes with players early in the year to build up their confidence. He seems to forget that April games are just as important as September games. He'll leave Olerud in because he doesn't want to put pressure on him. He'll go with Acker and Ward when they're going through terrible streaks, and, heaven help us, when Kenny Williams was here, he played him too much ahead of real major leaguers like Hill and Whiten.

Tony LaRussa (whose team is struggling right now) has it right. He has every one of his ball players attuned to the fact that there is nothing personal about changing players. His players all understand that every game has to be won every day with the best lineup possible. That's why he's been able to keep his team at or near the top through a bad spate of injuries. He manages aggressively and smartly. Cito manages conservatively and for tomorrow. But if you don't win the game today, tomorrow doesn't count.

◆ A BASEBALL ADDICT'S DIARY

◇ Post-Game Notes

Later in the game, I was stuck with a warm, tasteless SkyDome hot dog and a diet Coke. $6.03, please. Two weeks I ago I was at Buffalo's Pilot Stadium — a dream field — where the food court not only has variety, but some of the items are really good. Imagine, you can get everything from submarine sandwiches to Italian sausages to barbecued beef, cheese steaks, egg rolls, clams, corn on the cob, turkey dogs and chicken sandwiches. We tested it, and it was good. Trust me. Not only that, I was able to buy a grilled salami with cheese sandwich, an Italian sausage, two orders of fries, a loganberry drink and two diet Cokes for about $11.00. The real *smells* of the foods wafting through the downstairs concourse were terrific

◆ ◆ ◆

I was eager to see how today's papers would treat yesterday's Blue Jays game. Would they highlight Alomar's acrobatics and heroics? They didn't. They concentrated instead on Bob MacDonald's excellent outing. MacDonald's post-game interview yesterday gave some hope that he has the maturity to pitch in the bigs. He said he knew there would be days he wouldn't pitch this well, and then, bless him, when he used a cliché, he acknowledged it. He said, "*As we always say*, I just went out there trying to do my best and throw strikes."

Duane Ward can be one of the hottest pitchers in the league, but, as soon as he has one bad outing, he loses confidence. That's what happened Friday night against the Indians. He came into a laugher (8–4) and walked three out of the first four batters, bringing the tying run to the plate in the ninth inning. He has had a series of bad outings, and it may be another season of good Ward streaks and bad Ward streaks. Must be nerve-wracking even on a no-nerve manager like Cito, because you don't know which Duane Ward is sitting in the bullpen waiting to come out. Indeed, Duane Ward doesn't know.

◆ ◆ ◆

Some nice touches: Jerry Browne, banjo hitter but always a good guy to have around, has a two-for-three day. In the eighth inning, Carter, coming in from right field, arranges to arrive at the same spot as Browne coming out of the Indian dugout. Joe stops to tap him on the backside and have a chat.

Not so nice touch: Middle of the eighth inning, the scoreboard flashes the announcement that Joe Carter has been named American League Player of the Week. And so he should be! But why not *announce* it? So few fans saw it that there wasn't much applause. He deserved more. Carter stood in right field, not seeming to know what the very modest fuss was all about. Our stadium is known as the quietest emporium this side of Mirabel Airport. Exciting and chauvinistic opportunities such as "our Joe" being player of the week should not be missed. They should be seized aggressively and trumpeted.

◆ ◆ ◆

I give up. Gonzales made some great plays when he replaced Sprague at third late yesterday. And Sprague was terrible in the field today. I've changed my mind, Cito. You were right on this one. But, since you have Mulliniks on the bench, when you bring in Gonzales to replace Sprague and Gonzales comes up in a key situation in the eighth or ninth inning, we could send in Rance to pinch hit for him.

◆ ◆ ◆

It's 3:35 P.M. I'm still in the car, in the basement of my office, where I'll be changing from my shorts back into my trousers. Then it's a conference call set up to discuss our application for a Niagara Falls Class-A baseball franchise. (My son Robbie thinks they should be called the Banana Muffins.) Then a call to my starting pitcher for our own softball game tonight. And then deal with two pending crises and a presentation for clients. Way to ruin a great day.

◆ ◆ ◆

Final note. There was no one within a radius of two hundred seats I'd ever seen before. Were these all tourists who didn't have to work? Seems to me in Wrigley Field the truancy rate is a lot higher.

Knucklers and Faded Fastballs

Thursday, July 11, 1991			7:35 PM		Toronto SkyDome		
Pre-Game Standings							
	W	L	Pct.	GB	Ho.	Strk.	P10	Div.
TORONTO	49	34	.590	-	27-16	W-3	8-2	24-16
Boston	42	38	.525	5 1/2	24-19	L-1	6-4	17-21
Detroit	41	40	.506	7	23-15	W-1	7-3	20-19
Final Score: Blue Jays 2, Rangers 0					Attendance: 50,276		

B**ACK TO THE REAL WORLD.** The All-Star Game is over. Now comes that part of the season referred to as "the dog days." The games are slower and played more carefully. The fans (and players) are just a little bit more tense, and the players are melding into a "team."

Players generally are becoming familiar with their batting orders, with their teammates' quirks, with the rhythm of their games. They are settling into the stage where they have a mystical ability to sense when, say, Mark McGwire, in a huge hitting slump, is going to tank one out of the park. Or where a banjo hitter, say Jeff Huson, is going to get a key double. Or, on the other hand, when Jack Clark is going to pop out with a runner on third. They're sensing which relief pitchers are having "unconscious" years. The players know now that Angel Mark Eichhorn, a Blue Jays cast-off, hasn't walked a batter yet (unbelievable). That Duane Ward is in a great groove, similar to the one he was in in April and May. That Nolan Ryan is going to either throw a ten strikeout, low-hit game or lose. And they know the Expos are dispirited, the White Sox are without last year's chemistry and that Mark Langston is having a great year.

I think, too, they're sensing that Clemens is not unbeatable. And this is important. Whether he is or not, teams are now going to Boston with a different attitude, not conceding one game right off the top. This outlook entirely changes the confidence of a team going into a three- or four-game series against the Sox.

Yes, after the All-Star break everything, suddenly, is serious. The contrast is even sharper in Toronto this year, after the All-Star festival and the happy, jocular, casual atmosphere. Tonight, it's back to work. The boys mean business, and the boys have confidence. Even Cito in the pre-game show tonight sounded different. They're on a roll right now, and it doesn't look like the kind of artificial roll that Texas, Seattle or Minnesota had.

But who knows what I'll be writing three weeks from now.

◇ The Game

Before the Blue Jays take the field, Joe Carter walks through the Blue Jays' dugout, shaking hands and patting every player on the shoulder, cheering them on to start the second half of the season. Everyone seems to enjoy this warm encouragement, and, from Carter, it is genuine. As they come out on the field, the players look calmly confident as opposed to nervously edgy. They don't seem cocky; there's no Oakland swagger. It's more like the old New York Yankees certainty.

Texas — currently at the top of the AL West — is in for four. Poor Julio Franco's at second base, one of the best players in the game and selected to back up Alomar at the All-Star Game. He came in second in the voting, but way behind Robbie. Franco was unfortunate enough or foolish enough to indicate that he was the better ball player and should have been the All-Star second baseman. Needless to say, the Toronto fans booed him constantly and loudly during introductions at the All-Star Game, and his lack of good sportsmanship was criticized by the media across North America.

Tony LaRussa did not put Franco into the All-Star Game on Tuesday night. LaRussa hasn't said why, but Alomar was the only starter on both teams to go the whole nine. LaRussa couldn't simply have overlooked him, and there's just no excuse for this. Was

LaRussa trying to teach Franco a lesson? It clearly isn't fair to invite someone to the game, a front-line player, and not even allow him one at bat.

As luck would have it for Franco, his team is in town, so the Toronto fans have the whole nine innings to boo him — which they do, every time he touches the ball or comes to bat.

Candiotti starts. Although he is now 1–1 since he joined us after the gutsy trade with Cleveland that involved Hill and Whiten, he hasn't had a real game in a groove. And it looks bad again as the first two batters single. He then gets the heart of the lineup out on infield tappers and pop ups. He gives up only two more hits through the eighth inning, striking out ten and giving up no runs.

Kevin Brown, an inconsistent hurler, is pitching for the Rangers and chooses tonight to pitch to his potential. The book on Brown is that he's hard to hit the first time through the lineup, but, second time around, the teams tend to get his measure and hit him all over the park.

The Blue Jays eventually start to put men on base, but they can't bring them home. They have five or six hits before they put up a run. This better not become a habit! Finally we get a run on a Myers double followed by Olerud's single. Olerud goes three for four tonight to get his batting average way up to .240. If Olerud actually starts to hit, and if Devo, Robbie and Joe continue, this team will be out of sight.

An indication of why this could be *the year* occurs in the bottom of the eighth inning. The game's been scoreless into the seventh, when Olly knocks in a run. Then, with two out in the eighth, one of those incredible godsends occurs. Mulliniks hits a short fly ball to left field. For the Texas Rangers that spot used to be home of Pete (Cement Hands) Incaviglia. Canadian Kevin Reimer is the new left fielder, and he decides to play the ball like Inky used to, by letting it fall just in front of his glove as he tries to sprint in and catch it. He overruns it, and it goes through his legs *all the way to the fence*. Poor Rance sees this as he heads to second and he gasps for breath, knowing he'll be sent to third. He looks like "the little engine that could" as he hits third, only to see the horrifying sight of Rich Hacker waving him home! Rance rolls his eyes skywards, prays to St Jude and pushes his spikes along to home plate. He's safe … and alive.

When your team is not on a roll, and when it's not going to win the pennant, and when God hasn't decreed it or divined it, Reimer catches Rance's fly ball. The previous inning, Mookie took off at the crack of the bat from straightaway left and successfully snow-coned a deep fly ball on the warning track in left centre. In other years, he narrowly missed it — or George Bell missed it by a mile. The gods put that one *in* Mookie's glove and put Mulliniks's fly ball *under* Reimer's glove. This has got to be the year.

Gruber is back in the lineup. He can't swing the bat, going zero for four. I think there were too many articles written about his dogging it. He's coming back before he's ready. More careers than one have been ruined that way. And he could be a liability at third. We'll see what the next three or four days bring. Right now, Kelly's batting is abysmal.

We speculate that Pat Gillick has had a talk with Cito during the All-Star break. It is not the Blue Jays' style to interfere with their manager. Management runs the Blue Jays like a corporation: hire your people and then let them do their job. Not exactly the Harold Ballard school. But Cito is managing differently tonight. In the seventh inning, when Myers gets a key double, Cito brings in Derek Bell to pinch run. When Olerud hits that single to right field, it's to Ruben Sierra, one of the best arms in the game. Sierra charges it and unloads to the plate. Few Blue Jays would have made it, but Bell does, getting in just under the tag. Credit Cito … or Pat … with the key run.

BOXSCORE

Blue Jays..2
Rangers..0

TEXAS	AB	R	H	BI	TORONTO	AB	R	H	BI
Dwning dh	4	0	1	0	White cf	4	0	0	0
Plmero 1b	4	0	3	0	RAlmr 2b	4	0	0	0
Sierra rf	4	0	0	0	Carter rf	3	0	1	0
Franco 2b	4	0	0	0	Gruber 3b	4	0	0	0
Reimer lf	4	0	0	0	Mllniks dh	4	1	1	1
Gonzalz cf	4	0	0	0	Myers c	3	0	1	0
Bechele 3b	2	0	0	0	DBell pr	0	1	0	0
IRdrgz c	3	0	1	0	Brders c	1	0	1	0
Huson ss	2	0	0	0	Olerud 1b	4	0	3	1
Stnley ph	1	0	0	0	MnLee ss	3	0	0	0
MDiaz ss	0	0	0	0	MWlsn lf	3	0	2	0
					Ducey lf	0	0	0	0
Totals	32	0	5	0	Totals	33	2	9	2

Texas	000	000	000	- 0
Toronto	000	000	11x	- 2

E - Franco (12). LOB - Texas 6, Toronto 8. 2B - Palmeiro (26), IRodriguez (5), Myers (18), Borders (7), Olerud (10). HR - Mulliniks (2).

	IP	H	R	ER	BB	SO
Texas						
KBrown (L, 7-7)	7 2/3	9	2	2	0	6
Rogers	1/3	0	0	0	0	1
Toronto						
Candiotti (W, 9-7)	8	5	0	0	0	10
Henke (S, 17)	1	0	0	0	0	1

HBP - by KBrown (Carter), by Candiotti (Buechele). WP - KBrown.

In the first part of the year, Cito, for defensive reasons, absolutely refused to pull Mookie Wilson in the late innings. Mookie's arm is weaker than Jerry Zeidel's, my B'nai Brith second baseman. But incredibly, tonight Cito stuns us by putting in Rob Ducey in the ninth inning. Exactly right, Cito. Glad to see you playing for keeps. That's worth another two games the rest of the year.

Candiotti goes eight, Henke comes in for the ninth. Interesting to note that the Terminator has only eighteen strikeouts in twenty-one innings. That would be pretty good for most pitchers, but not for Henke. He usually has more strikeouts than innings pitched. The fact that he is falling behind that pace indicates his fastball's probably slowing and he's going a little bit on reputation and a little bit on his slider and forkball.

◇ Our Very Own Knuckleballer

Candiotti's performance was better even than it looks on paper. The batters were mostly missing the knuckler by six to twelve inches. Candiotti was mixing it up well, both speed and location. It was simply a great pitching performance by Candi. We began to see tonight why his earned run average is among the lowest in the league. It was no contest.

The knuckler is a baseball oddity. It is a pitch that relies on the wind, friction and fluff rather than on strength, control or guile. All other pitches spin on their axis as they travel the 0.4 seconds between the pitcher's hand and the batter's bat. Superb hitters can actually "read" the pitch by picking up the spin on the 108 red stitches on the Haitian ball (rubbed, I might add, in New Jersey soil). Why is a pitcher with a great curve — say, Bert Blyleven — not unhittable? Because, after a few innings, indeed after a few years, major-league hitters adjust to the size and angle of the curve.

A screwball spins in the opposite direction to a curve, and a slider spins horizontally rather than vertically. Don't ask me how a hitter picks all this up, but he does. Once he sees the spin, his instincts — his built-in book of experience — tells him what route the ball is likely to follow to the catcher's mitt.

Then there is the knuckler. It has its own mind. It goes where it and the wind and other elements want it to go. It's a real tough pitch to throw. The pitcher must bend his fingers at the knuckles and grasp the ball, not with the knuckles, but with the fingernails. Then, just at the moment of release, all fingers and the thumb must thrust forward towards the plate at exactly the same time so that there is absolutely no spin on the ball. Those 108 raised stitches create friction against the air, wind and humidity, causing the ball to follow an irregular and unpredictable path to the plate. Does the batter know where the pitch is going to go? No. Does the pitcher? No. Does the catcher? No. Does the umpire? No. Not a chance. Does it matter?

Till we had one, I hated knuckleballers and the knuckleball. I've watched Hoyt Wilhelm, Charlie Hough and the Niekros for years. They're all annoying. Like Hough, they all seem to be old, with wide waists and sloppy uniforms. They seem to need a taxi to get to the mound and find it impossible to work up a sweat. They remind me more of a shell game carney than an athlete. They trick the ball past you. The catchers need to use oversized mitts and even then they miss two or three times an inning. Base-stealing is easy because the ball takes such a long, slow journey to the plate. (I expect one day to see Cecil Fielder try to steal on Hough or Candiotti.) And, of course, there are plenty of walks and some dropped third strikes. It changes the style of play, the tradition of play and "purity."

Oh, yes. I do know that a knuckler, like the curve, the smoker, the screwball and the split-finger is just a different way to trick the batter, but somehow the knuckler floating in, dipsy-doodling, dropping and rising, just ain't fair. I swear it's nerf ball, not baseball.

But now that we do indeed have our very own knuckleballer, I've had a chance to study the knuckler carefully. While it is still a nerf, I like it. Candiotti is different, too. He looks like an athlete. He is younger — 33. He has some other pitches, including a fastball and a curve, to keep the batters off balance. Most other knuckleballers throw the knuckler exclusively.

Still, even our own knuckler does something to the rhythm of the game. It will be an awkward, unpredictable game. A Candiotti game is a far cry from a Stieb game or a Key game. But it can, I admit, be as effective. Or, dare I say it, it can be even more than that.

I always did love knuckleballers.

◇ Post-Game Notes

Sparky Anderson is the All-Star bafflegabber. At the All-Star Game he gave a typical sermon on the infallibility of the Blue Jays. It was his usual bluff, blarney and bullfeathers. He is saying it to take the pressure off his own team and to take the edge off our team. He never says anything that isn't partly strategic, partly tactical and partly red herring. Sparky assures everyone that the Jays can't be caught by anyone … especially his team.

◆ ◆ ◆

More about "rolls." I don't quite know how to describe the difference between the rolls. There's just something about this one that seems comfortable. One sometimes senses that a team doesn't know how much longer it can tiptoe down the streak. The Blue Jays seem to know that they control the winning streak (thirteen of the last sixteen), and that means the streak will be longer. When they lose a game they take it in stride. It's more like an accident than the end of the roll.

And tonight's crowd *expects* the team to win. It's a quiet confidence. Same as the team's.

◆ ◆ ◆

Meanwhile, in the Texas dugout, Bob Valentine is doing his number. He is known to be a firecracker. Explosive, intense and opinionated. He knows his own volatility and tries to control his emotions to such an extent that he spends most of the game walking up and down the dugout (imagine that, Cito), talking to his players, sometimes bouncing a ball, but always trying to smile and chew gum. I think he makes his players feel good, yet they're aware he's an intense guy underneath. Probably a pretty good mixture.

Texas looks serious in the dugout. Indeed, when my daughter tries to get backup outfielder and pinch baserunner Gary Pettis to give her a bat, he declines. When she tells him it's her birthday, he does ask how old she is and says to wait till after the game. Which we do, only to have him give us an autograph on an All-Star program. Sorry, Gary; not quite what we had in mind.

◆ ◆ ◆

After the game, which was well played and close, the umpires, as always, must go through the visiting team's dugout to get to their own dressing rooms. One of the umpires happens to be standing beside Valentine as they go down the stairs. Valentine fakes yelling at him as though it's his fault they lost. Valentine and the umpire both laugh as they go down the stairs. Well done, Bobby. You even looked like you're relaxed about the loss. He knows he's got to keep his team loose and not feeling any panic.

By the way, Bobby, you brought in Kenny Rogers to relieve Kevin Brown, and Rogers got out the one man he pitched to. But the stats, 6.99 earned run average, more walks than strikeouts — yikes.

◆ ◆ ◆

Boston is kind enough to blow a 2–0 lead to Minnesota and lose 7–3. The Blue Jays are up an incredible six-and-a-half. The Blue Jays are sixteen out of the last nineteen, and this is our big chance. Boston has a series of tough games for the next two weeks, while we have Texas (also tough) and then some dogs. If we can win three out of four here against Texas, we can bust this baby wide open. Give me nine or ten and it's a laugher. Call the fat lady.

Jays Ridin' High, Julio Ridin' Low

Friday, July 12, 1991   7:35 PM   Toronto SkyDome

Pre-Game Standings

	W	L	Pct.	GB	Ho.	Strk.	P10	Div.
TORONTO	50	34	.595	-	28-16	W-4	9-1	24-16
Boston	42	39	.519	6 1/2	24-19	L-2	5-5	17-21
Detroit	41	41	.500	8	23-16	L-1	6-4	20-19

Final Score: Blue Jays 6, Rangers 2   Attendance: 50,279

MY DAUGHTER MELISSA'S TWENTIETH BIRTHDAY. Fifty per cent of all second-year University of Western Ontario students are at our house to celebrate. It will, trust me, be noisier than the SkyDome. For her birthday, what more could I promise than the streak will continue.

Sorry, Julio. Even I may boo tonight. The *Globe and Mail* reports this morning, reprinting Pete Gammon's column in *Baseball America*, that Franco said "Toronto got rid of almost all their Latin players and said they had to for the chemistry as if the reason they didn't win was because they had too many Latins. I don't buy that and neither do Ruben Sierra, Juan Gonzalez or any of us." That doesn't make Tony LaRussa right in not playing you in the All-Star Game, Julio. It just makes us right in not cheering you. And, oh yes. The second baseman in the game, the one who whipped you in All-Star voting at second base, he's Latin American. So too, last time I looked, is our shortstop, Manuel Lee. And who is this pitcher who has thrown a whole bunch of shutout innings for us? Could his name be Guzman? Could he be Latin American, just like the Jose Guzman who's pitching for you tonight? Smarten up, Julio. You're good at playing second base; you aren't so good at some other things. I don't think you'll ever challenge Robbie Alomar for All-Star at second base, nor will you challenge Perez de Cuellar for secretary general of the United Nations.

As I walk by Rhodes restaurant, I see Terry Clark, entrepreneur, nice guy, extrovert, buddy of Roy McMurtry's, owner of a bunch of SkyDome boxes (he leases them out for a profit most years), sitting in the bar section with three of his buddies. The front window is wide open, as it always is during the summer, and Terry asks me how many games the Blue Jays are going to win by. I remind him there are about eighty games to go, and he shouldn't get carried away. One of his buddies is prepared to wager that the Jays will win by nine. With our five-and-a-half–game lead at the All-Star break, the mania has clearly settled over the city.

◇ The Game

The Blue Jays begin the game with their usual, new-found spark.

Devon White singles and, on the first pitch to Alomar, decides to take second base. He is testing the alleged cannon arm of the new Texas catcher, Ivan Rodriguez. Don't test it! Rodriguez guns him down easily. Rodriguez, by the way, is all of 19 years old. He's batting .365 in his first few weeks in the majors. You can bat .165 if you've got an arm like his. Wow!

The next time White is up, we see the kind of ballsy play that shows the confidence and desire vital to championship teams. White gets on base again in the third inning and immediately steals second — this time successfully. It is one of those in-your-face moves to tell the other team it's not going to get the upper hand. The odd thing is that, if White had been thrown out, it would have left Texas with that upper hand but still no sense of domination. But when White steals the base, it changes the momentum and lets the Rangers know that it's another night of aggressive, confident, station-to-station, winning baseball by the Blue Jays. I love it!

Into the second inning and Wells walks the second batter. The third batter, Steve Buechele, one of the weaker hitters in a tough lineup, takes the ball over the fence for a 2–0 lead.

The ball game slithers along with Jose Guzman of the Rangers putting lots of Blue Jays on base, but the Blue Jays are continuing their bad habit of leaving runners stranded. Carter strikes out three times by the fourth inning. The first time there was a runner on third; the second, with the sacks loaded, he looks at six pitches and swings at only one — strike three. Meanwhile, John Olerud, in his first two at bats, looks at nine pitches without swinging. Four of the first five are balls, but three of the last four are strikes. John, I know your batting average is improving and I know you're getting hits, but, last time I looked, the only way to continue getting hits is by swinging that piece of wood in your hand. The "sweet swing" has to be swung.

In any event, Guzman is in and out of trouble, but mostly out of it, and it's Texas 2–1 as we go to the seventh. It is beginning to look like this is one we might lose. Still, as we look at the out-of-town scoreboard, we don't feel we're out of it.

The board gives us hope, since Minnesota gets to Roger Clemens in the second inning to take a 2–0 lead. Then suddenly it's 2–2, 3–2, 4–2 Boston. We keep watching the board as we watch the SkyDome roof close. I guess Harold Hossein called in and reported that there was a sprinkle somewhere near Chatham, and so on this otherwise nice night, the roof starts to inch closed around the second inning, completing the crawl by 8:30. Just as the Blue Jays come to bat in the seventh inning, Minnesota finally ties it up at four.

The baseball gods are with us this year, and Alomar leads off our seventh with a stroke up the middle, which bounces off the pitcher's mound into centre field. Carter walks. Egad — what's this? — Olerud executes a perfect Alomar-like bunt. Our cleanup hitter not only is willing to bunt but also executes it perfectly, so the third baseman has to make the play and can't cover the bag. Carter and Alomar on second and third. Tabler is brought in to pinch hit for Mulliniks, and Kenny Rogers intentionally walks Tabler to load the bases and set up a double play.

Manager Bobby Valentine brings in the famous Goose Gossage to face Kelly Gruber. Gruber has been out, but not on the disabled list, with six different injuries to his right hand. After weeks of grumbling in the stands about his overly long "recovery," the media has begun to report on it obliquely over the last couple of days, with some references to his teammates' referring to him as "Mrs Gruber." (*They* said it, not me folks.) Gruber is feeling the heat and is in the starting lineup, although he's clearly not able to hit properly. He hasn't hit tonight and is up there now, facing the Goose and with the bases loaded in a key situation.

The Goose does what he usually does — pitch real hard and fast — but he is clearly working too quickly. He's not pausing between pitches and he seems to be out there playing quick pitch-and-catch with the 19-year-old catcher.

Surprisingly, Valentine does not come out to slow the Goose down. This is one of those instances where Carlton Fisk would make all the difference. Fisk would have popped up from behind the plate, stormed out to the mound and ordered his pitcher to slow down. Fisk would have moved so slowly between pitches and made so many "Al Widmar" trips back to the mound that Gossage couldn't have pitched quickly. The rookie catcher didn't. As a result, Gossage walks the half-crippled Gruber with the bases loaded. Tie game.

Now the right-handed Pat Borders is up facing Gossage, a right-handed pitcher. Notwithstanding our blandishments to Cito to bring in a left-handed pinch hitter (read Ducey), he lets Borders

BOXSCORE

Blue Jays..6
Rangers..2

TEXAS	AB	R	H	BI	TORONTO	AB	R	H	BI
Palmer lf	4	0	1	0	White cf	4	1	2	0
Pettis cf	0	0	0	0	RAlmr 2b	4	1	2	0
Plmero 1b	4	0	0	0	Carter rf	5	2	1	0
Sierra rf	3	0	0	0	Olerud 1b	3	0	2	0
Franco 2b	4	0	1	0	Mllniks dh	2	0	1	1
Gonzalz cf	3	1	0	0	Tabler dh	1	1	1	1
Dwning dh	4	0	0	0	Gruber 3b	4	1	0	1
Bechele 3b	4	1	2	2	Brders c	4	0	2	3
IRdrgz c	3	0	1	0	MnLee ss	3	0	1	0
MDiaz ss	3	0	0	0	Gnzles ss	0	0	0	0
					MWlsn lf	3	0	0	0
Totals	32	2	5	2	Totals	33	6	12	6

Texas   020 000 000 - 2
Toronto   001 000 41x - 6

DP - Texas 1. LOB - Texas 5, Toronto 12. 2B - Borders 2 (9). HR - Buechele (13). SB - White (20), MnLee (5). CS - White (5). S - Olerud.

	IP	H	R	ER	BB	SO
Texas						
JoGuzman (L, 4-4)	6	6	3	3	6	7
Rogers	1/3	0	1	1	1	0
Gossage	2/3	1	1	1	1	0
Jeffcoat	2/3	3	1	1	0	0
Rosenthal	1/3	0	0	0	0	0
Toronto						
Wells (W, 10-4)	7	5	2	2	2	3
DWard (S, 15)	2	0	0	0	0	3

JoGuzman pitched to 2 batters in the 7th.

hit. Borders, of course, is in a horrendous slump, batting about .225 with no home runs and five RBIs. Bases loaded, one out. The Goose throws ball one. Valentine comes out for a visit, finally. The Goose throws strike one. The Goose throws another strike. Borders, however, is looking for this fastball and drills it off the left-field fence for a double, clearing the bases and suddenly giving us a 5–2 lead. I *told* you not to pinch hit, Cito.

The boys in the middle, Carter, Tabler and Olerud, bunch a few singles in the eighth inning for another run. Ward pitches the eighth and ninth effectively. Six up, six down and 6–2 Blue Jays.

At almost exactly the same time, Minnesota puts up a fifth run to take a 5–4 lead, and Aguilera comes on in the ninth and strikes out two of the last three batters. Suddenly the Blue Jays are seven-and-a-half in front, having won seventeen of twenty and five in a row. Maybe Terry Clark's friend is right. 7 ½ !!! Heaven!!!

◇ Franco E-4

Lots of people in Toronto — in good, old, multicultural, liberal Toronto — have been mouthing the same line about the "Latins" as Julio Franco. The cocktail party and elevator chatter has focused on the "got rid of all the Latins" theme.

Now seatmates, law partners, friends and readers of this book all know that I do not think Paul Beeston and Pat Gillick and, more often, their managers are perfect. But I know Beeston and Gillick, and they are first-class. They haven't always been amused by my "Metro Morning" comments about Lloyd Moseby, Jimy Williams, Kenny Williams and Johnny Olerud, but they remain friends, they kid me about my comments and they accept the right of others to criticize and comment (at least I think they do). They also accept the fact that they are not infallible. Imagine! We in section 117, of course, are totally infallible, and the Blue Jays go out and hire a couple of guys who actually make mistakes. In any event, I'm not shy about disagreeing with Pat and Paul.

Indeed, that's part of the attraction of baseball. Given the pace at which it moves, we have a whole lot of time — not only between games but also during games, innings and even at bats — to second-guess or third-guess or fourth-guess the decisions that are made. For fans who are there to do more than buy a hot dog, admire the roof and laugh at goofy plays shown on the Jumbotron, part of the charm and allure of the game is that one can get involved. Most of the other major sports move too quickly, and the strategy isn't as obvious.

With baseball, however, you have lots of time to say, "Why is he letting Borders bat against Gossage?" "Why doesn't he go with a hot bat instead of worrying about batting right against right?" "Why isn't he sacrificing here?" "This guy takes too many pitches." "Why doesn't he have White stealing?" "He's got to bring in Henke to start the next inning." "Acker should be gone." Or, my own favourites: "Olerud needs to play in the minors." "Sprague needs more playing time." "The catchers have to block the plate." "Cito doesn't pinch hit enough." That's part of what makes it so much fun. It looks like a passive game, but it isn't. It's almost interactive because, although we can't actually pull the levers, we pretend we can and talk about how we would — during the game, after the game, and sometimes all winter.

All this is to say that I'm happy to take part in the century-old ritual of second-guessing management, even this first-class Blue Jays management (which in my view is the best and most successful in baseball).

As a sometime critic, do I accept what Franco says? Absolutely not. We are the only team to have a winning season every year since 1983. We have proven ourselves to be one of the best teams in major-league baseball, year after year, and we have won those games with players from several countries and of diverse cultural backgrounds. Among that mix have been a large number of superb Latin players. The Blue Jays have built their organization relying heavily on Epy Guerrero, their coordinator of Latin America player development and scouting, and his particular roots and reputation in the Dominican Republic. Some of their top players have been Latin American: Alfredo Griffin, Damaso Garcia, Tony Fernandez, Otto Velez, Luis Gomez, George Bell, Manuel Lee, Juan Berenguer, Jose Nunez, Juan Beniquez, Sil Campusano, Rico Carty, Junior Felix, Nelson Liriano, Freddy Manrique, Luis Sojo, Luis Leal, Victor Cruz and Hector Torres — to name just a few. Not all were front-liners, but they all made real contributions, and some of them were the heart of the team.

George Bell, of course, won the American League most valuable player award in 1987, as well as contributing some memorable single efforts, including one 7-RBI game and two 6-RBI games. The list of longest-game hitting streaks for the Blue Jays includes only two non-Latins: Bell twenty-two, Garcia, twenty-one, Moseby twenty-one, Garcia twenty, Griffin nineteen, Garcia eighteen, Fernandez eighteen, Mayberry seventeen, Garcia seventeen, Bell seventeen. Three Jays have hit three homers in a game. Two of them are Otto Velez and George Bell. Tony Fernandez has the highest single-season batting average for a Blue Jay (.322), and Garcia is tied for third, with .310. Look over almost every Blue Jays record, and you'll find a list replete with repetitions of Bell, Fernandez, Garcia, Griffin and other Latins.

Which brings us to the question of whether the Blue Jays are trying to end their reliance on Latins. Not a chance. Would you trade Fernandez (Dominican Republic) for Roberto Alomar (Puerto Rico)? You bet you would. You'd trade your rabbi for Alomar. Would you trade Felix and Sojo for Devon White? To this point in the season, it's no contest.

Was the dugout full of cliques? Sure it was, but was this the fault of the Latins? Was it unique to the Blue Jays? No and no. Who was the only player able to move comfortably among all the cliques? Answer: George Bell. Was he controversial? Yes. Did some players really have trouble with him? Yes. Did he have good close friends in every group? You bet he did. Would the Blue Jays have kept Bell if he would DH for a reasonable sum of money — say, a mere $2.5 million? I'm sure of it. Do they wish they had him instead of Tabler or Mulliniks down to DH for the last half of the season? You bet they do.

Are the Latins — God, I hate even to be writing this stupid generalization — unable to perform during pennant races? It is dumb, unfair, ignorant and intolerant of people to say so. As I write this, angrily, I'm obliged to fight on bad ground by categorizing people on the basis of race or nationality — something I've fought all my life. But maybe you have to do it. So I'll bite my tongue as I squeeze my pen and write the names of people like Perez and Martinez and Santiago and Carew and Cardenal and Campaneris and Rojas. And how about Clemente and Sanguillen and Concepcion? The list goes on. Many of these players have played on pennant-winning and championship teams, with lots of other Latins.

If there's a single franchise in baseball that can't be accused historically or today of playing colour, race or nationality games, it's the Toronto Blue Jays. Even as they trade away or lose some players from Latin America — players they were really fond of and would like to have today — they are scouting aggressively in those same parts of the world. They have scouts in the shortstop incubator of San Pedro de Macoris (Melvin Gomes), Santo Domingo (Ignacio Javier), Panama (Ramon Webster), as well as scouting supervisors based in Puerto Nuevo and Puerto Rico. The legendary Epy Guerrero continues his role. The Jays at this moment are planning to be among the first into Cuba to catch the wave of excellent players that will hit the States as soon as Castro discovers Khrushchev is dead. The Blue Jays also have a team in the Dominican summer league, the Santo Domingo Blue Jays. And I don't expect its purpose is to sell SkyDome tickets in the Dominican Republic.

I've seen lots of players who wanted to win and wanted to win badly. I've seen lots of players who would run through walls to catch a ball or break up a double play. But I haven't seen many who were more competitive or could do all of the above more willingly than George (Cause of "Bad Chemistry" on the Team) Bell. I could, but won't, list lots of disruptive and "bad chemistry" players throughout baseball who have not been "Latin." (Last time I looked, the single, most irritating element in the chemistry that was "bad" for the Blue Jays was Jimy Williams.)

The significant thing about the Latin ball players, to my mind, is how they got here. Go take a look at the New York–Penn League or the Eastern League or the South Atlantic League or the Pioneer League. Players in those leagues, regardless of their country of origin, are sent in their late teens to play for no money with teammates they've never met before, thousands of miles away from their families and friends. It's a lonely, bleak enough existence for an 18- or 19-year-old kid from New Jersey or New Mexico or even Los Angeles.

But imagine a little-educated, unilingual youngster who's never been out of the Dominican Republic and who finds himself suddenly — and sudden it is — playing in High Desert, Modesto, Salem, Hagerstown, Medicine Hat, Tacoma, Bristol, Batavia, Macon, Charleston, Savannah, Butte, Boise, Pulaski, Kenosha, Peoria or Cedar Rapids. These are not big multicultural communities. Many of them are monolithic, one-dimensional, English-speaking, white Anglo-Saxon Protestant. These kids are living in a new culture, with a total language barrier, if not an educational barrier, and rarely is there a major-league bilingual scout or coach attached to the team to help the youngster adjust. No, for the most part these Latin players have come up the tough way. The ones who make it have lots of determination. They need it to survive. They had far more pressure on them than their counterparts.

I may grumble at Manuel Lee when he swings at a third strike in the dirt, but I admire his courage and his dedication to the game. He and his colleagues fought their way up. Don't tell me these guys don't have heart, spirit, determination or a will to succeed. They do. And it's not *because* they're "Latin." Their spirit and determination come more from the cultural, language and distance factors that have made their climb so much tougher. They have been tested so much more than many of the other players, and they are real achievers.

Give me a kid who had to fight up the hard way through tough, hard discipline and dedication, whether he be a Pete Rose or a George Bell, and I'll take him a thousand times over a .400 hitter who was handed $1 million to sign directly out of some university in California.

◇ Post-Game Notes

More about Alomar and Franco. During a pitching change with Alomar on second, he and Franco chat like long lost buddies. Maybe we fans are the only ones mad at Franco. Robbie certainly isn't. The two of them stand, chat and laugh throughout the two long pitching changes.

◆ ◆ ◆

In its excellent nightly sports program, CNN announces: "It looks like a runaway in the American League East," as Boston falls seven-and-a-half behind.

◆ ◆ ◆

Nolan Ryan was walking through the dugout with a ball that was hit into it, and a couple of kids leaned over beside us, asking for the ball. Nolan, without a smile or a word, tossed the ball to the kid. I urged the kid to reject the ball unless he got an autograph. The ball is worth $8; a Ryan autograph on the ball is worth $70.

◆ ◆ ◆

The 2/3-tron. This is a big-time $7 million screen, seen by four million fans a year. Running a scoreboard simply is not complicated. You won't convince me it is. Yet today, we see the following on the tron:

- Carter's statistics are still on the board when Olerud is up batting fourth. Later, Devon White is up and Mookie Wilson's stats are showing.
- Between innings, the following sign appears: "Carter's home run sets a Blue Jay record for 4 home runs in 5 consecutive games." Huh? Carter hasn't hit a home run in the last two days. Did not hit a home run tonight. Was this left over from a previous wish, or does someone have a crystal ball? Why was it programmed into the computer? Why was that button pressed?
- Julio Franco is up in the eighth inning. The Jumbotron indicates a ground out, a fly out and a single to centre in his previous three at bats, which, in Jumbotronese, translates into "0 for 3" on the night. A single is a hit. Always has been, always will be.

Last night we were stunned to see that the new out-of-town scoreboard, which is still a rotating board requiring us to keep looking until it shows the Boston score, at least looked like a real major-league out-of-town scoreboard — it showed the uniform number of the pitcher currently on the mound for each of the out-of-town teams. When Rafe came by (if Cooperstown had a section for program sellers, he'd be in it), Sheldon and I decided to buy a program so we could identify the pitchers from their numbers. This is exactly the way it's done in every other major-league park in the United States and Canada (and probably Japan). Of course, when we get the program, we find that the numbers are not listed. All we know is that no. 47 is pitching for Boston against no. 26 for Minnesota. Come on, guys, can't we do it right? So tonight, we go back and find that this innovation is gone. The out-of-town pitchers' numbers are no longer shown on the board. It can't be *that* complicated. Every other park seems to know how to do it. And why does the out-of-town scoreboard need to rotate?

◆ ◆ ◆

A friend of mine said that Rance Mulliniks looks like a skeet shooter. As soon as he said it, I knew what he meant. Rance seems to have that dead eye-bat coordination. He glares down the barrel of the bat at the ball as he hits it as if he were a shooter looking down the sight of the rifle. I'll think of that every time I see Rance bat.

◆ ◆ ◆

It's clear why Texas is in or near first place in the American League West. There are .300 hitters all over the place, and hardly anyone's below .285. Everyone looks like he can clear the fence as Steve Buechele did tonight. Meanwhile, look through our lineup and it's almost impossible to find a home-run threat now that Carter may have cooled off. No matter. It seems impossible for us to lose.

We're seven-and-a-half up. If we drop back to five or five-and-a-half back, we are going to feel panicky because it won't look like such a big lead. Two weeks ago, when we were two-and-a-half and one-and-a-half up, all we wanted to do was make the All-Star break with any lead! Now, faster than Duane Ward breaks into a sweat, we're seven-and-a-half games up. A week ago tonight, a seven-and-a-half game lead would have looked like a mountain. But having *had* that, if we now drop to five we will start to feel nervous. At least the fans will. I know I will. But maybe the ball club, with its confidence and class, will not.

We will win the Texas series and that is the pattern we have to follow. If the Jays play .500, the Red Sox can say good night. For example, we're now fifty-one and thirty-four, or seventeen games over .500. With seventy-seven games to go, if we play just under .500 —

that is, win thirty-eight and lose thirty-nine — we will end up winning eighty-nine ball games. In the last few years, this number has been enough to win the AL East. Put another way, if in the seventy-seven games left we can go, say, forty-two and thirty-five — not a big deal — we would win ninety-three games. And that certainly should do it. To go forty-two and thirty-five means splitting the rest of our series and winning three of them by one game. The key, therefore, is to avoid a losing streak and to hang around .500. If we can streak for one more week, then it is indeed, Roger, all over.

◆ ◆ ◆

All sorts of All-Star Game leftovers in the dailies today. A bunch of players from other teams in the AL East saying how happy they would be just to play .500. But Cecil Fielder of the Tigers claims they are going to make a run for it. Wade Boggs mentions the sorry state of BoSox pitching.

◆ ◆ ◆

A word to the fan who sat along the row from us last night and felt obliged, absolutely obliged, to go out for a Coke in the eighth inning of a one-run game with runners on base and Kelly Gruber at bat with a 3–2 pitch coming. He not only couldn't wait till the end of the inning or the end of the at bat, but neither could he wait till the pitch was thrown. He pushed his way past nine people during the pitcher's windup so that he arrived dead in front of me (and dead he almost was) as the 3–2 pitch crossed the plate. The word to the fan ... think!

Chemistry and Confidence — and a Little Bit of Luck

Monday, July 15, 1991			8:35 PM		Royals Stadium		
Pre-Game Standings							
	W	L	Pct.	GB	Ho.	Strk.	P10	Div.
TORONTO	52	35	.598	-	30-17	L-1	8-2	24-16
Boston	43	41	.512	7 1/2	24-19	W-1	5-5	17-21
Detroit	43	42	.506	8	25-17	L-1	6-4	20-19
Final Score: Blue Jays 5, Royals 3								

THIS IS PAINFUL. The west coast games are the worst, but the midwest ones are second. When they go twelve innings, it's disastrous. A three-hour and forty-minute game against Kansas City. It's now 1:45 A.M. We played our softball game tonight, and I reinjured my groin going one for three and beat out a great bunt in the last inning to drive in our only run. Then home to ice up the 47-year-old knees, the groin and everything else, while we watch the Jays in Kansas City. Guzman against Boddicker.

This is the "snap back" game. It's the one I thought about a few games ago — the one following the first loss after the hot streak. They come out calm and unspooked, playing confident baseball, not feeling that it was based on magic.

◇ The Game

They lead off sensationally, with Carter showing that his bat has not cooled down after his two–home run performance yesterday. He doubles in the first inning. When Olerud, batting cleanup (I'm not convinced yet), follows with a single, Carter, a pretty good runner, comes around to score. Only one problem: Danny Tartabull in right field, who has a shotgun for an arm, charges the ball and plays it about as perfectly as an outfielder can. Unlike last week, when Rob Ducey hit Greg Myers with a perfect throw only to have Myers park it on the ground before turning to tag the runner, today, when the Kansas City catcher, Mike Macfarlane, gets the throw, he holds the ball and blocks the plate. Maybe he shouldn't have. Carter arrives at almost the same time as the ball and collides with Macfarlane's left leg, which is blocking the plate. So long, Mike. Bad ligament damage. See you in September. Carter is called out.

KC gets to Guzman for two runs in the bottom of the first. This is not surprising, since Guzman is pitching like Guzman in his first two starts, not his last three. What is surprising is that the camera close-ups show Guzman's face is relaxed; he's looking like a confident big-league pitcher. His three wins have done a lot for him, and he is beginning to believe he can pitch in the bigs. He's apparently not concerned about his wildness or about facing big-league batters. That's how his *face* looks. His motion, however, is back to that of his first two starts. He's falling way off the mound on the left-hand side after his delivery, and, while this movement is producing extraordinary speed (96 mph), it is also producing extraordinary wildness. He's behind almost every batter, often three balls and no strikes. Why isn't Cisco out of the dugout to tell Guzman what Buck Martinez just told him on TV? The ball is all over the place. He's not only wild high, he's wild low. Greg Myers looks more like Grant Fuhr than Yogi Berra. This is a dangerous way to live.

Guzman continues in trouble the entire five innings he pitches, getting out of innings that he has no right to. Cito visits him and leaves him in. Kansas City hitters were being very helpful by swinging at pitches out of the strike zone and popping up or grounding to Alomar. Incredibly, they got only four hits off a wild, out-of-control pitcher.

The Blue Jays put up two runs, thanks to God and Alomar. The second was thanks to the reopening of the Alomar clinic. Alomar hit a ball to left centre — a double for ninety-eight out of a hundred major-league ball players (and a single for Olerud and Fielder). Alomar does not break stride as he goes all the way to third base. Maybe he should have stopped at second, since there were two out and a fly ball wasn't going to score him. But Alomar decided that he was going to go to third. As he said in an interview a couple of weeks ago, he does those things only when he absolutely knows he can, because that's how his father taught him.

He makes his now familiar wide turn into third base so as to block off the relay throw from the shortstop to the third baseman. Nonetheless, it's going to be close. Alomar slides into third, head first, far to the left-field side, grabbing the base to stop his momentum. He is clearly safe but he would have been out had he made a traditional slide *to* the bag. (So much for my theory about sliding feet first.) Hacker, the third-base coach, knows Alomar's style and positions himself to show Alomar which side of the base to slide towards. Hacker is way down to the ground, indicating a slide with his left foot extended towards left field. Alomar picks up the message and executes. Needless to say, Carter singles to score him.

Anyway, the story of this game is much later, long after everyone's asleep, long after I should have been. The Blue Jays leave all sorts of runners and, by the end of nine, have two runs on fourteen hits. Regardless, we go into extras and the prologue doesn't matter. The upshot is that in the bottom of the eleventh it should have been all over. Kansas City loads the bases with none out (with help from Olerud hitting the runner with what should have been an easy throw to Alomar). This is clearly the end. Timlin is pitching, and, of course, he's become known as "The Vulture" since he's always in there at the right time to get the "W." Not tonight, though; his luck has run out, and he hasn't pitched well this inning. Sacks loaded, infield in, none out. It's just a matter of time.

Who's going to be the lucky player to drive in the game-winning run? First batter, ground ball to Lee, easy one. Throws to the plate to get the force. Next batter. Ground ball to Lee, easy play to the plate to get the force. Good grief! They're going to do it again! Any other year, any other time, those ground balls would have gone through a drawn-in infield, but this year they're pulled like a magnet to Manuel's glove. No great plays required; it's just going to go to his mitt. No sensational throw to the plate necessary; just a routine toss. It's what, for a double play, would be called room service. We order it up, and they deliver it.

The best is yet to come. Given the Blue Jays' magic this year, Timlin, incredibly and unexpectedly, unloads a wild pitch that sails right over Borders's glove to the backstop. Not good with the bases loaded in an extra-inning game. Still-well takes off from third and sprints for home. The ball, however, bounces hard off the backstop and right to a rushing Pat Borders, who grabs it cleanly, turns and fires to Mike Timlin, who's covering the plate. And in a play you'll see maybe once a year, Timlin tags out the runner for the third out. Wow! A play and a scene to savour!

It's exciting to see again enthusiasm in the Blue Jays' dugout. Last year, Fernandez would have been sitting in his usual position at the far end of the bench, talking to no one, not even standing up to shake hands with a home-run hitter. McGriff, wonderful ball player, nice guy, but a little laid back; Bell, exuberant, but exuding as many bad vibes as good ones; and prior to last year, the born agains — almost pathologically opposed to emotion.

BOXSCORE

Blue Jays..................5
Royals......................3

Toronto	AB	R	H	BI	Kansas City	AB	R	H	BI
White cf	7	0	2	0	McRae cf	6	0	1	0
RAlmr 2b	6	1	3	0	KGbson lf	6	0	1	0
Carter rf	5	1	3	1	Brett dh	5	2	2	0
Olerud 1b	6	1	2	0	Trtabll rf	4	1	2	1
Mllniks dh	4	1	2	0	Bnzngr 1b	6	0	2	2
Gruber 3b	6	1	2	1	Mcfrine c	0	0	0	0
Myers c	4	0	2	1	Mayne c	6	0	1	0
MWilsn pr	0	0	0	0	Pecota 3b	4	0	0	0
Brders c	1	0	1	1	Shmprt 2b	3	0	0	0
Ducey lf	4	0	0	0	Esnrich ph	1	0	0	0
Snyder rf	1	0	0	1	Stilwell ss	0	0	0	0
MnLee ss	6	0	0	0	Howard ss	3	0	0	0
					Crmrte ph	0	0	0	0
					Thrmn pr	0	0	0	0
					Seitz 3b	1	0	0	0
Totals	50	5	17	5	Totals	45	3	9	3

Toronto	000	110	000	003 - 5
Kansas City	200	000	000	001 - 3

E - Olerud (5). DP - Kansas City 1. LOB - Toronto 14, Kansas City 12. 2B - Carter (26), Olerud (11), Mulliniks (6), Myers 2 (20), McRae (12), Brett 2 (23), Tartabull (19), Benzinger (1). 3B - RAlomar (6). SB - KGibson (8), Pecota (3), Thurman (1). S - Ducey, Pecota.

	IP	H	R	ER	BB	SO
Toronto						
JuGuzman	5	4	2	2	3	5
MacDonald	2 1/3	0	0	0	0	1
DWard	2 2/3	2	0	0	1	5
Timlin (W, 9-4)	1	1	0	0	1	0
Henke (S, 19)	1	2	1	1	0	0
Kansas City						
Boddicker	6 2/3	10	2	2	0	0
SDavis	1 1/3	1	0	0	0	0
Montgomery	2	2	0	0	1	2
Crawford (L, 2-1)	1	4	3	3	2	0
Magnante	1	0	0	0	0	0

Crawford pitched to 5 batters in the 12th.
HBP - by Crawford (Borders). WP - JuGuzman 2.

This year, when Timlin makes the play at plate, he jumps in the air in excitement and happiness. The bench explodes in high fives, low fours, laughs and screams. And in the top of the twelfth, when the first Blue Jay run of the inning crosses the plate, the camera flashes to the dugout to catch Carter with his fabulous smile and the rest jumping around like kids.

The Jays add two more, to take a safe and sudden 5–2 lead to the bottom of the twelfth, and Henke slops to a 5–3 save.

Eight games up!

◆ Chemistry!

This happiness can go a long way. Never mind those who say chemistry is not important. I don't buy that for a moment. Chemistry and confidence are a part of a game in which a good number of the players on the team are at about the same level. This is particularly so in an era where there are no Koufaxes or Gibsons or Benches or Mayses. No player dominates the game today for more than half a season. Ask Roger Clemens.

Every team has a good half-dozen front liners. Every team has another ten to fifteen solid players (each making $1 million), predictably batting .250 to .275 and playing steady, not sensational, field. And every team has another half-dozen up-and-comers or once-weres, who contribute when the mood or enthusiasm strikes. The difference between teams is often pitching staffs plus confidence and chemistry. Of the three, the pitching staff is most important — no question here — but pitching staffs have a lot to do with chemistry and confidence too. It's a whole lot easier to throw a curve ball with the count three and two, or to throw a curve into the dirt with the count two and two, if you think your fielders will make the play or your catcher will be able to block the pitch. It's easier to unload that fastball straight down the middle to get the big strikeout if you know that, in the event the batter can get around on the pitch, Devon White is even money to pull it off the wall. The fielders will make these plays only if they are happy, alert, and intense but not too tense. If they just *feel* they are going to execute, they will.

This year's team has been shown by Alomar especially, but also by White and Carter, how to be into the game, happy to be there, and how to play. Other sports simply don't rely as much on split-second instinct as this team does. (Goaltending in hockey may be an exception.) Too many people talk about chemistry only in terms of one dimension — "happiness" or a "happy clubhouse" — and I think too many sports writers measure it in terms of the charm of ball players and their comfort with the media. But chemistry is something else, too. It is certainly happiness.

The guys have got to look forward to coming out to the park and playing with their teammates. I always felt Garth Iorg and Rance Mulliniks illustrated this spirit when they were platooning under Bobby Cox and Jimy Williams. They both were confident third basemen for the team at that stage. Each wanted to play every day, and there were certainly teams on which each could have played perhaps not every day but at least more games than they did for the Blue Jays. But one always felt they were genuine team players who rooted for each other and liked each other.

This year's team members seem to be comfortable with one another. Lots of friendships and no serious cliques. Everyone seems to be happy for everyone else. Mookie, who may be the ultimate team player, seems not to resent his lack of playing time but is simply happy to be around.

Borders, who thought he'd be catching a majority of games, clearly lost that position to Myers in the first half of the season and didn't seem to gripe about it or become a negative force. Myers has seemed to be equally supportive. Just watch the dugout. It's always fun to see who is sitting with whom, who is talking to whom.

Even though Ward was obviously disappointed at having to give the stopper role back to Henke after he replaced him so superbly in May, he has become, if anything, a better pitcher. You often see him talking and laughing with Henke in the bullpen.

But, in addition to the social chemistry, the chemistry that I think counts more is a chemistry of confidence. It's a chemistry that says "I can produce." It's a chemistry that says "I'm not waiting for the mistake to be made, or the break to go against me, or the bad umpire's call, or the bad ground ball. I believe I'm the best player at this position and I can produce. And I believe my manager is a great manager, and, even when I disagree with what he's doing, I won't use his decision as a crutch or an excuse. Ditto for the general manager."

Robbie Alomar displays that attitude on every play. He never lacks confidence; he never hesitates. He plays straight ahead and hard. Carter and White, to this point, have been similar.

Olerud lacks confidence. Gruber has suddenly lost the confidence he exhibited when he was on his incredible roll last year, particularly in the early part. He knew, you knew, everyone knew that he was a threat to take it over the fence. His injuries and the pressure of celebrity status, I think, have made him second guess and put too much pressure on himself.

Mysteriously, Borders and Myers still, in my view, are not confident of their big-league ability. Far too many passed balls (scored wild pitches) because they are tentative, afraid of making another error and feel that the pitchers are better pitchers than they are catchers. It's as if they feel honoured to be catching Key, Candiotti, Stottlemyre and Wells and are struggling to stay with them. The catcher is in many ways the quarterback, and I think the lack of confidence of the two catchers is a problem.

Cito Gaston's main strength has not been generalship, strategy and aggressive management on the field. It's been rather to instill the kind of confidence his players require. Cito has invested time, energy and patience in his ball players. His goal has been to make them comfortable with themselves, their position on the team and their ability. He's given some of them more playing time than they deserve, left them in games too long and failed to pinch hit for them so they'll know they have his confidence and will be confident in themselves.

So this is a nice, enjoyable, confident, friendly, easy-to-like team. But to go the route, give me a mean dude like Doyle Alexander even, or a menacing Jack Clark instead of Olerud at first. In fact, give me a Jack Clark hitting only with Olerud's stats, but give me his menacing I-hate-you-guys attitude. Then the chemistry would be perfect.

◇ Post-Game Notes

Detroit wins and Boston is kind enough to lose again, leaving Boston third and Detroit second, eight back. Eight. Can you believe it?

◆ ◆ ◆

Cory Snyder made his debut last night, actually making contact with the ball. In the key twelfth inning, he was sent in by Cito to pinch hit for Rob Ducey when Kansas City went with a lefty. I would have batted Ducey instead of Snyder. Snyder can't hit. A bad acquisition. When Texas was here last week and Bobby Valentine made one of his two dozen or so visits to our end of the dugout to cheer on his players, to burn off nervous energy or to try to steal some signals, I asked him whether Cory Snyder can hit. He smiled, shook his head "no" and then squeezed his nose with two fingers. I think that was his subtle way of agreeing with us.

Today Snyder hit a hard ball to third base. Kevin Seitzer, a below-average fielder, knocked it down but could do nothing more than pick it up and step on third, getting a force while allowing the runner on third to score. Sorry, folks; let's not applaud and call that a key hit or a key play for Snyder. It was a bouncing ball, hard hit to third, which a Kelly Gruber or, more to the point, a Bill Pecota, who moved from third to second when they brought in Seitzer, would have grabbed and fired to home, cutting off the run.

◆ ◆ ◆

Duane Ward, who I hated to see on the mound earlier in the year, continues to inspire as he threw at 97 mph and pitched some impressive innings, striking out an incredible number of batters. Henke, however, coming in at the bottom of the twelfth to "save" the game, got out of it but gave up a run. Henke is not the dominating "terminator" that once he was.

◆ ◆ ◆

With the acquisition of Snyder, I'm surprised that Ed Sprague has stayed up and Derek Bell has been sent down. It's surprising from the standpoint of developing Sprague, since he needs to catch in the minors and get at bats to improve his hitting. Nonetheless, there is some sense to Bell going down. Snyder plays excellent defensive outfield — better than Bell (must be something about the name) — and can't be worse at bat since Bell was clearly unable to handle big-league pitching at this stage of his career. I think Bell is one of those players who is caught in the middle. He can handle minor-league pitching so easily that he hasn't acquired the discipline to handle major-league pitching. I look at Sprague and think that he has had to work harder in the minors and, therefore, has developed more fundamentally sound mechanics and discipline. I hope that the Blue Jays are not resting on Derek Bell's batting average but will work with him in the minors to "mature" his hitting.

But folks, wouldn't you rather have George Bell back than Cory Snyder? If Bell were clogging up the middle of our batting order as DH, it would look like this: White, Alomar, Carter, Bell, Gruber, the hot-hitting Myers, Olerud (we could then tolerate his bat in that spot), Ducey and Lee. The top half looks very good in that scenario, but it's not going to happen. I do believe that George Bell, given what we have been reading in the papers, wishes it *would* happen and would come back here even if he had to drive Pat Gillick's car part time. But it won't happen. Cliff Johnson, yes. Al Oliver, yes. George? No. Too big a contract ... too much history ... too much crow to eat.

Managers and Other Masochists

Tuesday, July 23, 1991			8:05 PM		Comiskey Park		
Pre-Game Standings							
	W	L	Pct.	GB	Ho.	Strk.	P10	Div.
TORONTO	55	38	.591	-	30-17	L-2	6-4	24-16
Detroit	47	44	.516	7	28-17	L-2	6-4	20-19
New York	44	44	.500	8 1/2	22-18	L-1	6-4	23-13

Final Score: White Sox 3, Blue Jays 2

THIS GAME IS brought to you courtesy of CJCL, since once again we cannot actually see the ball game on TV. Instead, we are treated to a game that, I guess, just about everyone in Canada would want to watch: the Montreal Expos against the San Diego Padres in San Diego at 10:30 P.M. As the TV game comes on, you can see mostly empty seats behind Padre pitcher Andy Benes. Even the people in San Diego don't want to watch this game.

Seems like a year since the Jays left. Actually, it's been only eight days, but, in six games, they are three and three and have lost the last two (in Texas). This is the "cool off" time. Since the All-Star break, they are six and four, but it just isn't the same.

Okay, it's Candiotti against Fernandez in Chicago. Candiotti is now the American League leader in earned run average, at just over two runs per game. Meanwhile, Roger Clemens was the losing pitcher last night as Boston obliged yet again. Clemens is now a mediocre eleven and seven after getting off to a hot start. At the moment, he's just another pitcher. Still, with Boston fading, we've got to break our losing streak tonight.

◇ The Game

This game leads off with the breaks against us in the first inning. Alomar hits a wicked one to third base, but it's flagged down by Ventura, who makes a great play to get him out. In his next at bat in the third, Alomar is called out on strikes and slams his helmet to the ground. We know enough about Alomar now to know he has a temper and that he displays it only when he's really been robbed by an umpire. Bad call. Alomar will end up the day two for four, and it could easily have been four for four.

Meanwhile, in an unbelievable display of stubbornness, Cito starts Cory Snyder against right-handed pitcher Alex Fernandez. No way this should be happening. Ducey, a lefty, is hitting well. Snyder is hitting under .200 and, by his own admission, hasn't got his batting eye back (and never will). Nonetheless, Cito is going to do his "Kenny Williams" routine and play Snyder against all odds and against all sensibility.

Olerud leads off the second inning with a double and is left on third when Snyder grounds out. Serves you right, Cito.

The White Sox get a legitimate run in the third and an illegitimate run in the fourth, when a double is followed by two Candiotti wild pitches. It's 2–0 to the eighth. With one out, White and Alomar single and then move up a base on a passed ball. The White Sox walk Carter to load the bases. What's different this inning? Chicago manager Jeff Torborg took Alex Fernandez out after seven and brought in Donn Pall. He lasts four batters, three of whom get on base. Then Torborg goes to Scott Radinsky.

A lot of managers do these things. Fernandez threw 106 pitches, about the point at which current major-league starters *begin* to tire. At a pace of ten pitches per inning, he has shown good stuff all night and could have easily got through the eighth. He might have thrown a complete-game shutout. But in this era of automatic setup man/closer baseball — where managers operate on automatic pilot — Torborg does the predictable, and immediately pays the price.

Olerud comes up with the bases loaded and one out. Putting the ball in play to the outfield is vital. Olerud, sporting his silly .236 batting average but still batting cleanup, promptly strikes out. Which brings up Kelly Gruber. He's hitting .120 with runners in scoring position, the fourth worst in the American League at this point. Are you wondering as I am why he's batting fifth? Surprisingly, Gruber delivers a single to right, scoring White and Alomar to tie the ball game. Key hit, Kelly. So now Jeff Torborg is going nuts, having pulled Fernandez and brought in Pall, obviously the wrong move, then left in Radinsky, who succeeded Pall after the bases became loaded. He was tempted to go to Bobby Thigpen. After Gruber hit the clutch single, Torborg *then* decides, precisely one batter too late, to go to Thigpen. Thigpen comes in to pitch to Pat Tabler, who has been announced to replace left-handed hitter Mulliniks.

Cito, maybe now sensing that he shouldn't have Snyder in the lineup, pinch hits for the pinch hitter, replacing Tabler with Rob Ducey, who should have been in the game in the first place. Ducey, by the way, is hitting almost .100 points better than Cory Snyder at this point in the season. Nonetheless, as baseball goes, Ducey taps out to second on the first or second pitch to end the inning 2–2.

Cory Snyder leads off the ninth inning, taking a called strike three to end up zero for four through nine. I guess now he'll play in the next two games in the series. Just definitely stick with him until the Tigers catch us, Cito.

In the clutch top of the ninth inning, after Snyder goes in the tank, Borders singles. Then Manuel Lee bunts, trying to sacrifice him, and Thigpen fields it and goes to second but throws high (God bless him), allowing both runners safe berths at first and second.

Unfortunately, White then hits a roller over the pitcher's mound, and my buddy Ozzie Guillen makes a great play by fielding the ball, stepping on second and flipping it to first to catch the speedy White and end the inning on a double play. A week-and-a-half ago, that ball got through for a run-scoring single, or Guillen threw it late to first. One way or another, it wasn't a double play. This week it is.

Bottom of the ninth. I don't care if the Blue Jays win the division by ten games and the World Series four to zero. I don't want to hear any talk about Cito Gaston being manager of the year. In the bottom of the ninth, Carlton Fisk hits a chintzy little fly ball for a Texas-leaguer single. The next batter is Lance Johnson, who, everyone in North America knows, is going to lay down a sacrifice bunt. With Duane Ward and Bob MacDonald warming up in the bullpen,

◆ A BASEBALL ADDICT'S DIARY

Cito is a cinch to go to either MacDonald the lefty to pitch to Johnson (a lefty), or Duane Ward to increase the chances of a pop up. So, does Cito bring in either one? Of course not. He leaves in Candiotti. Now this is the same Cito Gaston who will pull out Todd Stottlemyre and David Wells, even when they are pitching a shutout and usually after six or seven innings. But Candiotti? After having left him in too long last week and allowing him to lose the game in the tenth, he of course leaves him in again. Lance Johnson then slaps a bunt hit — he chokes up to bunt but slaps the ball through the hole created by Lee covering second on the bunt. The ball trips into left field, where Carter bobbles it, resulting in runners on second and third.

BOXSCORE

White Sox...3
Blue Jays...2

TORONTO	AB	R	H	BI	CHICAGO	AB	R	H	BI
White cf	5	1	1	0	Raines lf	4	0	0	0
RAlmr 2b	4	1	2	0	Vntura 3b	4	0	1	0
Carter lf	2	0	0	0	Thmas dh	3	0	0	0
Olerud 1b	4	0	1	0	Pasqua rf	4	1	1	0
Gruber 3b	4	0	1	2	Fisk c	4	0	1	0
Mllniks dh	3	0	1	0	Krkvce pr	0	1	0	0
Tabler ph	0	0	0	0	Kittle 1b	2	0	0	0
Ducey dh	1	0	0	0	LJhnsn cf	1	0	1	0
Snyder rf	4	0	0	0	Huff cf	3	0	0	0
Brders c	4	0	2	0	Cora 2b	4	1	2	1
MWlsn pr	0	0	0	0	Guillen ss	3	0	1	1
Myers c	0	0	0	0					
MnLee ss	2	0	0	0					
Totals	33	2	8	2	Totals	32	3	7	2

| Toronto | 000 | 000 | 020 | - | 2 |
| Chicago | 001 | 100 | 001 | - | 3 |

E - Carter (5). DP - Chicago 1. LOB - Toronto 8, Chicago 8. 2B - Olerud (13), Cora (1). SB - Guillen (14). S - MnLee 2.

	IP	H	R	ER	BB	SO
Toronto						
Candiotti (L, 9-9)	8	7	3	3	3	4
Chicago						
Fernandez	7	4	0	0	1	4
Pall	1/3	2	2	2	1	0
Radinsky	1/3	1	0	0	0	1
Thigpen (W, 7-3)	1 1/3	1	0	0	0	1

WP - Candiotti 3, Fernandez, Pall.

In a tie game in the ninth with none out, the next batter is intentionally walked to set up a force play at home. After that, there is no doubt Cito is going to bring in Duane Ward. He's going to bring in Ward because, after having Candiotti go all the way, throwing slow pitches, it goes without saying that Duane Ward's 90-plus fastball is going to look even faster to the White Sox.

Gaston recently made the ludicrous statement that he likes pitching Candiotti in the first game of a series because he believes it confuses the opposition batters' timing for the entire series. I don't buy that for a second. These are major-league batters who adjust themselves to the starting pitcher each day. They do not adjust themselves Tuesday to the speed of Monday's pitcher.

Anyway, just to contradict himself, Cito leaves Candiotti in there. This is crazy for several reasons:

1. With the bases loaded, you do not want a wild pitch or a passed ball. This is exactly what you have with a knuckleballer on the mound.
2. You want to increase your chances of a strikeout in this situation. A strikeout would set up a potential double play to get out of the inning. Duane Ward has, I think, the best strikeout ratio in the league and is striking out well more than one batter per inning.
3. Candiotti has faced three batters in the ninth inning and they got on base, as did the second last batter in the eighth inning.

But no, Cito doesn't take him out of the game. Joey Cora, more likely to challenge Eddy Gaedel than Ty Cobb or Pete Rose, promptly singles to left field to win the ball game.

Don't forget this one, folks. This is a Cito Gaston loss. Look at Cory Snyder. Look at Candiotti staying in too long.

◇ To Manage or Not to Manage

Now some will say that it's easy for people like me to sit here, after the fact, and criticize the manager's decisions. It's true, but Cito should have felt this baby slipping away. It just felt like a game that was in trouble all the way.

I know Cito would have looked like a hero if Snyder had homered or Candiotti had got out of the inning. But they didn't, and Cito is paid $200,000-plus a year to manage the team, and we're paid nothing to sit here and comment after the fact. He's supposed to know what to do and to make the right plays and right calls and push the right buttons. If it were easy, they would let me do it (and I'd do it for nothing).

I guess I am hard on Cito. But that's because I care so much about this team and, like most fans, spend a lot of time second-, third- and fourth-guessing my own manager, as opposed to the other guys' manager. So let's stop and talk about the other managers a bit. One could categorize major-league managers in a lot of ways. I divide them into five categories:

- The Negatives
- The Eccentrics
- The Guerillas
- The Low Impacts
- The High Impacts

The Negatives. Doug Rader (Angels' manager, soon to be fired), Greg Riddoch (San Diego manager, to be fired at the end of the season), John McNamara (recently fired Cleveland manager) and Jimy Williams (you know who he is). These guys remind me of parents who take out their frustrations on their kids. When things go badly, they assume the players are striking out intentionally or hitting to the wrong side of second base intentionally or throwing wild pitches because they are trying to hit their mother-in-law sitting in the first row of the stands. They get frustrated at the team's failures, of which there will be at least sixty-five, and more likely seventy-five or so, in a season. Instead of working to build confidence (certainly Cito's strength) or to devise interesting ways to pull out games through on-field strategy (not Cito's strength), they simply get uptight and either explode or implode. They take the team that's tight and make it tighter. They take a team that's losing and make it so unhappy that it loses more.

The Eccentrics. Well, these guys are fun. I don't want them managing my team, but these are unpredictable guys. Don Zimmer (recently fired by the Cubs), Tommy Lasorda (manager of the Dodgers), Joe Morgan (manager of the defending AL East champion Red Sox) and Stump Merrill (soon-to-be-fired manager of the Yankees). These guys manage on hunches. They pinch hit, hit and run and bunt where you don't expect them to. Zimmer was notorious for doing odd-ball things in the year he guided the Cubs to the division championship. Lasorda will pull a pitcher with a 1–1 count on a hunch. Joe Morgan and Stump Merrill? Well, just look at them. Even their own players complain. They are admitted characters, interesting chaps, but they don't provide the sense of security, stability, reliability, predictability and confidence that good management of any organization requires.

The Guerillas. Whitey Herzog, Dick Williams, Billy Martin. None of them is currently managing, and poor Billy Martin — he's currently chewing out some ball player who got picked off second in the fourth inning of a game between the Saints and the Sinners in the dome in the sky. These guys were the General Pattons of their teams. Give them twenty-five ball players and they would push, cajole, shove, exert, exhort and "tough" their players to ten more wins than their talent warranted. They did whatever was necessary to win, and they invariably produced above-average seasons for their teams, especially in the first year they took over. The intensity and excitement and professionalism and knowledge of these experts — well, *commanders*, inspired their troops. They could get the extra mile out of guys through an incredible love/hate relationship, and they usually burned out themselves and their players after a couple of years. You just can't go at that pace, with that intensity, and fire 162 games a year for more than a couple of seasons. Just ask a bunch of Oakland A's whose pitching-arms were burned out by Billy Martin in the mid-1970s. But all of these managers produced teams that were great to watch.

The Low Impacts. The late Walter Alston (who was patiently coaching the Saints against Billy Martin's Sinners), Roger Craig, Tom Trebelhorn (of the Brewers) and our very own Cito Gaston. These are managers who basically believe that you make a team feel good, you respect the professionalism of the athletes, and you try to encourage them to execute the basics — and then sit back and watch. They don't play aggressively on the field or in the clubhouse. They won't win many games with their managing, and occasionally, by lying back too long or by going too far to build up confidence, they'll lose some. It will be hard to measure the ones they win because they'll have won them by making a Manuel Lee, a Greg Myers, a Mookie Wilson, a Rance Mulliniks, a John Olerud feel better than his statistics warrant. When one of those players produces, it will look like luck, coincidence or a bad pitch by the other team, but it will be due, to some degree, to the manager's patience and confidence and stroking. Why do I call them low impact? Because they seem to accept what they've been given and kind of let it roll. They don't try to take control of a game so much as let the players do the best they can. In most years, they allow a good team to perform not *above* its skill level but *at* its skill level. This style is okay, except for those years when another team in the division is having a career year, when it is streaking, or when it has just hired one of the guerilla managers.

I think if the Blue Jays had had a manager out of the guerilla category, they would have gone all the way in one or two of the last five or six years and, unquestionably, this year. But they would have gone from ninety-five wins to eighty-four wins and back to ninety, as opposed to winning consistently around eighty-six to ninety-three games a year.

The High Impacts. Buck Rodgers (recently fired, of course, by the deservedly hapless Expos), Bobby Cox (now managing the Atlanta Braves to an above-average season), Jim Leyland and, of course, Tony LaRussa. These are managers who seem to do it all. Every single year they get their teams playing above their capabilities. They've taken teams with injuries and produced. They've taken teams with "bad actors" and difficult-to-manage players (Canseco, Pascual Perez, Oil Can Boyd, Lonnie Smith) and made them positive and contributing factors. They've consistently got rookies and brought them along quickly (Glavine, Avery, DeShields) and handled veterans skilfully (Rickey Henderson, Dave Henderson, Dave Parker). They've adapted their managing style to the team. They've changed onfield strategy to suit the players, the injuries and the opponents. They're innovative with their batting lineups. They're not afraid to pinch hit. And they control the game. Their players respect them. They are direct and forceful, but not foolish, unfair, star-crossed or prone to temper tantrums. They understand that running a team is like running a company. You've got to earn trust: if you can't control your own temper, others won't allow you to control them. They demand professionalism and they give professionalism, and you can only do the former if you provide the latter.

Give me any of these guys running our team and we would have gone all the way two or three times out of the last six years.

Oh yes, there is a final category I didn't mention, and that's the Sparky Anderson category. It really pains me to say this since his mannerisms are irritating. He drives me nuts when I see him walk out to the mound and jump, skip or lie down to avoid stepping on the white lines on the field. Between innings, he goes down the runway at the end of the dugout and lights up his pipe so that the sweet

smell of the tobacco wafts across our noses. He announces that every one of his players is the best prospect he's ever seen (remember Darnell Coles?), and he gets the player to believe him — at least for a while. He takes these retreads and makes them believe they are major leaguers still (Incaviglia). He takes bad apples and gives them new life (Doyle Alexander). He takes journeymen and makes them Cy Young winners (Willie Hernandez). He gets key home runs from players you wouldn't have in your outfield (Larry Herndon).

Then there are, of course, the mind games he plays with the other teams. Every other manager is the best manager since Joe McCarthy. In every city his team plays, he is happy to talk to the local media about what a "fine young team" the home team is, or how he thinks the team is the best in the league and will probably win it easily. Every other team is a cinch to win it all.

And then there's his uncanny ability to pull out the right pinch hitter at the right time. This is all you can see, but there's something else — there's got to be something else. Year after year, he gets teams to perform not only above their ability but way above their ability. Write off a Tiger team and you might as well underestimate your ex-spouse's lawyer. Everyone had to pick the Tigers this year for fifth or worse, strictly on merit. But Sparky is going to challenge us all year. Some years he has had jackrabbits, some years seasoned pros like Whitaker, Trammell, Gibby, Petry, Morris, and this year he's got old strikeout kings — Deer, Incaviglia, Tettleton — and a team that makes errors and strikes out when it isn't hitting homers. And a pitching staff that should struggle in Syracuse. Their pitching has been near the bottom of the league all year, and so has their overall hitting. But Sparky will dipsy-doodle them through all that and get the right mixture of pitching and hitting, mainly home runs, in the right number of games to produce a lot of runs.

Yes, he's annoying. I couldn't tolerate listening to him every day with his blarney and BS. But, with the team we've got, I know for sure I'd be watching games in mid-October. I don't understand it.

Look at him right now. He's sitting a few games behind us with a team with no starting pitchers and only one reliever (Henneman), who, along with his catcher, his first baseman and his shortstop, I'd take over ours. But that's it. Five, maybe six, plus Tony Phillips. Yet there he is, and he's going to tail us all the way.

I've picked five categories plus Sparky. You could create seven categories, but there'd still be a separate one for him.

◇ Post-Game Notes

Tigers have pulled to within six. Still a good, solid lead, but now that the Blue Jays have lost three in a row, that old stomach feeling is rumbling about. This was one of those points when the Blue Jays could have busted it all open and made the entire season a laugher instead of letting the others stay close. It's embarrassing to be watching the Tigers. When they come in here next week, suddenly we're in a pressure situation where we have to play well or else the six-game lead will be three or two before we know it.

◆ ◆ ◆

The Expos' uniforms with the circus stripe down the sides and the eighteen-colour hats are the second worst in major-league history, only after the short-panted Chicago White Sox uniforms of the late 1970s. The Expos' uniforms were always hokey, but, when someone decided to add those stripes, it made the players look like clowns.

◆ ◆ ◆

Save me from the TV producer who thinks he's covering something between the Caribana Parade, the Charles and Di wedding and the Olympics as he moves the cameras to get a close-in-picture of everything sports fans don't want to see just when they don't want to see it.

How many times have you seen the cameras miss a key play as they pan to the crowd? Or how many times have you seen the last play in the World Series or a Stanley Cup and then have the camera ignore the celebration of the overjoyed athletes to show some half-corked fans hugging one another in the stands? I want to see the ball players at the moment of the victory — the ones who are constrained, the ones who are laid back, the ones who cry, the ones who pray, the ones who wave to their wives — not while they're pouring champagne over one another in the dressing room.

Turning-Points and True Grit

Sunday, July 28, 1991   3:05 PM   Toronto SkyDome

Pre-Game Standings

	W	L	Pct.	GB	Ho.	Strk.	P10
TORONTO	57	41	.582	-	31-18	L-1	4-6
Detroit	50	46	.521	6	30-18	L-1	6-4
New York	46	47	.495	8 1/2	24-21	W-1	5-5

Final Score: Royals 10, Blue Jays 4   Attendance: 50,291

WELL, NO WAY SHOULD YOU LOSE two out of three to the Royals at home. Today is a "must win" game.

As it happens, the game is a perfect example of what's happened to the Blue Jays. The intensity is gone. When the intensity goes, the breaks go. When the breaks go, the umpires' calls go against you. Candiotti is pitching. He's had five starts for the Blue Jays, and the Blue Jays have scored only ten runs to support him. The result — a two-and-three record.

This game will end up looking like a blow-out, but it was in fact just one close game in a long season. If the Blue Jays had executed at some key turning-points, they would have won it.

◇ The Game

Turning-Point No. 1
In the Blue Jays' first, White and Alomar go out quickly, and Carter is hit by a pitch. He glares not at the pitcher and not at the Kansas City dugout but, for some reason, up into the stands behind home

plate. He does this almost all the way to first base. He is clearly upset. I guess yesterday's failure with the bases loaded in the ninth is bothering him. I like to see a ball player who cares, but he seems a bit rattled. After one pickoff throw to first, Gubicza, the Kansas City pitcher, is standing on the mound when Carter breaks for second. Maybe the easiest pickoff in history. Gubicza throws to first baseman Warren Cromartie, who throws to second so quickly that Carter turns and comes back to first. The Crow tags him. End of inning.

Turning-Point No. 2
In the second inning, Gruber comes up with Olerud on second and lines the pitch back at Gubicza. Gubicza — in what we've seen too much of this season — tries to knock down the ball with his bare *pitching hand*. I know this is a reflex action, but it should be drilled into pitchers' heads that under *no* circumstances should they play a ball with their bare hand, particularly a line drive back up the middle. Gubicza slaps it and gets away without an injury. The ball tails off for an infield hit.

With runners on first and third, Mulliniks walks, bringing up Borders. Borders, who's getting another start against a right-handed pitcher, still has no home runs and is batting .243. The bases are loaded, and no one is out. He has a chance to blow this baby open. He can't do it. With two strikes, he at least shows excellent bat control by hitting the ball to second base, allowing Olerud to score easily.

One might question new KC manager Hal McRae's strategy here. He's got Gubicza against Candiotti, which ought to mean a low-scoring game. In spite of Candi's rough start, he probably won't give up many runs. So why not play the infield "in," hoping to cut off a run, particularly since the bottom end of the Blue Jays' batting order is coming up. Instead, he leaves the infield back and Borders hits a routine ground ball for a fielder's choice, moving the runners up and scoring a run.

Manuel Lee is up next. A single could bring in two runs, a walk could load the bases. He swings wildly at three Gubicza pitches in the dirt to strike out.

This is one of the key at bats in the game, though it doesn't look it at the time. It's fascinating how an experienced player like Lee (among others) can absolutely *know* that Gubicza is going to throw stuff that breaks late and hits the plate and still swing. Lee does it three times. Three strikes. Not even close. This is an at bat that two weeks ago would have been a single. Wilson pops to first base, and a promising inning turns into one run scored on a fielder's choice.

Turning-Point No. 3
Candiotti gets to two out in the fifth easily. He's now set down six in a row and nine of the last ten. Then he walks Seitzer and the roof falls in. Seitzer's walk is followed by a Cromartie triple, a walk to Tartabull, a wild pitch — which I call a passed ball on Borders for the third catching error in five innings — and a single to Eisenreich. The wild pitch/passed ball puts Tartabull in scoring position, and Eisenreich's single brings in a run. Benzinger pops to second to end the inning. Three runs on two hits and two walks. Through five innings, Candiotti has given up five hits and four walks. A sure formula for disaster. He's lucky to have given up only three runs.

Turning-Point No. 4
The Blue Jays show some fight when Borders leads off the bottom of the fifth with a solid single to left. It looks like a double, but Kirk Gibson charges the ball hard (unlike Wilson later in the game) and fires to second, holding Borders to a single. This proves to be another key play when Manuel Lee hits a two hopper to the shortstop, who easily runs a double play.

How important was that double play? Mookie Wilson singles next. Borders would have been on second and Wilson's single would have scored the second run, making it 3–2, one out, one on. Thanks to Gibson, the run doesn't score, and you've got two out, one on, none in.

Gibby finishes the day zero for four with two walks but, through his defensive hustle, makes a key contribution to the victory.

Turning-Point No. 5
Contrast that with what happens next. In the top of the sixth, a catcher named Spehr, just up since Macfarlane was injured in the home-plate collision with Joe Carter last week, doubles to lead off.

Shumpert lays down a sacrifice bunt, but Olerud and Candiotti both move slowly. It was an excellent bunt down the first-base side, but Olerud, tentative as always, simply gets in too late and, by the time he picks it up and turns, can't get the runner at first. So the Royals now have runners at first and third with none out, instead of one out with a runner on third. Shumpert decides to try to steal second, which is not a bad play given Borders's bad day in the field. But, in this case, Borders guns him down, leaving the Blue Jays where they would have been had Olerud made the play at first. One out, runner on third.

Someone named Howard, batting .171 and inexplicably in the lineup, is 0-2 on the day. He promptly doubles against Candiotti, who entered the game with the second-lowest earned run average in the league. Cito finally figures out that since Kansas City had two out in the fifth with no runs and none on and Gibson up, the next eight batters but one got on base. Through that stretch, there were two singles, two doubles, two walks and a triple. So he goes to Bob MacDonald.

MacDonald comes into a key situation. The game is 4-1, but we're not out of it yet. MacDonald, however, opens with four straight high pitches to walk Gibby. Seitzer, who walked in the first and the fifth, is up, and MacDonald promptly walks him again.

At this point in the game, the Blue Jays have given up six walks in six innings. Cromartie then singles to knock in Howard and Gibson. Tartabull and Eisenreich are out, but big damage has been done. Take this game back to that point in the fifth with two out and none on and the Blue Jays leading 1-0. Here's how it went:

Seitzer–walk
Cromartie–triple
Tartabull–walk
Eisenreich–single
Benzinger–out
Spehr–double
Shumpert–single
Howard–double
Gibson–walk
Seitzer–walk
Cromartie–single.

Through that stretch, the Royals sent eleven men to the plate, ten of whom got on base and only one of whom got out. That was the ball game.

Turning-Point No. 6
After all this damage, the Blue Jays come up in the bottom of the sixth, down 6–1. You have to feel they're out of this game. They've lost their edge and everyone's unhappy in the ballpark. Still, another key inning is coming. It will be long forgotten, along with Gibby's play a couple of innings back.

Alomar leads off with a classic at bat. On the first two pitches, which are outside to Alomar batting left, he swings softly and accurately, wanting only to get the ball into play. He fouls them down the left-field line. The third pitch is on the inside corner, and, concentrating on making contact, Alomar fouls it down the right-field side. He almost *carries* the ball to the side of the field in which it's pitched. The fourth pitch is over the plate down the middle, and Alomar taps it into centre field for a base hit.

Carter comes up, and you can tell he senses that this is an important at bat. Unlike yesterday, he tears into the pitch and knocks it to deep centre field. Lots of fans start to scream, anticipating a two-run homer, but we know this one hasn't got the legs. Eisenreich makes a routine play on the warning track. Another ten feet and this ball game could have turned around.

Turning-Point No. 7
Alomar is still into this game. Although we are down five runs, he tags up on first and takes second on the fly ball. He could have done the casual thing, which was just hang around between first and second, watching the play. Or he could have taken off, presuming it might fall in for a hit. But he knew that it likely would be a routine fly to deep centre. So he tagged up and took second. It would be a fatal error to get nailed at second in a game where you are down five runs and need base runners. But Alomar knows the field and the game so well that he's sure he can grab second with no risk.

Olerud is hit by a pitch, so the Blue Jays have runners on first and second, with one out. Another turning-point. Kelly Gruber is up. If he can knock both of them in or hit a home run, this is a brand new ball game. Gruber strikes out after getting one bad call and one good pitch. The bad umpiring cost him his concentration, and he's gone.

Turning-Point No. 8
Mulliniks walks, loading the bases for the Jays for the second time in six innings. This brings up Pat Borders. At this point, Hal McRae surprises us by going to the bullpen for Storm Davis. Davis has lost his spot in the starting rotation and is now a middle reliever/setup man out of the KC bullpen. We are delighted to see him replace Gubicza.

You had to figure it was a certainty that Cito would bring in a left-handed batter to replace Borders. But oh no, not Cito. As always, he's going to wait till later, later, later, later. He has Rob Ducey on the bench, and Ducey, although his bat has cooled off, is having a better year than Borders. (*Mulroney* is having a better year.) And Greg Myers, who is *certainly* having a better year, batting 40 points higher with better power stats, is also on the bench. It's an automatic easy switch, but, needless to say, Cito switches neither Myers nor Ducey. In another key at bat, Borders swings at the first pitch, bounces it meekly to Seitzer, who lobs it to second for a fielder's choice, ending the "rally."

Turning-Point No. 9
End of six, Kansas City 6–1. Blue Jays strand six runners in six innings.

In the bottom of the seventh, Manuel Lee leads off with a single. Mookie grounds to second, moving Lee up, and then Devon White, with a chance to get a real rally going, strikes out. Robbie Alomar, still intense, singles — scoring Lee to make it 6–2. Joe Carter now comes up and, incredibly, on a low change-up or off-speed pitch from Davis, strikes out for the second time in four innings.

Turning-Point No. 10
Cito now throws in the towel. He's down 6–2 and any team down four in the eighth is unlikely to win … particularly our team, the way it's been going. But Cito tosses in the towel by bringing in good, old Jim Acker.

Turning-Point No. 11
Acker has stated many times that he's embarrassing himself with his pitching this year. Right again. After getting the first two batters out, he goes like this:
    Cromartie – double
    Tartabull – walk
    Eisenreich – single
    Benzinger – single
    Spehr – double.
Three runs on four hits. This puts the ball game out of reach.

◆ ◆ ◆

The Blue Jays make an effort in the bottom of the ninth, with Wilson, White, Carter and Olerud all getting singles to score two runs: 10–4.

The Blue Jays were in this game at key times. Potentially they could have won what looks like a blow-out. But they didn't come through in the clutch, Cito didn't manage aggressively and the over-the-hill boys — Acker and Henke — gave up the throw-away runs.

Meanwhile, the Red Sox managed to lose two games, 10–8 and 7–4, to the White Sox. Thank you.

◇ True Grit

This game is a good example of the "quiet" and unseen plays that are barely noticed when they occur, that are hardly mentioned in the post-game commentary and that are totally forgotten in twenty-four hours. They are never referred to as turning-points in the season,

BOXSCORE

Royals..10
Blue Jays..4

KANSAS CITY	AB	R	H	BI	TORONTO	AB	R	H	BI
KGbson lf	4	1	0	0	White cf	5	1	1	0
Thrmn lf	0	0	0	0	RAlmr 2b	5	0	2	1
Seitz 3b	3	2	0	0	Carter rf	4	0	1	1
Crmrte 1b	6	2	4	2	Olerud 1b	4	1	2	1
Trtabll rf	2	1	1	1	Gruber 3b	5	0	1	0
McRae cf	1	1	1	1	Mllniks dh	2	0	1	0
Esnrich cf	6	1	2	2	Brders c	4	0	1	1
Bnzngr dh	5	0	2	1	MnLee ss	4	1	1	0
Spehr c	5	1	3	1	MWlsn lf	4	1	2	0
Shmprt 2b	5	0	2	0					
Howard ss	5	1	1	1					
Totals	42	10	16	9	Totals	37	4	12	4

| Kansas City | 000 | 033 | 031 | - | 10 |
| Toronto | 010 | 000 | 102 | - | 4 |

E - Borders (3). DP - Kansas City 1. LOB - Kansas City 13, Toronto 10. 2B - Cromartie (7), Tartabull (23), Spehr 3 (4), Howard (1), Olerud (14). 3B - Cromartie (2). SB - Seitzer (4), MWilson (6). CS - Shumpert (7), Carter (8).

	IP	H	R	ER	BB	SO
Kansas City						
Gubicza (W, 6-5)	5 2/3	5	1	1	2	4
SDavis (S, 2)	3 1/3	7	3	3	0	3
Toronto						
Candiotti (L, 9-10)	5 1/3	8	5	5	4	2
MacDonald	1 2/3	2	1	1	2	1
Acker	1	4	3	3	1	1
Henke	1	2	1	1	1	0

HBP - by Gubicza (Carter), by Gubicza (Olerud). WP - Candiotti. PB - Borders.

as are grand-slam homers, "Bill Buckner" errors or bases-loaded walks. But they are the moments that distinguish a championship team from a .500 club. Moments of execution where performance under pressure or simple delivery makes the difference. No one will look back on this game as one of the "winnable" ones because the turning-point was not a glaring error or hit or managing decision. But there are far more games in a season that are "routine" than there are games determined on one play. Given that pennants are generally won by two or three games, it's important to have a team that can execute both in the field and at bat and not give away free outs, hits or baserunners.

It's the reason the Yankees couldn't win while paying top buck for the best-known heavy-hitter free agent. It's the night-after-night quiet, efficient, routine execution. It's what the Twins — and to some extent the Braves and the Cardinals — are doing this year. Baseball being baseball, every team is going to put up seventy wins, more or less, every year. If a team can execute and deliver, it'll turn a seventy-win season into an eighty-five–win season.

It's no secret that I'm not a fan of Cito's (non-) managing style. But what he's trying to establish among his players is a kind of quiet confidence that playing simple, straight-ahead, fundamental baseball will deliver a "quiet" pennant.

Tonight we ended up with a big loss instead of a possible narrow win. We'll never know if someone other than Acker would have done better or if pinch hitters could have delivered better than Lee. For that matter, Manuel will deliver on other nights. The question is, can Cito get his players back to the calm, confident state they were in three weeks ago?

I picked up a real appreciation for the many turning-points of games when I started to score them, batter-by-batter, a long time ago.

These turning-points are, in my view, the real reason this team — which could be ten games up — is going to be in a tight one right to the end. It's one of the reasons I'm not an Olerud fan. He seems somehow too indifferent to the game situation. If patience, balance and "maturity" are assets, they also can be liabilities. Faith in one's long-term ability can take the edge off. It's not all that different from the born-agains who have faith in a higher authority. It's a fatalism that writes off circumstances to "long-term averages" or to "just staying level." But staying level means that you don't sharpen the edge. One never gets the sense that Olerud is keyed into the particular situation in a game. Every at bat is a carbon copy of the previous one. He's as willing to take a pitch and show his notorious "patience" with a one and two count in the ninth inning with two on as he is in the second inning with none out and no one on. He seems as unfazed by a two hopper to second as he does by a double off the wall in left field.

Contrast that with our buddy George Bell. The crouch would always get a little more pronounced in clutch situations. The bat would be waved over his right shoulder a little quicker and a few more times. He would walk with purpose towards the plate. His eyes would open somehow wider and his lips close tighter.

The same is true of Jack Clark and Will Clark and Bonilla and Bonds and Cal Ripken and Canseco and McGwire (except for this year) and Dave Parker and Dave Winfield and Rickey Henderson and Dave Henderson and Kirk Gibson. Wait a minute. Do I sense a common factor here? Do a bunch of these guys play for the Oakland A's? Yep. And that's part of the reason they've been American League leaders. That's the difference between Alomar and Fernandez, White and Felix, Carter and just about anyone except Bell.

Funny thing about Rance. I love him — everyone's got to love him — and he does get keyed into the game situation. But the problem is that although he pulls the trigger, the gun doesn't go off like it used to a few years ago — neither as often nor as loud. Give me his heart in a bunch of other ball players and I'd be a happy guy.

And that's what explains Pat Tabler hanging around a .500 batting average with the bases loaded and over .300 with men in scoring position. No one can explain it, but it is somehow an ability just to "get the juices going."

And over the course of this year, I've come to get a feeling for who I want up in these quiet but important situations. You know I don't want Olerud. And it's funny, but I don't want Kelly, even though he's hit a couple of key runs. This year he seems to be so eager to match last year's numbers that he's first-ball hitting and bouncing out. I sure want Carter, though he's struck out in a couple of these key situations.

I know I want Robbie up, and Devon's made me a believer. I don't want Manuel. Funnily, I don't mind Mookie. Like Rance, he's not going to give you the pop or the noise. But he's such a damn gamer. You get the feeling that if he has to take one in the helmet, the groin or the knuckles, if he has to beat out a bunt, he's damn well going to get you something in the clutch situation. I don't want Snyder; he was far too spooked about his own problems to produce in a clutch situation. But I sure do want Sprague.

Pitchers. Ward's the funniest case of all. I really hated him at the start of this year, because he blew so many save opportunities last year. Truth to tell, if he had kept his act together last year, we would have won the pennant. And I can't deny that this year he's gone sky high a couple of times again. But when he comes out of the bullpen, he's storming. It's like he wants that ball real bad. He wants to be in there, and he wants to strike the sons of bitches out. Contrast that with Acker, who's hoping to luck past another batter.

Our starters are, overall, pretty good clutch guys. This year, Todd Stottlemyre seems to love the pressure situation. He seems confident and has the courage to throw inside and to knock guys down and play eye-for-an-eye baseball.

Cito is part of all this. Like Olerud, too patient, too accepting, too "long haulish." I hate to see the Lou Piniella/Billy Martin type of argument with the umpire. But, gee, I wish Cito would give us some emotion. Maybe by really blowing his cork once in a while. I hate to say that I think it counts and I even hate to see it. It slows down games, it trivializes the situation, and, of course, it isn't going to change the umpire's mind. But there's something about not taking a bad call lying down.

Pete Rose? You may not like his attitude, personality, friends or hobbies. But when he came up to bat he waved that stick with one single focus, and that was on smacking that ball out of the infield. You wanted him up in that clutch situation, and he got that mean little smile on his face when he was in it. A bulldog.

So the season is made up of a thousand of these turning-points, and chemistry is more dependent on "gamers" than on "sweet swingers." We didn't convert tonight, but we've converted in a lot of games so far this season.

◇ Post-Game Notes

The Jumbotron continues to give us academic and useless information. For example, when Mookie Wilson came up in the bottom of the fifth, just after Lee hit into a double play to leave two out and none on, it told us that Mookie is hitting .327 with runners in scoring position.

On the day, the Blue Jays show as having committed one error. In my view, you have to add MacDonald's error on the Cromartie infield grounder, Mookie's error on Howard's double to the wall, two passed balls/wild pitches and Olerud's failure to convert a sac bunt into an out at first. Five plays that could have been made in the field by the Blue Jays.

♦ ♦ ♦

As Carter came up in the key situation in the sixth inning with Alomar on first, the crowd was hushed, except for a vendor hawking something called "slush." He comes by three times a game, and every time I wonder about the marketing genius who named this hunk of flavoured crushed ice. It may be good and tempting on a hot day, but I could never bring myself to buy something called "slush." How about "crushed ice," "snow cone," "frozen cone," "freezicles," or "igloos"? Even "Jaysicles." Anything but "slush." Slush is what I find under the left rear wheel of my car when yesterday's snow is dirty and melting.

♦ ♦ ♦

Galen Cisco made two trips to the mound to try to settle down his pitchers. Each time the pleasant, warm, typically quiet SkyDome afternoon was shattered by the irritating sounds of "Cisco Kid Was a Friend of Mine." Must bug the pitcher at least as much as it irritates us.

♦ ♦ ♦

The Kansas City players are always a friendly lot, despite the addition this year of Kirk Gibson. Gibson doesn't seem to talk to teammates, let alone fans, and he always looks like he would just as soon punch you as speak to you. We remember Gibby from four years ago, when he was with the Tigers. He stopped in front of the dugout to argue with some fans beside us. I was getting ready to do my own imitation of Ben Johnson when that argument started. Gibby is one of the few major-league players (Albert Belle and Rob Dibble are others) who might actually come into the stands for a tête-à-tête.

Terry Shumpert, a good young ball player with a thin batting average and a wide smile, yesterday tossed a ball to me to give to the little boy beside me.

Bret Saberhagen is a two-time Cy Young award winner — good looking, real nice guy. He spends most of the game at our end of the dugout, sitting on the step or leaning against the railing. He'll often fool with the camera lens beside him, putting the telecast out of focus, and will almost invariably chat with fans. My buddy Les Sherman brought his three-and-a-half-year-old son, Stephen, down to sit with us and the kid asked Saberhagen for a ball. After Saberhagen told him several times to wait till the end of the game, the kid asked why he couldn't have one now, and "where are the balls anyway?" Sabes smiled, gave up and tossed the kid a baseball.

Warren Cromartie is with the KCs after having spent six or seven years in Japan. He seems to be a relaxed ball player now that he's back: blowing bubbles, smiling and spending an inordinate amount of time looking up at the stands and talking to his teammates.

George Brett, in contrast, used to be a friendly, easy player. Now, whether or not he's in the lineup, he seems far less communicative.

◆ ◆ ◆

What's happened here? MacDonald has had a bad outing today. Timlin had a bad outing yesterday, and Henke had one on Friday. The bullpen is struggling, the starters are fading. This is a team that relies on pitching, not hitting. It must help out its hitting by making acquisitions. Or it must pray that our pitching, unlike any other team's, can perform at the level it's been at for an entire season. Unnoticed through the winning streak and through the pitching stats is the fact that we just are not producing runs.

If I were the Blue Jays, I'd be trading Henke right now, before there is any more proof that he's lost it. Two months ago you could have traded him and got a real outfielder (not Cory Snyder). Now you couldn't. He's in his thirties and he's lost his fastball. A trade to the National League may give him an extra year until it gets used to him, but I think he's gone.

◆ ◆ ◆

It mystifies me. Almost every major-league ball player has clauses in his contract outlining the things he can't do. Things like skiing, waterskiing, cutting down trees. But leave it to baseball players. In the off season, there are invariably instances of players slicing their pitching thumb with a hedge trimmer (Bob Ojeda) or annihilating their knee ligaments on a snowmobile (Carney Lansford). During this season, innumerable pitchers are throwing up a bare hand to stop a line drive, like Gubicza did today.

Dozens of position players when they're on first base put a hand in front of their helmet in case the pitcher's throw to first goes wild. I'm not sure, but I *think* they're wearing the helmet to protect them against just that. And this particular reaction will just ensure that the player ends up with three or four broken fingers and on the disabled list.

I feel the same way about the latest trend in baserunning — the head-first slide. Rickey Henderson's been a marvellous innovator, but he introduced this really dumb move. You take ball players who are paid $3 million to work half a year; then you put them on the base paths and say "go ahead, slide head first, and risk countless injuries." Feet-first sliding seemed to work for the first 130 years of baseball history. It gets you there just as quickly and you can hook slide, as well as using high-flying spikes to intimidate. I don't understand it.

Strike Zones, Cyclops and Shaker

Friday, August 2, 1991   7:35 PM   Fenway Park
Pre-Game Standings

	W	L	Pct.	GB	Ho.	Strk.	P10	Div.
TORONTO	59	44	.573	-	33-21	W-2	4-6	26-16
Detroit	52	49	.515	6	32-18	W-2	6-4	20-19
New York	47	51	.480	9 1/2	25-25	W-1	3-7	23-13

Final Score: Red Sox 5, Blue Jays 3

THE SLIDE CONTINUES. After the White Sox swept us 12–4 and 8–7 on Monday and Tuesday, Cleveland arrived. Of course, the way we're going, nothing comes easy. We won both games — 3–1 and 7–5 — but as the media described it, we "won ugly."

Some incidents from this week show exactly what happens to a team in a bit of a panic:

- Against the White Sox Tuesday night in the ninth inning, Devon White singled and on the first pitch to Carter promptly broke for second, long before the pitcher even thought of starting his move to the plate. He got picked off and killed the last gasp.
- Against Cleveland on Wednesday. With the bases loaded, Greg Myers hit a deep fly ball to right field. Mark Whiten climbed the wall in right field and made an enormous catch. With only one out, he knew Olerud could tag and score from third and therefore simply fired hard to second. Gruber foolishly was hung up between second and third, and Whiten's throw doubled him off.

While all this was happening, Olerud loped even more slowly than usual towards home. He crossed it so late that it appeared at first the umpire had called the third out before Olerud hit the plate. The run stood, but it shouldn't have been close.

- On Thursday afternoon, with runners on first and third, Olerud hesitated on a ground ball towards first. By the time he decided what to do, the runner on third scored. If Olerud had come up throwing, the runner would easily have been out. In the same game, Albert Belle singled, driving in a key run past Manuel Lee's outstretched glove. Tony Fernandez would have made that play. Four weeks ago, Lee would have made that play.
- Thursday again. After Acker was inexplicably called into the ball game by Cito, he gave up a double, a walk and a wild pitch. The walk was to Mike Aldrete, who is a terrible hitter. Jim Acker chose to walk him and then wild pitch him to second. Runners on second and third, none out. Tie game, infield in, when the batter hit a little tapper towards third base. Acker charged it, and could have thrown it to first or to home to hang up Aldrete easily. He dropped the ball.
- Still Thursday. Devon White was up with Mookie Wilson on second. Down two strikes, he took a half-swing and the ball zipped past the catcher to the backstop. Wilson alertly went straight to third, while White stood there thinking it was a ball. Cleveland catcher Joel Skinner presumed it was a swing for strike three and threw to first before White twigged. In fact, White never left the batter's box until the third-base umpire confirmed that it *was* a full swing and he was out. Instead of one out, runners on first and third, we ended up with two out, runner on third.

All of this brings us to what may be one of the pivotal games in the season — Candiotti against Clemens, the Blue Jays at Fenway Park ... and Friday night TV.

The Blue Jays are coming in to probably the most important ten days of the season, three games against Boston in Boston, three games against Detroit at the SkyDome, followed by four more games against Boston. I'm busy worrying big about the Blue Jays right now, but I'm trying to keep some things in perspective. First,

Detroit and Boston are well behind. For them a split or even a narrow win in the series is not enough. They've got to sweep. If Boston wins five of the seven games (God forbid), they'll pick up three games only and still be seven back. If the Blue Jays win just three of the seven, then the Red Sox pick up a grand total of one game. Detroit is looking at a three-game series in Toronto. If they win 2–1, they'll cut the lead (presuming it's still six) to five. On the other hand, if Detroit can sweep three, they'll pick up three games. Hence the pressure.

◇ The Game

Clemens tends always to be at his best against the Blue Jays. We can't expect an easy time tonight, and it's not. But it starts that way.

The Blue Jays come on the field looking better than they have recently. Confident and relaxed. I think they're happy to be away from home and getting a fresh start. In the second inning, Kelly Gruber hits a solo home run just above the green monster in left field. 1–0, Blue Jays. Spirits are up, we're all feeling good. I foolishly feel the Blue Jays are going to win this game and stop the slide. The next batter, Mulliniks, hits a grounder to third. This is Wade Boggs's territory, but last night he pulled a groin muscle and is unlikely to play in this series. In any event, "Psycho" Steve Lyons is playing third. Lyons is a front-line flake and a fourth-string third baseman, and he lets Rance's grounder zip under his glove for an error.

Notwithstanding Psycho, the Red Sox get out of the inning partly helped by a one-out, two-on strikeout by Rene Gonzales. Cito has decided to play Gonzales tonight because he apparently "is a good, high fastball hitter" (this from Buck Martinez on TSN). With a lifetime batting average of .217, it's hard to believe that he's a good anything hitter. Mookie then comes up with two out and two on and hits a liner at third. Sure enough, Psycho makes a great diving catch to end the inning.

Candiotti pitches a sloppy second inning, but he gets out of it.

In the top of the third, the Blue Jays continue their confident play, with Alomar getting a single and Joe Carter homering seconds after Buck Martinez announces that Carter is having trouble seeing

Clemens's fastball. Blue Jays 3, Boston 0.

The Blue Jays are playing more heads-up ball than we've seen in the last week-and-a-half. When Psycho hits a foul ball into the first row of the stands on the third-base side in the third inning, Gruber leans into the stands and makes the catch. Unique in this day and age is the fact that Kelly actually uses two hands to make the catch. That's exactly the way Sheldon taught me and exactly the way Pete Rose always caught the ball. There is no conceivable reason not to use both hands whenever you *can*. But it's uncool. Everyone from Rickey Henderson to Devon White has to make the good-looking one-hander.

Blue Jays carry the 3–0 lead into the bottom of the fifth, and I'm breathing easy, even taking a moment to go downstairs to get a diet Coke. But leading off the fifth, Candiotti walks Luis Rivera and commits two fatal errors on one play:

- He walks the number-nine batter in the lineup — an absolute no-no.
- The batter leads off the inning.

Todd Stottlemyre's father, Mel, a great pitcher for the Yankees years ago, did some homework last year as pitching coach for the New York Mets and discovered that 70 percent of leadoff walks come around to score.

Jody Reed, the number-one hitter, then doubles, and, after Psycho pops to the shortstop, Candiotti issues his fifth walk in five innings. A formula for disaster. The bases are loaded and up comes Jack Clark. On Wednesday, Clark hit three home runs, including a grand slam, in one game; on the opening day of the season at the SkyDome, he hit the grand slam that beat the Blue Jays.

With the bases loaded, it would now be reasonable to expect a pitching change. But we know Cito will hardly ever pull Candiotti from a game in any circumstance, no matter how bad the situation. To be fair, Mike Timlin was put on the DL yesterday. David Weathers, a double-A pitcher with an excellent earned run average but a poor win/loss record, has been brought up to replace him. In any case, there is no one warming up in the bullpen, so Cito has not given himself the option of changing pitchers. Only when Clark is actually in the batter's box does Cito get Bob MacDonald and Weathers warming up. When did you first sense there was trouble, Cito?

Clark hits a ball deep to right-centre for an easy sac fly. Not only does Rivera — that fatal number-nine hitter — leadoff-walk-score, but Reed and Quintana both tag up and move up a base. Now we have two runners in scoring position and a single will tie the score. Mike Greenwell comes up next and shows that we needn't worry about a single. He drills a Candiotti pitch to deep right field, well over the fence. Boston 4, Toronto 3 in the blink of an eye.

It's my fault. I should never have gone for that Coke.

The next batter, Tom Brunansky, lines a back-to-back homer over the left-field fence. Boston 5, Blue Jays 3. Unbelievably now, the camera switches to the Blue Jays' bullpen. Both MacDonald and Weathers are *sitting down*! Cito apparently decided that Candiotti, having given up two walks, a double and two home runs in the inning, was now out of the woods because, I guess, no one was left on base. Candiotti does get out of the inning with a strikeout.

Suddenly, the Blue Jays are behind, and this is the point in the game where it is vital to snap back quickly, to regain the momentum and to show you're not about to let down or be beaten. In this kind of circumstance, the last thing you want is a quick inning. The batters should be coming up taking pitches, stepping out of the batter's box, doing anything to slow down the momentum of the game, to slow down the pitcher and to regain control. What the opposition wants after a big inning is exactly the reverse. They want to run out on the field and get the other team out — one, two, three.

Just watch it. The pitcher rarely will step off the rubber, go for the resin bag, or even spit or grab himself. He will play a quick game of pitch and catch with the catcher and try to get his team back up to bat while they're feeling that they can hit every ball out of the park. Carter, Olerud and Gruber are coming up and one would hope that experienced people like them would drag out the inning while doing everything they can to get on base. But Carter flies to deep right on the second or third pitch. Olerud takes his nightly called third strike, and Gruber bounces out quickly third to first.

The Red Sox don't score again, but they don't have to. Roger Clemens gives up only one hit after Carter's home run in the third: a single to Borders in the seventh. The seventh was the last chance the Blue Jays really had to get back in the game. Clemens set down the side in the fourth, fifth and sixth to record eleven outs in a row. He then gave up a none-out walk in the seventh to Rance Mulliniks. And this run should score because it's a leadoff walk. Pat Borders follows with his second single of the night to put runners at first and second with none out.

Here's where Cito again has to take responsibility, in part, for the outcome. The runner at second is Rance Mulliniks, one of the slowest Blue Jays and a DH. Rob Ducey should have been sent in to pinch run for him. We're in the seventh inning, we've got a rally going against one of the best pitchers in baseball and you've got to strike while the iron's hot. But not Cito. He does not pinch run for Mulliniks. There are runners at first and second, and reliable Rene (Mediocre Glove, Bad Bat) Gonzales is up.

There are a dozen possibilities, all of which represent a better chance for a base hit or even a successful sac bunt than does Rene Gonzales. If Ducey weren't going to pinch run, he could have been brought in here. Or Pat Tabler. Or even rookie Ed Sprague. But no. Gonzales comes up and is asked to sacrifice the runners. He chokes up to bunt but fails to make a move on either of the first or second pitches — both strikes. Now *I'm* choked up. Then he makes a half-hearted move at the third pitch, which of course is strike three. Mookie Wilson, another player Cito will never pinch hit for, is allowed to hit, and he flies to short centre field, bringing up Devon White, who has struck out three times already. Devon makes it four in short order.

BOXSCORE

Red Sox 5
Blue Jays 3

TORONTO	AB	R	H	BI	BOSTON	AB	R	H	BI
White cf	4	0	0	0	Reed 2b	4	1	1	0
RAlmr 2b	4	1	1	0	Lyons 3b	4	0	0	0
Carter rf	4	1	1	2	Qintana 1b	1	1	0	0
Olerud 1b	4	0	0	0	JClark dh	3	0	0	1
Gruber 3b	4	1	1	1	Grnwl lf	4	1	3	3
Mllniks dh	3	0	0	0	Brnsky rf	4	1	2	1
Brders c	4	0	2	0	Burks cf	4	0	0	0
Gnzales ss	3	0	0	0	Pena c	2	0	0	0
MWilsn lf	3	0	0	0	Rivera ss	2	1	0	0
Totals	33	3	5	3	Totals	28	5	6	5

Toronto   012 000 000 - 3
Boston   000 050 00x - 5

E - RAlomar (11), Lyons (3). LOB - Toronto 4, Boston 5. 2B - Reed (23), Greenwell (14). HR - Carter (24), Gruber (12), Greenwell (8), Brunansky (13). CS - Greenwell (3). SF - JClark.

	IP	H	R	ER	BB	SO
Toronto						
Candiotti (L, 9-11)	7	5	5	5	5	2
Weathrs	1	1	0	0	0	1
Boston						
Clemens (W, 12-7)	9	5	3	3	1	9

WP - Clemens.

On the night, the Blue Jays leave four runners. All four were left by Gonzales and Wilson. Understandable in the second inning, but, in the seventh, it is not.

Had the Blue Jays been able to beat Roger Clemens in a game in which they were beating the Red Sox by three runs, they would have broken Boston's hearts and backs. Clemens is, of course, Boston's best (or only) pitcher. As it is, the Blue Jays lose their early confidence and their chance to gain momentum through lazy managing and a seeming willingness to go down easily to Roger Clemens's fastball.

◇ "Cyclops"

Tonight Clemens is clearly the beneficiary, as are most front-line pitchers, of generous calls from the umpires. Everyone knows that the Nolan Ryans, the Roger Clemenses, the Orel Hershisers all get the benefit of the doubt from the umpire. The umpires believe they can hit the corners, and they give them the corners even when they've missed them. Equally, the great hitters — the George Bretts, the Wade Boggses and the Don Mattinglys — get the benefit of the doubt when they take a pitch. If these guys take a pitch, the umpire presumes that they know the strike zone, and you hardly ever see a called third strike.

Baseball junkies revel in all of this. The announcers, particularly the former players, will say, "Well Ryan, of course, has the benefit of the wide strike zone," or "Boggs has such a good eye, you know if he takes the pitch it's unlikely that the umpire is going to call it on him." Here's one fan who thinks that is all oxtrailings. That is how it's called, but I can't think of another sport where there are tough line calls to make, including tennis, where the benefit of the doubt is given to a star player. Picture this: You've got Manuel Lee batting .228 in against Roger Clemens. If Lee is batting .228 overall, you can imagine what the odds are of his getting a hit against Clemens. And here you have an umpire who is then going to tilt the odds even further in favour of Clemens.

Why? Well, there can't be too many explanations. Let's try a couple.

One: Clemens is a star and deserves the benefit of the doubt. No. Stars have proven they can do it under any circumstances. Stars don't need the edge. I have trouble imagining that Babe Ruth asked for or expected an edge. And for sure, the meanest dude of all, Ty Cobb, wouldn't have. No. It shouldn't work that way. But it does.

Two: In a marginal situation where a pitch is on, at or has just missed the outside corner of the plate, the umpire is more likely to be right if he relies on the judgment of a seasoned, patient hitter like Wade Boggs. This argument has some validity. Having watched both Wade Boggs and a bunch of umpires, I agree that Boggs is often more likely to be right. But that isn't the point. Umpires, like hockey referees, linesmen, football field judges and all other arbiters in sport, are paid to be objective and fair. To call it the way they see it. The umpire has absolutely no right to rely on Boggs's judgment. He should be calling them exactly the same, whether it's Boggs, Bonilla or Buddy Biancalana at bat. The umpire should be absolutely oblivious to who's up to bat, save for measuring the strike zone depending on the distance between the batter's knees and "numbers." To allow the personality, hitting record or "eye" of the batter to affect the pitch call is to destroy the symmetry and objectivity of a game built on fairness.

Were some of Hank Aaron's 755 home runs the result of umpires giving him a smaller strike zone later in his career? Were some of Nolan Ryan's incredible numbers in both wins and strikeouts a function of being given a wider strike zone than Jim Clancy? For that matter, do umpires call the game differently in the eighth inning of a no-hit bid than in the second inning? Count on it.

All of that will and should become academic in our lifetime. Even today, there is no need to rely on balls and strikes being called by an umpire. Electronics will replace all of this and establish what the real strike zone is in every game.

"Cyclops," the electronic line judge, has already entered the game of tennis. Of course, that doesn't stop John McEnroe from arguing against the "beep," nor will the electronic Joe Brinkman stop Jack Clark from yelling and screaming when he strikes out on a "Cyclops"-called third strike. But at least the machine won't be able to howl back at him.

We will hear, when the time comes, all the same silly comments we hear from the NFL luddites who don't like the instant replay on certain calls. But folks, please, these sports addict us. Never mind the players whose livelihoods depend upon winning or losing, who spend six months a year trying to win a championship and who want it determined on skill and ability, not on one umpire's stupid call. What about me? These sports suck me in. They tease me, they addict me, they make me listen to the Tigers games through static, they make me care about someone named Carlos Quintana, they make me memorize the good and bad umpires, they make me growl at my wife when my teams lose. All I ask for is that I be given a break. I'm busy enough being angry at Cito for not pinch hitting, at Ward for losing his cool, at Gruber for first-pitch hitting, at Gillick for losing Bell and at Cito (again) for using Jim Acker. It's not fair to make me rail at an umpire's call that I damn well know was made because Roger Clemens and not Joe Hesketh is pitching and because "Cyclops" isn't umping.

But I don't promise not to be aggravated by "Cyclops" either.

◇ Post-Game Notes

The trading deadline is now past. I predicted on CBC's "Metro Morning" last Wednesday that Tom Henke would be gone. I still believe he was shopped around the league. I still believe his fastball has abandoned him, but I'm happy to report that he mopped up against the Indians yesterday and did one of his old Henke performances, getting three out quickly in the ninth, including a last out strikeout. On the other hand, it was against the Indians.

◆ ◆ ◆

Once again the Blue Jays have taken me up the rollercoaster early in the game by jumping into the lead. Once again they let me down. To make it worse, Detroit is hitting their usual number of home runs, with Whitaker and Fryman going over the fence and Cecil yet to be heard from. Even Lloyd Moseby gets a long triple. It's 7–2 for the Tigers over the Yankees by the seventh inning, and tomorrow our lead is going to be only five over Detroit. By the time Detroit gets here, it could be three. Not quite the scenario I talked about two hours ago, and not quite the scenario that we saw at the All-Star break. If the Tigers catch us and win the pennant, I swear I'll give up baseball.

◆ ◆ ◆

Only Robbie Alomar continues to have his head in the game. In the Wednesday night game with Cleveland leading 1–0, he tripled to the wall in right field on a ball that, for many players, would have been a double. The next batter hit a grounder to third. The third baseman, Manto, alertly checked Alomar to make sure he was still near third base and not going for home. The instant the third baseman released the ball, Alomar took off, and by the time the first baseman, Martinez, relayed the throw home, Alomar had slid in (head first, of course), safe under the tag. A key run, and one that required split-second timing, courage and speed. Unlike White and Olerud and Lee in the last couple of days, Alomar was still in the game.

Trying to keep the Blue Jays' slump in perspective, Pittsburgh, probably the best team in baseball and the team with the best record, currently at sixty and forty, has lost six games in a row. And, like the Jays, they're four and six in their last ten. On the other hand, San Francisco, which spent a good part of this year unexpectedly in last place in the NL West, has now won eleven in a row. Streaks over a 162-game season are what baseball is all about.

Meanwhile, it is aggravating to see the Detroit Tigers hanging in there. Sparky Anderson was quoted in the paper today as saying that the Tigers are not capable of catching the Blue Jays. My late mother would call Sparky an *"uction"* — Yiddish for stubborn, irritating, a pain in the butt. Cito responds both properly and accurately: "Ah, you know that darn Sparky. He thinks he can grab a little edge by lulling us." Sparky is simply trying to take the pressure off his own team by keeping them loose and telling them not to worry about the Blue Jays. Just keep hitting home runs.

◆ ◆ ◆

I'm going to take Shaker for a walk now; not Lloyd Moseby, need I say, but my dog. In 1984, we decided to get a family pet and chose a wonderful Kerry blue terrier. While at the ball game with friends, watching the Shake have one of his rare good seasons, my kids decided to name their new pet "Shaker." Thanksgiving Day 1984, of course, was the very day that Shaker arrived in our house and that Bill Davis said goodbye to his as he announced his retirement as leader of Ontario's Progressive Conservative party. This was what one might call a fairly busy day in my home, since:

- Shaker arrived.
- I resigned as chairman of the SkyDome in order to
- run for the leadership of the Party, which was
- won in the following January by Frank Miller,
- all of which resulted in our losing in the subsequent election that May.

I'll leave it to you to decide which of the above I regret the most.

◆ ◆ ◆

Since Lloyd Moseby's fortunes went as well as my Party's over the next three years, we wanted to do an Albert (don't call me Joey) Belle, a Manuel (don't call me Manny) Lee, or an Ahmad Rashad or a Karem Abdul Jabbar and change Shaker's name to Junior (Felix), then Mookie, then Devo. But my dog's smarter than some baseball experts. He still answers only to Shaker, and so Shaker it is.

During our walk, my shattered nerves were tested when the dog that lives next door to my neighbour — the NDP Minister of Community and Social Services — decided to jump out and bark at Shaker, who barked right back like an AL umpire. If only I had Cito's temperament (not to mention his job).

Spooky Sparky in Virgin Territory

Thursday, August 8, 1991   7:35 PM   Toronto SkyDome

Pre-Game Standings

	W	L	Pct.	GB	Ho.	Strk.	P10	Div.
TORONTO	62	46	.574	-	35-21	W-3	5-5	29-18
Detroit	55	52	.514	6 1/2	35-19	L-3	5-5	23-22
Boston	50	57	.467	11 1/2	28-29	L-4	4-6	19-22

Final Score: Tigers 4, Blue Jays 0   Attendance: 50,307

WITHIN EVERY SEASON of 162 games, there are three or four that become etched in my memory. The rest fade into a series of great catches, big homers, dumb pitching changes or even brawls. One forgets the day, month and sometimes even the opposition, but the incident, the highlight and the circumstances stand out among a blur of fly balls, singles and double plays.

Every season leaves a general impression. 1984 — spirit, hope and Roy Lee Jackson. 1985 — Bobby Cox managing aggressively, Doyle Anderson pitching meanly and Al Oliver. 1986 — lethargy and a late run and Duane Ward's first start in Boston late in the season. 1987 — George Bell, Madlock injuring Fernandez, the choke in the last week. 1988 — Bell-as-DH-disaster, malcontents, and Stieb's two near no-hitters. 1989 — Mookie's spirit, Williams's firing, a happy club, bad basics and Rickey Henderson. 1990 — Brunansky's catch, more bad basics and Kenny (Wrong Way) Williams.

1991? Can't tell till December or January what images will linger and what broad general impression the year will bring.

But within all that, there are a half-dozen games that will be remembered for years. They may not be typical of that year — indeed, they may stand out because they are not — but tonight was surely a memorable game. Having won the first two games of the series, we had the Tigers back by six-and-a-half games and ready to close them out. Seven-and-a-half would do it for sure. The media made it easy for Sparky to motivate his troops. I suppose he didn't have to say anything when his players saw the Toronto headlines: "Done Like Dinner," "Where's the Tiger Power?" and all sorts of other premature obituaries.

I was at my eye doctor's waiting room, surrounded by senior citizens with various ailments. Neither physical condition nor mother tongue could inhibit them from discussing loudly the state of the Blue Jays and "good old Kelly," and "Mr Henke" and "that nice man, Mr Gaston."

It was finally my turn to see the doctor, who put some messy guck in my eyes. This dilated my pupils to the extent that my eyes were a cross between Rick Moranis and a solar eclipse. The doctor said that although it would take a while for this effect to disappear, I should be okay in an hour, more or less.

My left eye behaved, but it wasn't till the fifth inning of the game, some five-and-a-half hours later, that my right eye ceased delivering fuzzy images. I think I'd been seeing the game the way Cory Snyder'd been seeing the ball. Or perhaps I felt like the Tigers facing Candiotti tonight.

For the third time in three days, the stadium was muted. No pennant excitement, no fever, no tension. The Tiger dugout for the third day running was unusually laid back. If anything, it was a little on the depressed side, unlike the first two games when the players seemed passive but interested.

◇ The Game

Candiotti is due for a class outing and we just know it. So, I think, do the Tigers.

He strikes out Cuyler and Whitaker and then issues his usual first-inning walk to Bergman before striking out Fielder. Small problem, however. Greg Myers misses the third strike and it goes back to the screen. Cecil Fielder, who needs a lift on an eighteen wheeler when he's in a hurry, makes it to first, beating the ball there easily. Maybe "beat" isn't the right word — "lands ahead of" is more appropriate.

Just kidding, Cecil. You can play on my team anytime ... again.

Tettleton then walks, so, after five batters, Candiotti has struck out three, walked two, has the bases loaded and is still in the first inning. This is really hard to do. Travis Fryman, who homered yesterday, is up. But again it's one of those times we simply don't think we're in trouble and we're right. He flies out to right field.

Poor Greg Myers is having trouble catching Candiotti. He misses eight pitches in the first inning. This, of course, is good news, not bad, because it indicates that Candiotti's knuckler is really floating and moving tonight. Myers is playing goal more than catching ... happy to block the ball successfully. By the end of Candi's seven-inning stint tonight, Myers will miss twenty-six pitches. Rough. He does a really fine job of blocking the ones he doesn't catch though, keeping Candi out of trouble.

Meanwhile, Bill Gullickson is pitching for Detroit. He is this year's Storm Davis — bad stats everywhere but in the "win" column; 4.22 earned run average, fourteen and six. Compare this with Candiotti, who is 2.49 and nine and eleven. The difference? Tigers score an average of six runs per game for Gully, while Candiotti's teams, the devastating Indians and the Toronto Blue Jays, have given him barely two per game, the lowest in the majors.

Gullickson is not about to threaten anyone for the Cy Young. But watch tonight. Devon White leads off, as he always does, by getting on base. Today it's a double. Yesterday it was a homer. But Gullickson, remembering that the SkyDome is Cy Young territory, then goes to the first hitter in the fifth without giving up another hit.

Candiotti is pitching a different but great game. Top of the second, John Moses (acquired yesterday by the Tigers), who is 33 years old at the start of this game but will be 34 at the end, strikes out. Deer walks. Livingstone strikes out. Nine batters so far; five strikeouts, three walks. Cuyler singles and the Tigers have had five runners in two innings, but Candiotti still appears to be in command.

This brings up Lou Whitaker, the veteran Jay killer, who lines a single to short right centre. Carter charges it and we anticipate a play at the plate, but, no, in one of the moments that will mark the 1991 season, Carter flashes out of nowhere. And, instead of playing it on a hop, he dives to make a backhanded catch right before the ball hits the ramp. Third out, saving at least one run.

Carter is a gamer. After he made a just marginally more sensational catch to save the game last weekend in Boston he said:

- "You do whatever you have to do to catch the ball. If you have to hit the wall, if you have to get beat up, you do it."
- "Look, this is the fun time. This is the pressure time. I've never played in pressure games before. I want to play in them now."
- "Games like these you see what you're made of. You make that diving play because that's what it's all about."

Joe's bat has cooled off (temporarily, I think), but his spirit and his body haven't. It's an old baseball cliché that batters slump, but not runners and usually not fielders. If anything, Carter's cool bat will motivate him to push his customarily good fielding up a notch. He's just a guy who's going to contribute in every way he can. This catch is his third great one in four nights. I figure this will be the play of the game, giving the Jays momentum and killing off the Tigers. But I am forgetting history, hexes and the baseball gods.

Carter's enthusiasm and heroics are not enough to wake up our bats early. Only Devo can get on base between his leadoff double and the fifth. When he does, it's by way of being hit by a pitch. Devo continues to display speed, smarts and hustle when, with two out, he intends to steal second. We know it, Sparky knows it, Gullickson knows it and Tettleton knows it. Gullickson throws five times to first to hold him on, and, when he finally throws to the plate, it's a pitch out. White is going all right and swipes the ball successfully. This is right out of the Rickey Henderson in-your-face school of baseball. But, like Carter's great catch, it isn't enough to fire the Blue Jays, since reliable Robbie Alomar strikes out to end the inning.

The Tigers also exhibit good baseball. Every team charts opposing teams and their players. They know how often Olerud will hit an inside pitch to the right side and how often he will pull it to the right side. The infielders will all watch the catcher's signal and glove placement so that if he calls for an off-speed slider, they'll take an additional step or two towards the first-base line. What looks like a routine easy out is often a result of lengthy research and analysis, the catcher remembering what pitch to call on whom and the infielders watching the catcher's fingers and positioning themselves accordingly. So, when Olerud hits a ball hard to deep second base in the fourth, he is out easily — but only because of pre-execution by the Tigers. They knew where to play him on that particular pitch, and Whitaker was sitting there waiting for the ball's arrival. They do the same to retire White in the sixth, but this time it's with the second baseman two or three steps in the other direction.

In both cases the ball went right to Whitaker — a routine catch, due to solid, thorough (but unseen) managing and scouting.

In tonight's ball game we get to see some bad baseball too. Mulliniks leads off the fifth with a single for our second hit, but Myers tries to sacrifice him to second in an 0–0 game and bunts like a pre-1991 Blue Jay: too hard and too close to the pitcher. Gullickson grabs it and fires to second to get Mulliniks. Is this important? Well, Ducey is up next and promptly singles. Had Myers executed the sac bunt successfully, Mulliniks would have scored.

Mickey Tettleton, the catcher the Tigers stole for Jeff Robinson (now in the minors), reaches way out over the plate in the sixth to hit a textbook bat-control double. Unusual for a power hitter and for the Tigers in particular, whose bats are about as disciplined as Lou Piniella's temper. More great baseball. Fryman, the next batter, lines the ball down the third-base line. Gruber jumps high to grab it. If he doesn't, Tettleton scores easily. Great play, Kelly, and great positioning too.

As we go through the sixth still 0–0, Robbie's getting frustrated. The player who may be the most disciplined bat-control man in the league failed to hit to the right side after White's leadoff double in the first and struck out in the third with White on base. After he grounded out in the sixth, he slammed his helmet on the dugout steps. Unusual. Bad news — he's showing his temper. Good news — he cares. Robbie will go on to single in the eighth, tenth and fourteenth.

After Carter singles, we see Olerud up with one on and two out. He does what he has become notorious for doing: taking pitches, including third strikes. The kid has a — are you ready for it? — "sweet swing." He has patience, obviously. He is said to be a good student, easy to teach. So tell me why he won't swing at a third-strike pitch? You simply have to swing at anything that could be called when you have two strikes ... unless you are Brett, Mattingly or Gwynn. Olerud isn't, and I'm afraid he will not be. Unfazed, Olerud ends the sixth with his bat on his shoulder.

Candiotti is still in control. Strikes out Deer for the second time (on an "Olerud" third strike) and then, in a night when we'll see everything, Cuyler tries a two-strike bunt. Candiotti gets his twelfth and last strikeout.

There is something happening in almost every half-inning now, and Gruber leads off the Blue Jays' seventh with a single, bringing a slumping Mulliniks up with one of the key at bats of the game. He does the logical thing by laying down a bunt after getting up 2–0, but it isn't a good one. Have I seen this before? This one goes, you guessed it, straight back to Gullickson, who easily gets Gruber at second. It could be a replay on the Jumbotron of Mulliniks and Myers, but, no, this is Gruber and Mulliniks with the same act. Myers follows with his daily deep fly to centre field.

Ducey uppercuts a pop to the catcher. After seven, it's scoreless. A tense, exciting game now. An exhibition of great pitching and managing with some poor execution mixed in. But the mistakes provide a chance to study and appreciate what ought to have been done and how plays should have been executed. In the top of the eighth, Cito makes a little-noted move, which turns out to be a grave mistake and one that will haunt him later in the game.

Candiotti has gone seven innings, striking out twelve batters (to tie a Blue Jays' record for even nine-inning games), giving up no runs on only four hits. Even when he walked a runner on, he was in complete command of the game. Cito had been leaving Candiotti in games too long. Tonight, when Candiotti is not even remotely struggling, he surprisingly sends Bob MacDonald out to start the eighth.

MacDonald is a lefty, as is the scheduled batter, Dave Bergman. Sparky, of course, pinch hits Skeeter Barnes, a right-handed batter, even though it's third spot in the batting order, and he flies to centre field. Are you listening Cito?

The big mistake is yet to come. Gaston does it by pulling MacDonald after one batter. Why? Why in the eighth inning does he bring in a new pitcher to pitch to one batter — and not a particularly difficult out in a key situation — with none on? Never seen that before.

David Weathers comes on to finish the eighth easily.

This will go fourteen innings, and Cito will have used one of his relievers, who could have given him two or three innings, to pitch to one batter. Or if he didn't need him to pitch two or three innings, he could have used him later in the game for a key out against a left-handed batter. But he didn't. He used him in a none-out, none-on situation against a bad batter in the eighth. The result is that all the bullpen arms will end up stretched tonight, with the Red Sox series coming up this weekend.

Weathers stays in the game until he walks the bases loaded in the ninth inning. Nice touch in a no-score game.

When we see Jim Acker start to walk in from the bullpen, we too want to walk — out. Picture this: Jim Acker pitching to Jay killer Whitaker with the bases loaded in the ninth. He gets him.

Blue Jays' ninth, 0–0. Henneman, Detroit's best pitcher, on the mound; strikes out Gruber and Mulliniks. Myers and Rob Ducey single. Only a crummy little Texas leaguer is required to win this game. But Manuel Lee is the batter. *Everyone* would pinch hit here. Lee has batted .211 in the last month. The game is on the line. There are lots of possible pinch hitters, including Sprague batting .279, Wilson and Borders batting around .250 and Tabler batting about the same as Lee but with a sensational career batting average with runners in scoring position. Give me any of them instead of Manuel Lee against Detroit's best reliever. But no, Cito lets Lee bat and he grounds out to end the inning. This is a team that has trouble scoring runs. It gets a few chances to score, and, when it does, it must. As in so many other situations, Cito simply will not pull the trigger with runners on base. And he must, because they simply aren't there too often.

Into extras unnecessarily. In the tenth, Alomar is up with one out. After smashing his helmet when he went zero for three through the sixth, he singled in the eighth and is eager to hit in the tenth. Alomar is now suddenly two for five. With Alomar on, the new Detroit pitcher, Jerry Don Gleaton, the ultimate journeyman, throws to first a half-dozen times to hold Robbie close. The fans boo. Why? Robbie will steal if he has half a chance. Gleaton is a lefty, so he can see the runner better. What else should Gleaton do?

Gleaton, indeed, is able to keep Robbie close, long enough for Carter and Olerud to fly out to end the inning. After ten, our cleanup hitter Olerud is zero for five and has left five runners on base. Cito is stuck with Acker now that he's used up MacDonald and Weathers in one-and-two-thirds innings.

Acker, a mediocre pitcher having a terrible year, finishes his sterling performance in the twelfth, and on comes Henke in an unusual situation for him. He has been perfect this year in save situations, although neither dominating nor terrorizing opposing batters. Henke comes in to finish the Tigers' twelfth, and he strikes out the side in the thirteenth, followed by the first batter in the fourteenth. Not a bad performance. Five batters, four strikeouts. Easy.

But Henke has succeeded this year in part — as Sparky Anderson pointed out the other day — because Duane Ward has been so effective in getting the Blue Jays through the seventh and eighth, allowing Henke to be called upon only in the ninth inning and usually with none on. This means his arm is not tired; he can come in in less difficult situations and work his arm to its capacity for only one inning.

Now, because of the length of the game and MacDonald's one-third of an inning, Henke is into his third inning and his sixth batter. That batter is Milt Cuyler, who doubles. Henke then walks Lou Whitaker, bringing up Skeeter Barnes.

Sparky and the Virgin Hex strike. Sparky pinch hits Mark Salas, a left-handed, pathetic-hitting journeyman catcher. Now, I have to say it. If Cito had brought in a Mark Salas, batting .067 — yes, .067 — no homers and four RBIs — yup, count them, four — to pinch hit for anyone in any kind of situation, I would have gone crazy. An .067 batter? Mark Salas? Spooky Sparky not only does that, but he pinch hits him for the number-three hitter in the lineup. The Blue Jays, on the other hand, seem to have a pathologic aversion to pinch hitting for anyone above number seven in the order (or pinch hitting at all, for that matter).

In one of those moments I'll remember long after this season is over, Mark Salas hits a three-run homer over the right-field fence.

Of course, he does it because (a) it's Sparky, (b) it's the Tigers versus Toronto in a late-season game and (c) everyone hits his first home run of the year here. We call the SkyDome virgin territory. There must be a dozen players who had no homers either in the season or in their careers who broke the donut here. Tonight, it's Salas. If it matters, Henke strikes out Fielder before letting Tettleton hit a Fred McGriff to the fifth deck in right field. He then strikes out Fryman. So Henke strikes out the side in the thirteenth and the fourteenth, getting six of seven outs on strikeouts while allowing four other batters to score on two home runs. A strange, sad outing.

Blue Jays go quietly with only Alomar still in the game in the bottom of the fourteenth as he delivers his third single.

A tough loss, 4–0 in fourteen.

BOXSCORE

Tigers....................4
Blue Jays................0

Detroit	AB	R	H	BI	Toronto	AB	R	H	BI
Cuyler cf	6	1	2	0	White cf	5	0	1	0
Whtker 2b	6	1	1	0	RAlmr 2b	7	0	3	0
Brgmn 1b	2	0	0	0	Carter rf	7	0	1	0
Barnes 1b	3	0	0	0	Olerud 1b	6	0	0	0
Salas 1b	1	1	1	3	Gruber 3b	6	0	2	0
Fielder dh	7	0	1	0	Mllniks dh	4	0	1	0
Ttlleton c	6	1	3	1	Tabler dh	2	0	1	0
Frymn ss	5	0	0	0	Myers c	4	0	1	0
Moses lf	5	0	0	0	MWlsn pr	0	0	0	0
Deer rf	4	0	0	0	Brders c	1	0	1	0
Lvnstn 3b	3	0	1	0	Ducey lf	4	0	2	0
Phillips 3b	2	0	0	0	Snyder rf	2	0	0	0
					MnLee ss	6	0	0	0
Totals	50	4	9	4	Totals	54	0	13	0

| Detroit | 000 | 000 | 000 | 04 - 4 |
| Toronto | 000 | 000 | 000 | 00 - 0 |

DP - Toronto 1. LOB - Detroit 14, Toronto 15. 2B - Cuyler (7), Tettleton (10), White (29). HR - Salas (1), Tettleton (21). SB - White (26). S - Moses.

	IP	H	R	ER	BB	SO
Detroit						
Gullickson	7 1/3	6	0	0	1	4
Henneman	1 2/3	2	0	0	0	3
Gleaton	3	3	0	0	0	1
PGibson (W, 5-5)	2	2	0	0	1	2
Toronto						
Candiotti	7	4	0	0	3	12
MacDonald	1/3	0	0	0	0	0
Weathers	1 1/3	0	0	0	3	2
Acker	3	2	0	0	2	1
Henke (L, 0-1)	2 1/3	3	4	4	1	6

HBP - by Gullickson (White). PB - Myers 2.

◇ Post-Game Notes

In tonight's fourteen-inning game, only one beer trip was made. Was everyone else down the road drunk, tired or perhaps — dare I say it — into the game? I hope so.

◆ ◆ ◆

When Gleaton complained about a first pitch that was called a ball, the ump clearly stiffed him by calling the next pitch, which was right down the middle, ball two. Gleaton got the message and didn't say a word. Gullickson became one of the few opposing pitchers to get a decent round of applause as he left the game in the eighth inning. Even though it was the Tigers and an overrated Gullickson, I was glad to see it.

♦ ♦ ♦

The roof was open tonight, even though showers were predicted, and, in fact, it sprinkled during a few innings between 8:26 and 9:01, and 9:42 and 9:45. Finally, at 10:00 the newly adventurous operators of the roof decided to close it. It took twenty-four minutes. They are really getting daring, and no doubt they're going to get caught.

♦ ♦ ♦

While the Tigers were taking batting practice before the game, Pat Gillick came out on the field from the Blue Jays' dugout and walked around to the right side of the batting cage, looking for the Shaker, Lloyd Moseby. They chatted and laughed for about five minutes. Gillick left the field without talking to any other player. Obviously, the affection the two of them were reputed to have for each other was real and lasting. That's good to see, although I hear that the true story behind the famous 1988 George Bell spring training problem is that the Shake stirred up the controversy after Bell had agreed to DH when he got his $2 million contract. It was only in spring training when Sil Campusano (can you believe it?) was going to take over centre field with the Shake moving to left that this became an issue.

♦ ♦ ♦

When Henke got Tettleton on a ground ball to Olerud to end the twelfth with two out and Barnes on first, it was by-the-book baseball. In extras, you usually guard the lines to prevent an extra base hit, thereby conceding any singles up the middle. Olerud is standing right near the line, holding Barnes on, when the ball is hit hard. If he's not, it's a double, but because of the game positioning it's a routine ground-ball out.

♦ ♦ ♦

I think we saw Stottlemyre in the bullpen warming up in the fourteenth. Blue Jays certainly would have had to find another pitcher because Henke couldn't have gone much longer, even if he had survived. If you had to guess which Blue Jay starting pitcher would volunteer to come in, you would have bet on Stottlemyre. No word about it in the media, but I'm sure that's what happened.

◆ ◆ ◆

This game was exhilarating and exhausting. Had we won it, it might have been another turning-point in a season in which we're grasping for turning-points daily. It was a morale booster to the winner, a heartbreaker to the loser. Most of all, it was a "classic." I enjoyed (almost) every minute of it.

But, beyond the art in artistry, the concerns linger. Fourteen innings, no runs against weak pitchers — terrible pitchers, in fact. The bullpen is tired. Four games coming up against the Red Sox, and we're going to need "quality starts" from Wells and Stottlemyre over the next two games. And we've got to start hitting. We finished with the unusual line of no runs on thirteen hits — not an easy thing to do. All but White's leadoff double were singles. This shows how quiet our bats are and that Cito needs to go back to basic station-to-station ball. Alomar should have been bunting to third in the first. Myers had to execute the sac bunt in the fifth, and Mulliniks had to execute the sac bunt in the seventh. Lee should have been pinch hit for in the ninth. Alomar should have stolen in the tenth. Snyder should not have been batting for Ducey in the eleventh or in the thirteenth. He left four runners on base in two at bats in extra innings. Lee should have been pinch hit for in the eleventh with two out and two on if he hadn't been pinch hit for in the ninth. Tabler should have been able to bunt Gruber to second in the thirteenth.

◆ ◆ ◆

Baseball — men and boys, athletes and children. A 10- or 11-year-old boy sits near us daily but always in different seats. He's a nice-looking, pleasant boy, and today we finally ask him how he gets his seats. "Do you sneak down from the bleachers?" "No, Sir," he says. "We find out which hotel the players are staying at and we go there in the morning and ask them for tickets. They always give us some."

He goes on to explain that he lives in the Moss Park area and his mom can't afford tickets, but he loves baseball and all the players are "really nice."

Baseball bridges generations, borders, cultures and income levels. Baseball!

◆ ◆ ◆

I have to wonder about Turner Ward down in Syracuse. He was quietly acquired in the Candiotti trade as someone to fill in, I would guess, in a now depleted outfield in Syracuse. But, while we go with the terribly struggling Cory Snyder, Ward has just finished a seventeen-game streak, hitting in nineteen of twenty since coming from Cleveland, for a batting average of .337 with four homers and eighteen RBIs.

◆ ◆ ◆

Finally, it was a very long game, lasting five hours and twelve minutes. Yes, it was 12:45 A.M. when it ended, but it was a keeper! Yet at the end I guess there were only eight thousand fans left in the park. The place was so empty that we could hear the umpires' calls after almost every pitch. It's a shame, folks. You sat through a good movie and left before the ending. You read a good book and threw it out before the last chapter. Or do you really only go to the movies to buy the popcorn?

It'll take me and Shaker a long walk at 1:15 to unwind. It'll probably take the Jays a long week.

"Rickey, did you see that California Angel *rookie* wearing *my* number?"

Ken Kaiser, "If you show that replay, I'll put you in a headlock!"

Oakland's finest eyeing the fans. Scares the heck out of me.

This Oakland fan could teach Cito how to juggle his playoff pitching rotation.

A full out-of-town scoreboard. All games – plus pitchers' numbers. (*Note*: Scoreboard operator tells Canseco he loves him with a little "33" beside Baltimore's "1.")

Unbelievable! 4 million fans *and* they used the full tron!

The top of the rollercoaster.

Simply the best.

Gold glove, velvet style.

Please come to Toronto – the seagulls forgive you.

Joe congratulating Devo.

Jose congratulating himself.

America's funniest home videos: The Yankees video each player's at bats on individual cassettes.

The second time the roof was open in the rain – no costumes were ruined this time.

Who was throwing *this* scuffer?

A wad of chewing tobacco wrapped in Bazooka bubble gum – courtesy of Ruben Amaro Jr.

Our best DH had only one at bat at SkyDome this year ... and in the wrong uniform.

The White Sox DH was a great fullback.

Two of my three favourite fans, Melissa and Robbie. (Jamie is on the front cover sitting next to me.)

Who are these good-looking people on the *full* tron? An excellent lawyer, his wonderful daughter, his cousin (by marriage) Susan, and his cousin (by baseball) Sheldon.

Beanballs in Tiger Town

Sunday, August 18, 1991   1:35 PM   Tiger Stadium
Pre-Game Standings

	W	L	Pct.	GB	Ho.	Strk.	P10	Div.
TORONTO	64	54	.542	-	35-26	W-1	2-8	31-26
Detroit	62	56	.525	2	39-21	L-1	6-4	27-25
Boston	58	59	.496	5 1/2	29-30	L-1	8-2	26-23

Final Score: Blue Jays 4, Tigers 2

THE BLUE JAYS stumble, literally stumble, into Detroit, having let them and even Boston back into the race. A week ago, Boston was out of it. Now, after the Jays blow four games to Boston and lose two more to Milwaukee, the Red Sox are hanging around five or six games out — far too close for comfort.

We've lost seven of eight. Each night during the Boston and Milwaukee series, we kept saying, "Well, that's it. It can't get worse than this. We're still in first place. We're all right."

It reminded me of my two years in hell as Leader of the Opposition. Every time an opinion poll came out showing that we had dropped a few more points in public support, we would say, "Well, the good news is we finally bottomed out." And we meant it and believed it ... at least until the next poll came out and we'd lost a few more percentage points.

Are the Blue Jays at the bottom? Well, this series could do it. Funny the way the Detroit Tigers always pop up, early season, mid-season or late season, exactly when you don't want them to. We always arrive in Detroit at the wrong time, and this could be the wrong time.

Sheldon and I had talked a couple of months ago about going down to the Detroit series, when it looked like a nothing series. Every season for the last six or seven, we have made this trek. Some have been memorable. One was during the leadership campaign in late 1985, when the Blue Jays were chasing (successfully, as it turned out) the AL East championship, and I was chasing (successfully) the PC leadership (in the consolation round). Just as the Blue Jays went on to lose the league championship series, so my party and I went on to lose the 1987 election. I managed to lose bigger than the Jays.

Anyway, as we were both chasing the qualifying championships, I visited Tiger Stadium after an afternoon all-candidates talk-a-thon in London. We flew to Windsor in time to see the game prior to campaigning in Windsor the next morning (always at the "Chicken Court") and working our way through southwestern Ontario back to Toronto.

My most memorable visit didn't involve the Jays, but the Tigers and the San Diego Padres in the 1984 World Series. Andy Brandt, our MPP and cabinet minister from Sarnia, was and is a lifelong Tigers fan. He was a well-liked member of our caucus and an important ally for a leadership contender to have. In the first leadership campaign, I was one of the four contenders for the right to succeed Bill Davis (as opposed to 1985, when it was the consolation round to succeed Frank Miller as Leader of the Opposition). I had reason to believe that Andy would support me, and this backing was fairly important since Miller already had thirty or so caucus members supporting him. My campaign organization, upon hearing that Brandt had invited me to join him at a World Series game in Detroit, paid for a private plane (a 1940 vintage one-and-one-half engine, piston-driven, noisy former soapbox-derby vehicle with wings), and I flew down to go to the game.

That game turned out to be the final one of the Series, with Detroit winning, which caused an enormous riot outside Tiger Stadium after the game. There were serious injuries, and Brandt and I moved just quickly enough to get out, grab a cab and get to the airport.

Andy's tickets, which he assured me were good, turned out to be last row of the first section, right under the overhang, eliminating all view of fly balls. I couldn't have cared less whether the Tigers or the Padres won, but I cared a whole lot about whether *I* was going to win. My mind was elsewhere, and the only true victory I had was avoiding the riot.

Small footnote to history: Brandt supported Miller.

The annual trek to Detroit is one of the fun times, given the Tigers/Jays rivalry over the years. This year, though, my father had taken seriously ill, and I cancelled out and spent Friday night watching (and scoring) the game at home over late dinner, listening to it in the car on the way to the hospital (pulling over to record every at bat) and watching the rest with my father on the tiny TV set hanging over his bed at the hospital.

◇ The Games Friday and Saturday

Friday night, the Blue Jays play the Tigers even through seven with Key on the mound. Then the Duane Ward of previous years shows up to give up two singles and two walks in the eighth inning to produce three runs and a 5–2 win for Detroit. The Blue Jays' three errors cost them the win. It's a game that they don't ever seem to be in, even when they are tied 2–2.

The most memorable part of the night is a mixup in the eighth inning on a foul ball down to shallow right field. On this play, Alomar and Carter collide and the ball drops, something we've not seen this year. It was foul, and the batter ultimately grounded out short to first, but having our two best players collide and miss a routine foul fly ball to right field is really demoralizing.

Immediately after that play, five of the next six batters get on base, putting up three runs.

On Saturday, the Blue Jays surprise us by putting up seven runs on eight hits to beat the Tigers 7–2. Maldonado and Olerud homer, and, like the previous night, the key to this game seems to be a play by Carter. This time, unlike the previous night, the ball is fair and affects the outcome directly. In the fifth, with two on and one out, Cecil Fielder hits a boomer to right field just barely over the fence. Carter, angry over last night's embarrassment, simply will not let that ball go out, as he runs to the fence, watches carefully and leaps with his glove to turn a three-run homer into a sac fly. The contrast with the previous evening is significant and the blocking of a Fielder home run doubly significant. It was Joe saying, "no, Cecil, I will not let you beat us."

What is disturbing for the Blue Jays is the fact that they let the Tigers back in the game with five runs in the fifth and sixth, after being up 5–0 in the fifth.

Pat Borders is not charged with any passed balls, but Buck Martinez, the good, former defensive catcher doing the TSN broadcast, continues to point out that those wild pitches should be called passed balls, which Borders should be blocking. Nonetheless, when Sparky goes to a right-handed pitcher in the eighth, Cito has Mulliniks pinch hit for Sprague (Mulliniks batting about twenty points lower than Sprague), but then lets Borders (batting .247) bat for himself.

The final good news in this game is that Henke arrives in the ninth and strikes out two out of three, including Fielder and the famous Mark Salas, to end the game. A big win. We will leave Detroit in first place, no matter what happens on Sunday.

On Friday night we got the feeling we weren't in the game, even when it was 2–2. On Saturday, up 5–0, we are scared the whole time. On Sunday though, we feel that the series should be ours. If it's not, it'll be a setback; if it is, yesterday's momentum will continue.

◇ Sunday

The next three hours on Sunday afternoon watching the game will be the only ones that I have at home, away from my father's side at the hospital. But a Blue Jays/Tigers game in Tiger Stadium is no way to unwind.

Just as I settle down in my weariness and angst, Devon White and Robbie Alomar hit back-to-back homers to lead off the game. Another moment that will outlive the season. Two pitches, and both hit easily out of the park. Bill Gullickson, the Detroit pitcher, as expected throws an inside pitch to the next batter, Carter, but then, as not expected, throws the next pitch farther inside and higher to bean Carter right on the helmet. In one of those scenes that everyone will always remember, Carter takes a couple of steps towards the mound with bat in hand, then realizes that he will be suspended for sure if he continues. He stops and appeals to the umpire to throw Gullickson out. All hell breaks loose, with Tettleton grabbing Carter. When the dust settles, Gullickson is thrown out of the ball game.

In an incredible display of leadership and courage, after Carter got on first, he immediately stole both second and third base, just to show the Tigers that he was neither intimidated nor out of the game. Nor was he grinning or chatting up the Detroit infielders as he usually does.

This is our chance to bury the Tigers for good, but Olerud, Gruber and Mulliniks all pop out. Jerry Don Gleaton, the journeyman, mediocre, knockaround ball player who closed us down in the Mark Salas game in Toronto, has been brought in to replace Gullickson and proceeds to pitch like Cy Young until he is replaced in the fifth. Meanwhile, in the bottom of the first, Tony Phillips keeps doing it to us by leading off with a single against Candiotti, stealing second and scoring on Trammell's single. So, suddenly, after a hot two-run start, we've only a one-run lead.

In the second, Cuyler, Phillips and Whitaker are all issued consecutive walks. When Cuyler tries to steal second, Myers decides to

BOXSCORE

Blue Jays..4
Tigers..2

TORONTO	AB	R	H	BI	DETROIT	AB	R	H	BI
White cf	5	1	3	1	Phillips 3b	3	1	1	0
RAlomar 2b	4	2	1	1	Whitaker 2b3	0	0	0	
JoCarter rf	4	0	1	0	Trammell ss	4	0	1	1
Olerud 1b	2	1	0	1	Fielder dh	3	0	0	0
CanMldnd lf	3	0	1	0	Tettleton c	4	0	1	0
Gruber 3b	4	0	1	1	Bergman 1b	4	0	0	0
Mulliniks dh	2	0	0	0	Incaviglia lf	4	0	0	0
Tabler dh	1	0	0	0	Deer rf	3	0	0	0
GMyers c	2	0	0	0	Cuyler cf	2	1	0	0
Borders c	2	0	0	0					
ManLee ss	2	0	0	0					
Ducey ph	1	0	0	0					
RGonzals ss	1	0	0	0					
Totals	33	4	7	4	Totals	30	2	3	1

Toronto   200 001 100 - 4
Detroit   110 000 000 - 2

E - GMyers, RGonzales, Cuyler. DP - Toronto 1. LOB - Toronto 8, Detroit 5. 2B - Gruber. HR - White (9) (off Gullickson), RAlomar (6) (off Gullickson). SB - JoCarter 2 (17), Phillips (10), Cuyler (31). SF - Olerud.

	IP	H	R	ER	BB	SO	HR
Toronto							
Candiotti (W, 10-11)	7	3	2	1	4	6	0
DWard	1	0	0	0	0	1	0
Henke (S, 28)	1	0	0	0	0	3	0
Detroit							
Gullickson	0	2	2	2	0	0	2
Gleaton	4	0	0	0	1	0	0
Kaiser (L, 0-1)	1 1/3	3	1	1	2	1	0
Gakeler	3 2/3	2	1	1	1	5	0

Gullickson pitched to 3 batters in the 1st.
PB - GMyers. HBP - by Gullickson (JoCarter).
SO - Tor: RAlomar, Ducey, White, RGonzales, Borders, JoCarter. Det: Cuyler, Phillips 2, Bergman 3, Deer, Incaviglia 2, Tettleton.

throw the ball to Devon White in centre field, allowing Cuyler to go to third. This is followed by a Candiotti wild pitch or, as I call it, a Myers passed ball. After two innings, the game is tied. The Blue Jays have two runs on two home runs. The Tigers, two runs on two singles, three walks, a passed ball and a stolen base.

The Blue Jays just don't know how to beat up on anyone. After Gleaton, someone named Kaiser comes in for the armless Tigers in the fifth, followed by Gakeler in the sixth. This change is a godsend. Gakeler walks Olerud, singles Maldonado and doubles Gruber, producing the go-ahead and, as it turns out, the winning run. We put up another run in the seventh when Alomar walks and is running with the pitch as Carter singles to put runners on first and third. He scores on an Olerud sac fly. 4–2.

Ward relieves Candiotti in the bottom of the eighth, and the Blue Jays — why do they refuse to win one without making me sweat? — commit an error with two out in the eighth. Trammell hits a routine ground ball to shortstop, exactly where Manuel Lee booted a key ground ball in 1987, costing us a run. Talk about déjà vu. We're sailing along and Gonzales does an instant replay with Cecil Fielder coming up. Right between his legs, same as Manuel in 1987. Cecil has done nothing in this series except one sac fly, and this is a perfect storybook error home-run scenario to tie the ball game. Thank you, Cecil, for not converting it! Henke comes in, and, just to prove how right I have been about his being over-the-hill, he strikes out Tettleton, Bergman and Incaviglia to clean out the ninth and give us the win.

◇ Beanballs

I love the game. Its skill, grace, consistency, oddities and inconsistencies. And I love/hate tight, hard-fought clutch series, when a double clutch on a ground ball, a missed call by an umpire, a gust of wind, a ball hit foul by a half-inch, a failed sac bunt, a 3–0 home run can take you up or down in a millisecond. When your euphoria feels temporary and your gloom permanent. A vital series is an addict's torture chamber.

This series was not a classic. It was not terribly well played. It was not in September. And it did not win or lose the pennant. But still it was the most important to date, and it was nerve-wracking.

Why am I so angry? Because I am caught up talking about the beanball. Why will Gullickson's beaning of Carter be one of the memorable moments of this great season of great baseball? I hate it. I resent it.

For years, I have been railing about the fighting and violence in hockey, such as hitting from behind and cheap intent-to-injure bodychecks. In football, there is no doubt that linesmen intend to hurt, injure, maim, intimidate or at least scare the quarterback when they hit him after each passing play. It fascinates me that the NFL would allow its marquee players — Montana, Marino, Esiason, Sims, Kelly, Kosar, Moon — to be the targets on every play of a 300-pound steroid giant trying to bust ribs or break ankles. All of them have missed parts or entire seasons because of hooliganism on the gridiron. The NBA is the only league smart enough to protect its marquee players.

Baseball? It goes through the motions. There are situations in which it is obvious that the pitchers throw at — not just near — the batter. Perhaps the two most obvious are the homer retaliation and the eye-for-an-eye retaliation. For decades, pitchers have hit or brushed back the next batter following a home run. It's a dumb move, because they don't do it after a 430-foot triple to deep centre field in Tiger Stadium, but may well after a 310-foot short porch and wind-blown fly-ball home run down the right-field line in the same stadium.

It's more an act of frustration. Every ball player batting after a home run looks for the beanball; every umpire expects it. It doesn't accomplish much, and it reminds me of, say, a Dave Manson who would slam Brett Hull to the ice after he puts the puck in the net, or of a goon tackler for one of the many Canadian teams named the Rough Riders who would tackle the Rocket long after he scores a touchdown.

The second type is the eye-for-an-eye retaliation. This occurs after a player has been hit and the other team's pitcher wants to protect his players. The rule is simple: hit my right fielder, and I'll hit your right fielder. This play too is really easy to spot since, in order to send the message, the pitcher does in fact hit exactly the same position player on the other team.

Now the Gullickson/Carter incident was, of course, a "homer retaliation" beaner. Carter expected to be pitched inside, and he was. What made this one even more obvious was that the first pitch to Carter was inside and did move him back off the plate. But Gullickson wanted more, so he threw it farther inside and it hit him on the head.

The leagues could and should stop this. Several stars have had their careers effectively ended (Tony Conigliaro) or severely affected (Dickie Thon, Don Zimmer) by beanballs. Some beanballs are accidental, but some are, shall we say, more intentional. Gullickson's looked more like the latter. But his immediate expulsion from the game is an exception. He may or may not be further suspended. When Jack McDowell hit Mark Whiten early in the year, he missed *one* game, hardly a suitable punishment.

Some of the best pitchers in baseball never used intimidation. They tested their skill against the skill of the batter. My first baseball hero was Robin Roberts of the Philadephia Phillies in the 1950s. Roberts is a Hall-of-Famer who won 286 games with a mediocre or poor team and pitched 45 shutouts. He was a control pitcher who threw at batters neither intentionally nor accidentally. Consequently, he gave up a lot of homers, but his skill allowed him to win twenty games, six years in a row (and nineteen the seventh year!).

Jimmy Key is one modern-day pitcher who relies on skill and control, not intimidation and fear, to get batters out.

I want to see Wayne Gretzky's skill and not his willingness to risk his eyes, teeth and arms by going to a corner with a big goon defenceman.

Equally, I want to see Joe Carter, Wade Boggs, Kirby Puckett, Rafael Palmeiro and Robbie Alomar measure their hitting ability against the best fastballs and curves of Clemens, Erickson, Candiotti, Swindell, Saberhagen and others.

To keep baseball a "kinder, gentler" game than other games, to keep it out of the category of brute strength, baseball ought to deal severely and immediately with beanballs.

Sad to say, however, the beaner is a fact of life. It's a weapon. It causes confrontation that is riveting while repulsive. The fact is that the Gullickson beaning incident was important. It angered the Jays. It reminded them how important Carter was to them and how much they liked him personally. It also gave Carter an opportunity to show what a heads-up, team-oriented ball player he is.

It was a turning-point — one of many — for the Jays this year. I am disappointed and angry that an ugly, improper, unfair, violent incident should be so significant — or significant at all. But it is.

The paradigm that I am caught in is that in 1989, when Tony Fernandez was hit by Cecilio Guante, the Blue Jays took it lying down, and I didn't like it. That group of Jays did not have enough fire, togetherness or fondness for Tony to retaliate, let alone get angry. I hate retaliation, I hate beanings, but, if the league won't stop it, I want Todd Stottlemyre pitching for me because he plays tough and he'll get even.

It's kind of like the Ben Johnson fiasco. If you believe that Ben Johnson was the only world-class sprinter on steroids, then you believe that Manuel Lee will win the batting title. If you believe that the East Germans excelled in international competition only because of skill and training, then you believe that Pat Borders may one day block the plate.

It must be something about playing in Canada — land of conservatism, propriety, kindness, fair play and "peace, order and good government" — well, peace and order, at least. The old definition of a Canadian, someone who can make love in a canoe, fits. We need a fire-eater, not an intimidator like Sal Maglie but a gang of I-want-it ball players.

When I coach minor hockey, I always tell my kids to have the attitude that "it's my puck, damn it. I want it and I want it all the time. If you've got it, I'm going to get it back and now."

Ban beanballs. Don't let them scare or dominate a memorable series. But if they're not going to be banned, if there's not going to be a crackdown, then, like I said, I want Stottlemyre.

◇ Post-Game Notes

When Phillips scored in the first inning, it was a close play at the plate. Myers, once again, was in front of the plate instead of blocking it. If he had been in the right position, that run would not have got in. The other night, I saw Gary Carter, a great but elderly catcher, blocking the plate for the Dodgers against a runner who was out by maybe ten feet. He made the runner take a detour to the on-deck circle to get around him. It didn't matter where the ball was or how much the runner had the ball beat by. Carter was going to block the plate. Myers leaves the gate wide open all the time.

◆ ◆ ◆

An example of how Sparky Anderson plays this game better than most. I think he told his players that they had a better chance looking for walks and wild pitches against Candiotti than trying to hit that crazy knuckler. Thus, in the first two innings, they drew four walks and produced two runs. Knuckleballers are also easy to steal bases on, and, in those two innings, they swiped two. That's Sparky. Specific game plan. Always thinking.

◆ ◆ ◆

Joe Carter came up in the seventh inning with Alomar on base and, when the first pitch was inside to him again, clearly not intentionally this time, Joe turned and laughed with his buddy Tettleton, with whom he had wrestled in the first inning. It reminds me of the spirited and genuine arguments we would have with members of the Opposition in question period in the legislature. Twenty minutes later, walking down the hall with the same members, we would be laughing or chuckling while the media was rushing the videotape of the argument to the studio.

See You in September

Saturday, August 31, 1991			1:30 PM		Yankee Stadium	
Pre-Game Standings						
	W	L	Pct.	GB	Ho.	Strk.	P10
TORONTO	72	58	.554	-	38-29	L-1	6-4
Detroit	69	60	.535	2 1/2	42-22	L-3	7-3
Boston	65	63	.508	6	33-30	W-1	6-4
Final Score: Blue Jays 5, Yankees 0						

LABOUR DAY WEEKEND. It's been a tough summer for me. Lots of work commitments and my father's illness have left me with time for only one day off, one weekend visit to the cottage and plenty of sadness. The exhilaration of the Blue Jays' run in June and July and the All-Star Game are high points. The family and I have escaped to the cottage for today and tomorrow to give me a chance to get a little bit of rest and to clear my obviously cobwebbed mind.

As I've been up here only once this summer, I'm determined to spend the afternoon on the deck or on the dock, if not in the water. (Lake Simcoe is colder than Kelly Gruber since he came off the DL.)

But after lunch, I notice it's 1:25 P.M., five minutes before the CTV coverage of the game from Yankee Stadium. It's been a long and enjoyable week of baseball, and the Blue Jays have settled into their pre-slump solid pitching and fielding and their hitting has improved. After beating the dogs in Baltimore, including a Candiotti/Henke ninth one-hitter, they open a four-game stand in Yankee Stadium with a really important game. Wells, who hasn't had a good outing since long before he volcanoed to Cito a couple of weeks ago, pitched a solid game to go nine innings on Friday night, beating the Yankees 5–0. With Cito hospitalized for his back problems, Gene Tenace has taken over as interim manager. He was smart enough to pull Candiotti the other night to allow Henke to pitch the ninth, and wise to leave Wells in to finish the game Friday night as a confidence builder. Good managing.

Forget yesterday's 9–2 blow-out by the Yankees. Detroit has started to lose on the coast, and you're allowed to get blown out once in a while. Atypically, the Blue Jays won a couple of games comfortably this week (scores: 5–2, 6–1, 3–0, 5–2). All of this makes me think they don't require my presence in front of the TV to root them home this afternoon.

But I have to drift into the family room and turn on our old Motorola, which is connected to *nothing* and so picks up only Channel 3 (Barrie). With my tea beside me, I hook up a pair of rabbit ears (clearly invented by someone who wanted to watch Milton Berle in 1953). It's a relief, after fiddling for a minute or two, to find out Melissa's right and that it can't tune in Channel 9, which is carrying the game. I am relieved, but then just decide to check one more time before I go out. As luck would have it, I fiddle with the copper rabbit ears for a mere moment before hearing Tommy Hutton and Fergie Olver come through loud and clear. The TV screen makes it look like snow in New York, but I can see Devon White strolling up to bat. (For those of you who are wondering, I got the game by angling the two ears at 45 and 270 degrees, respectively.)

Now, it's hard to call a game against the Yankees a key game. Since I can cover in depth only a couple of dozen of 162 games, you might wonder why I would select this one. Well first, having got this bloody game through the snow, I can't get away from it, and, if I'm not going to enjoy the sunny afternoon, I'm damn well going to write about the game.

Second, having won five straight and then getting blown out, the Jays must bounce back quickly and easily to keep the momentum going and to show the Tigers and the Red Sox that things are back to "normal."

Third, it did turn out to be an afternoon full of everything that baseball and this team are about — Devon White, the Alomar clinic, pinch hitting, good pitching, bad umpiring and luck.

◇ The Game

It's Jimmy Key against Eric Plunk. Plunk is a better pitcher than he's ever got credit for being. His career has been muddled by being traded for Rickey Henderson several times and by having too many managers who've tried to use him in too many ways.

While Key gets through four innings giving up no hits and only one walk, the Blue Jays splatter the bases with runners. Poor Joe Carter, who was hot in June and early July, cooled off and then heated up and now is ice cold. He comes up in the first after Alomar triples (a double for anyone else), with an easy chance for an RBI. Although Carter homered last night, he's not happy and is fishing for every ball thrown at him. He pops up to Mattingly, leaving Alomar at third. I continue to believe that, if the other teams were more worried about Olerud coming up after Carter, Carter would be seeing better pitches. Olerud, now back down to around .253, is still showing a little power (fifteen homers, fifty-one RBIs). He just *feels* like an out to opposition pitchers, and so they're throwing junk to Carter. In my view, having Maldonado bat cleanup every day after Carter would be worth three or four points on Carter's batting average.

Olerud can't score Alomar either but accepts a walk, and Maldo strikes out. This establishes a pattern that the Blue Jays will follow through to the sixth inning. In the second, Myers singles between three Blue Jays' strikeouts, but in the third we see this team's style as epitomized by White and Alomar and the problem it's having bringing them home. We also see several turning-points where a single would have made all the difference.

Devon White, with about as hot a bat as you can get, doubles to lead off the third, and Alomar singles. White gets a late start, since he is unsure whether the ball will fall in for a single and so has to hold at third. But when Mel Hall, a good-hitting right fielder for the Yankees, overthrows the cutoff man, Alomar sees it in an instant and ends up on second.

Runners on second and third with the heart of the order coming up, but Carter, Olerud and Maldonado all pop up to the infield. This happens to every team, but six weeks ago it was not happening to us. It seemed every baserunner was going to get home. Carter, Olerud or Maldonado with a cheap little single could have made it a 2–0 game. There's an instant replay in the fourth when the first two batters, Gruber and Mulliniks, get on base with a single and a walk.

Now here's the difference between Alomar and Gruber. Alomar knows everything that is happening and he's playing all-out, alert baseball all the time. Gruber singles when he hits a difficult pop into short left-centre field. The Yankees' shortstop Espinoza makes a fabulous play, running back and diving at the last instant only to have it pop out of his glove as he hits the ground. Gruber jogs around first and is just a half-dozen feet off first base when the ball rolls away from Espinoza. Alomar would have sensed that Espinoza either was going to catch the ball or, if he missed it, the time elapsed would allow him to get to second. *Cecil Fielder* could have got to second! But Gruber ends up with a single. He ends up on second anyway when Mulliniks walks, but Myers strikes out, as does Manuel Lee on a three-and-two pitch that was clearly down in the dirt.

Again an example of how a player who is not expected to and won't hit over .235 or .240 could simply make himself a more valuable hitter by showing discipline. Lee's swinging at high pitches (and Plunk knows it) and swinging at low pitches (the league knows it). Seems to me the Blue Jays should simply ask Lee to take a lot of pitches, look for a lot of walks and discipline himself to do two things: swing only at really good pitches, and bunt. If Lee had accepted a three-and-two ball for ball four, he would have loaded the bases with one out and White and Alomar coming up. As it happens, White walks on four pitches. Who knows if Plunk would have walked him if the sacks had already been loaded? Still, it's a distinct possibility. He was obviously going through a wild streak. Again, this is a place where silent, smart baseball would have put up a run. Now Alomar is up with the bases loaded and, unaccountably, first-ball swings to ground out second to first. It's a cardinal rule that you sit there and take a couple when a pitcher's wild.

Two innings of missed opportunities and the Blue Jays have no runs on five hits through four-and-a-half when the Yanks come up in the bottom of the fifth. Now we're into that make-or-break situation. At the end of five at bats, the Blue Jays have left eight runners on five hits and three walks. This is tough to do, and it's exactly the kind of game where the other team gets a walk, a cheap single and a couple of sacrifices and you're suddenly behind and completely frustrated.

My son Robbie, not addicted but a fan, and smart enough to want to go water-skiing instead of watching snowy Yankee Stadium, has come in to ask for some money (are you surprised?) and sees the stats at the end of four-and-a-half: Yankees with no runs, no hits and no errors.

He plunks himself down and says, "Do you think Key's thinking about a no-hitter yet?" The question mark is barely off his lips when Mel Hall singles to right field. Robbie says, "Damn it. God-damn it. That's my fault. I just blew it. It's like last year, when my hockey team had a shutout with fifteen seconds to go and someone on my bench said, 'we've got a shutout' and then the other team scored."

I am not, repeat not, superstitious. I follow no routine when we're winning. I don't park in the same spot when they're on a winning streak or change it on a losing streak. I do change my clothes. Sometimes I sit in seat three and sometimes in seat four. Nothing I do is going to affect the outcome of the game. But never would I mention a no-hitter during a no-hitter. This is not superstition. It's tradition and I'm obliged, as a true baseball fan, to honour it. When a pitcher is pitching a no-no, his teammates do not talk to him on the bench late in the game. *No one* says a word to him. The pitching coach doesn't ask how his arm is, the fielders don't say "great pitching" and nobody cheers him on. He sits there alone and lonely.

The unfair fans on the opposing team may yell out, "hey Dave, you're pitching a no-hitter," but not the *real* fans.

Robbie knows the superstition — oops, tradition — and he blew it. Fortunately, Key was less spooked than Robbie, struck out the next batter and got out of the inning after one more hit.

Now this was a potential turning-point in the game as well. The Blue Jays had left all those runners on base through five. Yankees had only one baserunner and no hits. But Jimmy Key, calm and back in form and throwing some wicked stuff on the corners, just works through the inning.

In the sixth, Robbie, having blown the no-hitter, decides he's going to take the thirty dollars I gave him to go buy gas and needs some help taking the boat out of the boathouse. This is clearly going to be one of those 1–0 games, and, since I've royally screwed up the afternoon, I decide it's a good opportunity to get some sun and some air. So we go down to the boathouse and manage to get the boat off the marine railway into a typically late-summer shallow Lake Simcoe. It takes me several batters to get back up, and Melissa has taken over the scoring for me while I'm gone.

I stroll up to get some confirmation that it's still a no-score game. Melissa reads her copious notes to me. Having watched five innings of scoreless ball, I arranged a run for the Blue Jays by leaving as Silly Stump Merrill replaced Plunk with Greg Cadaret, a lefty, and Gene Tenace (who I'm getting to like) did something Cito wouldn't have done. He brought Tabler to pinch hit for Mulliniks as early as the sixth inning. Tabler doubled and then Borders, pinch hitting for Myers, also doubled, knocking in the first run. Manuel Lee then bunted Borders to third, bringing up Devon White with one out and the second run sitting right there at third base. White flew to right field on what should have been a sac fly, but Hall's throw home got there at about the time that Borders did and Geren clearly missed the tag. Melissa's notes say "no way — disgusting call." She's absolutely right, as I see on the replay. Borders was safe, but Chuck Merriweather calls him out. "Disgusting" was not in fact Melissa's word but came from the admittedly biased but usually reserved Blue Jays' announcers Hutton and Olver.

More examples of how things are straightening out for the Blue Jays. Key leaves after five with his narrow 1–0 lead, and Timlin picks up where Key left off by easily retiring the Yankees in the sixth and seventh. It is vital for the Blue Jays' starters to know that Timlin can once again be counted on to get them from the fifth to the seventh (Ward territory) if necessary.

In the eighth, Mulliniks and Tabler again combine with a single and a double to produce another run. The difference between a 1–0 game and a 2–0 game is huge. When you have Henke and Ward waiting in the bullpen, a two-run lead is more than double the size of a one-run lead.

In the ninth, White and Alomar continue to show why they have been key forces in the Blue Jays' success so far this season. White singles and Alomar doubles to lead off the ninth. On the day, the two of them combine for two singles, two doubles, a triple and a walk. White is two for four plus a walk. He surely should have been two for three since his fly ball to right produced that terrible call at home and changed that sac fly into an out. Alomar almost hits for the cycle and goes three for five.

With runners on second and third and the Blue Jays threatening to turn a close game into an easy win, Carter comes up and, to complete a zero-for-five day, bounces one to our friend Randy Velarde at third, who commits his nightly error against the Blue Jays to load the bases. A sac fly, a walk and a double (by Gruber) later, three runs are in: 5–0 Blue Jays. An important win.

It's important because the team is showing signs of what's needed to win. Leadoff batters White and Alomar getting on base, the manager pinch hitting and the pinch hitters producing. Great pitching (a three hitter); smart, aggressive baserunning. Tabler scoring on a short double by Myers sliding in under the tag and Carter moving from first to second on the fly to centre. Great defence, with White continuing to put on an academy for superior centre fielding.

There is still evidence, of course, of problems. Too many runners left on base, especially in the early innings. Gruber's lack of

BOXSCORE

Blue Jays..5
Yankees...0

TORONTO	AB	R	H	BI	NEW YORK	AB	R	H	BI
White cf	4	1	2	0	Wllams cf	3	0	0	0
RAlmr 2b	5	1	3	0	Sax 2b	4	0	0	0
Carter rf	5	1	0	0	Mttngly 1b	3	0	1	0
Olerud 1b	3	0	0	1	RKelly lf	4	0	0	0
CnMldo lf	3	0	0	0	Hall rf	4	0	1	0
Gruber 3b	5	0	2	2	Mulens dh	2	0	0	0
Mllniks dh	1	0	0	0	Maas dh	1	0	0	0
Tabler dh	3	2	2	0	Espanza ss	3	0	0	0
Myers c	2	0	1	0	Geren c	2	0	1	0
Brders c	2	0	2	2	Shrdn ph	0	0	0	0
MnLee ss	3	0	0	0	Velarde 3b	0	0	0	0
					PKelly 3b	2	0	0	0
					Nokes c	1	0	0	0
Totals	36	5	12	5	Totals	29	0	3	0

Toronto   000 001 013 - 5
New York   000 000 000 - 0

E - Velarde (15). DP - Toronto 1, New York 1. LOB - Toronto 11, New York 5. 2B - White (34), RAlomar (35), Gruber (13), Tabler (5), Borders 2 (16), Mattingly (29). 3B - RAlomar (10). S - MnLee. SF - Olerud.

	IP	H	R	ER	BB	SO
Toronto						
Key (W, 14-9)	5	2	0	0	1	2
Timlin	2 1/3	0	0	0	2	0
DWard (S, 17)	1 2/3	1	0	0	0	1
New York						
Plunk	5	5	0	0	4	6
Cadaret (L, 6-5)	2	2	1	1	0	1
Habyan	2	5	4	3	1	2

aggressiveness and his problematic hitting. Olerud and Carter zero for eight and Lee striking out three times. But these problems, these failures and shortcomings, can be found in every game. The question is, are other players picking up the slack or are they all going into the tank the same day? The last month has been everyone, everyday into the aquarium. Now the balance is coming back.

Perhaps it's the cottage, perhaps it's the nice weather, perhaps it's being sucked in by five out of six against the dogs. Whatever it is, I'm feeling good and comfy about things these days.

Have they sucked me in again?

◇ September

It's September. Every month of the season is different. April is cold, irrelevant, surprising. May is the month of exaggerated stats — a bad team off to a good start. A couple of batters batting at or above .400 who will end up batting about .240 the rest of the year. A player or two with fifteen home runs and ahead of Ruth's and Maris's pace and a pitcher off to a quick five and 0 and looking like he's going to beat Denny McLain's thirty-one wins. June is when this year's all-stars develop. Since the All-Star Game is in July, it is essentially a measure not of a year's best players but of less than a half-season's. In the middle of June we begin to take note of those whose stats are still up — the Scott Ericksons, the Joe Carters — and those whose stats are down (Raines and Strawberry this year). July is the All-Star month and a month of easy, confident play, while August rolls into the dog days, the slumps, the winning streaks and the shake-outs.

September. Ah! September! That's strictly pennant race. It's scoreboard watching for six or eight teams. For those teams and their fans and their media, it's a time of chauvinistic, nail-biting, invigorating paranoia and jubilation. Yes, around Labour Day the horses take the final turn and head for home. The weather gets a little cooler and the pressure is on. It's only fun when it's over. It sure ain't fun while it's happening. It's agony, angst, aggravation ... and maybe ecstasy.

In September the day's appointments, obligations and responsibilities will be only fillers between visits to the Dome or the TV.

Every out will cost us the pennant. Every run will be "the most important run of the year." We'll etch players in our minds as "ultimate chokers" or "pressure players."

Every September I'm frustrated by what has become, I suppose, a necessary evil. On September 1, major-league teams expand their rosters from twenty-five to forty players, calling up players from their minor-league affiliates. While this isn't done in any other sport, in baseball it has been an important part of player development. Now, we really do look forward to seeing some of these players, and some of them come up and have hot months.

But this is a pennant race, and pennant races are won by a game or two. When you go into town, you don't know whether you're going to be playing the Baltimore Orioles or the Rochester Red Wings, the Chicago White Sox or the Vancouver Canadians, the Seattle Mariners or the Calgary Cannons, or the California Angels or the Edmonton Trappers. This is not fair. This distorts the pennant race.

I think the Blue Jays will be the ones to benefit this year as the "swing team" in September. Minnesota surprisingly seems to have the West locked up. In the tough West we will now see some double-A and triple-A pitchers either starting or in the game in the fourth or fifth inning, and a bunch of the players will be playing for their own stats, not for team wins.

Is this worth, say, two or three games to the Blue Jays on their western swing? For sure. They are just not going to be seeing the same teams and the same players they would have been seeing if Oakland were trying as hard to catch Minnesota as Toronto is to stay ahead of the Tigers.

All of this presents an unfair situation that, I wish, the leagues would address. There are several ways to proceed. They could require that the lineups be filed with the league president two days prior to each game from September 15 on. They could require that the starting rotation of each team be kept intact unless there's a proven injury. And so on.

Now how about the Jays this September? Well, their previous Septembers are legendary. They have good Septembers about as often as the post office has good union negotiations. Everyone knows the Blue Jays have a history of cold bats (G. Bell, '87), bad luck

(Fernandez and Whitt) and bad play (grounder between Lee's legs, Ward's start in Boston).

Do I think Carter is going to stay as spooked all September as he is now? No. Do I think Alomar is through his — for him — rough patch? Yes. Do I think White will stay hot through all of September? No. Will he cool *right* off? No. On the other hand, I don't think Gruber or Olerud will improve. If Gruber would, it would mean, in my view, a division championship, a pennant and a World Series. Do I think the pitching staff is back? You bet I do, and I don't think it will fold. I think the fact that we've been up and then down has given them more confidence, not less. I also think it's better that they're playing the West — sort of minding their own business, doing their own job and, as I've said, playing against a bunch of triple-A ball players.

The other thing to be said is that Gene Tenace is running the club, and it looks like he'll be running it for some time. He professes to be doing it the same way Cito would, but he is a different cat. As of today, he is seven and four since he took over, a pace that, if we are lucky enough to maintain it all the way, would give us an easy first place.

He is more creative than Cito. He is pinch hitting more often and earlier. He is talking to his ball players far more often in the dugout than Cito does. He is not sailing on automatic pilot, but is pulling Candiotti when he is doing well and leaving Wells in to go nine to build up his confidence. He's got Hacker sending Tabler home in a tight situation where ordinarily they'd play it too safe. I don't think Tenace is nearly ready to be a full-time major-league manager. He simply has not had enough experience. But I do like his style. Why, he will even argue calls with umpires. There is also something about the way he watches a game that makes me feel he's more intense.

And finally, it was so refreshing to read his comments the other day: "Now I sit there and see guys do certain things and it frustrates me." "Lack of communication in the outfield ... not anticipating a ball being hit to you in the infield ... a catcher not shifting his body (to block a pitch) ... can't get the bunt down." "Some of the mistakes, for this level, they're inexcusable. We're just making too many of them, especially for this time of the season."

If this isn't enough to snap Cito's bad disc into place, then nothing will. The reason I like his saying it is that he's saying what the players already know. It just seems to me better to say it and deal with it than to keep pretending that what's happening isn't happening.

I must say that I'm not as pessimistic this Labour Day as I usually am. Maybe it's just the peace and calm of Lake Simcoe. Maybe it's the good solid baseball they played this afternoon. Maybe I've just been fooled by the trip through the dog pound. But I think Detroit's odyssey is over. They've been hot and playing above their heads now for two months with the best record in the American League since the All-Star break. No, they've had their streaks and we've had ours. Both of our streaks are now over, I believe. Each team will settle back to its normal level, and our norm is simply a hell of a lot (or at least three games) better than theirs. I'm not quite convinced the Red Sox are dead, but they do have a lot of ground to cover. I think if Tenace keeps playing the game the way he's played it but uses his call-ups as the supplements that they ought to be, and if there are no injuries, we will be just fine. For Detroit, you may have thought it was fun while it lasted. But as my friend the late Richard Hatfield once said to me, "Too bad it lasted longer than it was fun." Sparky, the fun is over. Say good night.

Hope I haven't just done a Robbie.

◇ Post-Game Notes

With Don Chevrier covering the Canada Cup, Fergie Olver makes his return to the CTV telecasts doing play-by-play. He and Tommy and the producer combine to give us a close-in view of a hot dog vendor and launch into a short discussion of whether or not they like mustard on their hot dogs. But kudos to CTV for simply being sensible enough to give us four Blue Jays games Friday through Labour Day Monday. Baseball, especially this time of year, is what everyone wants to see. And when we get to see the whole series in New York, we've got to be happy.

◆ ◆ ◆

Not only did umpire Chuck Merriweather make a "disgusting" call against the Blue Jays in the sixth. Not only did he have a ridiculous day last week during the Yankees series in Toronto with a strike zone that seemed to be fluid and as wide as Lake Superior. But he also capped it all off by ruling that the first-pitch passed ball to Roberto Kelly with Don Mattingly on second in the ninth inning was in fact a foul ball off of Kelly's bat. No way.

◆ ◆ ◆

One of my favourite ball players is Don Mattingly. Let me say it quickly: if he were here DHing or playing first or both, we'd have this pennant won. Last week he was in a stupid controversy. The Yankees demanded he get his hair cut. The debonair Stump Merrill was dispatched by Gene Michael, the general manager (who, when he was playing for the Yankees, used to wear his hair longer than Mattingly does today), to bench Mattingly until he got his locks cut. Mattingly is only batting .302 and remains one of the best hitters and fielders in baseball, but that isn't good enough for the slumping Yankees who somehow feel that, if Mattingly got his hair cut, they would be in first place. If he looked like Olerud, he might end up playing like him. Don't cut the hair!

I remember Mattingly best from two years ago when, after he exploded in the dugout, ripping up things and yelling at fans on a Saturday, I saw him just after batting practice, about half an hour before the next game. A youngster I didn't know had come down to see if he could get a baseball from Mattingly — "Don, how about a ball?" Mattingly went into the dugout and brought out not a ball, but a bat.

I Spent a Week in Cleveland One Night

Friday, September 6, 1991			7:35 PM		Cleveland Stadium		
Pre-Game Standings							
	W	L	Pct.	GB	Ho.	Strk.	P10	Div.
TORONTO	76	60	.559	-	40-30	W-2	7-3	41-33
Detroit	71	63	.530	4	42-23	L-2	4-6	27-26
Boston	69	64	.519	5 1/2	35-31	W-2	6-4	29-23
Final Score: Blue Jays 7, Indians 4								

I'VE HAD A TERRIBLY DIFFICULT AND SAD WEEK. My dear father passed away last Sunday. Our family has spent this week in mourning (*shiva*). One of the last times my father was aware and alert enough to share with me was watching the Yankees/Jays game on TV four days before he died. He asked me to leave him a copy of one of my diary manuscripts for him to read. Unfortunately, he wasn't well enough again to read it. It is difficult to get back to life, work and this diary, but I must have his courage and carry on.

After the tension and sadness of the last month and week, I am exhausted and eager just to settle down in the den, unwind and watch the Blue Jays beat up on the Indians. I need it more than they need it.

It has been a pleasant week for the Blue Jays on their visit to the kennel. They are meeting and beating the dogs. Unable to stand prosperity, they ended up splitting four with the Yankees in New York and then coming home to beat the Orioles two out of three before going to Cleveland's municipal mausoleum. There, on Thursday night, the Blue Jays had — would you believe it? — a laugher. A laugher for us this year has been 4–1 (about the equivalent of a soccer laugher). But, last night, they put up thirteen big ones while Jimmy Key gave up only one run. Gruber actually had two doubles, as did Mulliniks. Big Joe seemed to be getting his swing back, hitting his thirty-first home run in a two-for-five night, scoring two and cashing in two.

They were so far ahead that by the end of the game, Robbie Alomar, at second base, found himself surrounded by the infamous Cory Snyder at first, Eddie Zosky at short, Ed Sprague at third, Ducey in left, Derek Bell in centre, Turner Ward in right, Randy Knorr catching and the Canadian, Horsman, pitching. The Canuck did well, one-and-a-third innings — no hits, no walks, two strikeouts. Robbie must have thought he was in Syracuse. This was a welcome relief, giving the team some time to relax, resting some of the key players and, most of all, just relieving some pressure. Meanwhile, Detroit lost to Oakland, so we're sitting at seven and three in our past ten on a two-game winning streak, four games up going into the second of four games in Cleveland. Not a bad spot to be in.

As we sit here, however, I remember the fact that early this week, when we beat the Orioles while the Tigers were beating Seattle, it was on balance "advantage Detroit," as tennis players would say. We still have to go through the West, while Detroit comes home to the kennel. That means our four-game lead only appears to be four. I'd say it's about a one-game lead at this stage. The Tigers have a ridiculously weak schedule from here on, and we face twenty-three final games against the West — five against the Mariners, six against the Athletics, six against the Twins and six against the Angels.

The race in the West is all but over, and so we'll be seeing lots of triple-A players, but the East is all but over for the four bottom teams, and the Tigers are not going to be playing merely the weaker East, but the weaker, weaker East.

I love laughers as long as they are in our favour. There's enough tension in real life. I don't need a 3–2 or 5–4 game, nor do I need Jim Acker finishing a game with the bases loaded and the winning run on third, to have a good time. If winning is good, winning big is great, and I love it when my team lambastes the other team. I never leave a Blue Jays blow-out early. Remember the night we had ten home runs at Exhibition Stadium? Hit homers, steal a bunch of bases, someone hit for the cycle, let Cory Snyder go three for four, let everyone in the lineup get hits and RBIs and, while you're doing it, remind the pitcher to throw a shutout, please. A perfect ball game.

I get into shorts and a t-shirt, settle down in the den, take my score card out and sit down to the equivalent of a two-and-a-half-hour body massage.

◇ The Game

They don't let me down. You remember Salas, one of two palindromes? Well, the other one, someone named Otto, is pitching against us tonight. Otto, realizing my emotional state, is kind enough to go through the first seven Blue Jays batters as follows:

White — single
Alomar — fielder's choice
Carter — triple
Gruber (batting cleanup surprisingly) — single
Maldonado — single
Tabler — sac fly
Sprague — strikeout

After one, 3–0 Blue Jays. In the bottom of the first Juan Guzman scares the hell out of me by issuing walks to the first two batters, but then Baerga hits into a fielder's choice and Albert Belle hits into a double play. I know things are going to be okay. Even when Guzman is going bad, our luck is good and he can't give up a run for trying.

In the top of the second with two out, White gets on by way of an error. Felix Fermin forgets that White runs slightly faster than Cito Gaston, and he throws a late one hopper to first. Alomar then follows with a single to the left-field wall, which he thinks he can stretch into a double easily. Albert Belle throws him out at second to end the inning.

In the third, the Blue Jays give me exactly what I wanted:

Carter — single
Gruber — ground out
Maldonado — double
Tabler — single (wild pitch)
Sprague — walk
Borders — sac fly
Lee (of all people) — double
White — ground out

Four runs, Blue Jays 7, Cleveland 0 after three. Guzman walks the leadoff batter in the third, but he's eliminated on a play they must have practised in spring training. The second man up, Fermin, hits a hard ground ball towards first, which Ed Sprague plays like Bill Buckner. Only this time it hits Sprague's ankle (Buckner should have been so lucky) and bounces to Alomar. Alomar fires the ball back to Sprague, who's alert enough to be on the first-base bag to get the batter. From Fermin through to one out in the sixth, Guzman retires ten batters and doesn't give up a hit. Then, in the sixth, two batters after Don Chevrier has violated the rule and told us twice that Guzman is throwing a no-hitter, Alex Cole singles.

Not to worry. Going into the eighth with our 7–0 lead, Gene Tenace puts in the Syracuse Chiefs to finish it off. We started the game with what I consider to be maybe the best hitting lineup we've seen all year: White, Alomar, Carter, Gruber, Maldonado, Tabler, Sprague, Borders, Lee. By the eighth, it is: Bell, Zosky, Ducey, Gruber, Maldonado, Wilson, Sprague, Borders, Gonzales.

No problem, except the substitutes didn't get a hit after the third, and the Blue Jays will finish the game with the same stats with which they finished the third inning: seven runs off nine hits. When you let Cleveland pitchers go through six innings without giving up a hit, you have, boys, gone south.

End of the eighth, Tenace replaces Guzman, who has pitched shutout ball through seven innings, giving up only two hits. He brings in Mike Timlin, a move I don't understand since Tenace ought to be having a look at all these young arms up from Syracuse. Anyway, Timlin comes in, and the odds and gods of baseball take over. It's incredible. Another Gonzalez (Jose), who's about twelfth on a depth chart of ten Cleveland outfielders, leads off with a double. After that, Fermin gets an infield single, which Zosky should have been able to convert. Cole hits a slow, high infield bouncer to Zosky, so slow he can beat it out. After three batters, they have two infield hits, and one runner scores. Fortunately, Mike Aldrete (formerly of every bad team in baseball) hits a seeing-eye ball between Gruber and Zosky for a single to left. After these cheap, lucky singles, Carlos Baerga hits a decent one over Zosky's head for the fifth consecutive hit. This takes Timlin out of the game and gives Cleveland two runs.

This is typical baseball. You're sitting there, the game is home and cooled out. You've got a good pitcher against a weak-hitting, maybe minor-league team, and he's throwing decently. Two batters, Fermin and Cole, don't hit the ball out of the infield. They swing and barely hit the ball onto the grass, making it bounce so slowly they can beat it out. This is a function of good pitching and bad hitting, which results in lucky high hoppers to the infield. Then Aldrete's tunnel ball that could just as easily have gone to Gruber or Zosky, but turned into a run-scoring single. Ditto for the next hit. Timlin pitched well, in fact, but his record will show that he got none out, faced five batters and gave up five hits.

Henke comes in, strikes out Albert Belle (his third strikeout of the night) and then kindly gives up a double to Martinez to make the game 7–4.

Why is this happening to me? No one has made a mistake. Tenace took out Guzman when he should have. Timlin threw ground balls, which is his specialty, and mediocre Cleveland hitters hit them poorly. But the odds of baseball are when you hit a ball into play, on a certain number of occasions, they are going to end up fair through no particular talent or skill. The odds also say that sometimes all these things are going to happen in the same inning.

Now my world is falling in again. Instead of relaxing as I watch the game, I hunker down and start to live with every pitch. Suddenly I realize that with Detroit winning 11–2 over Oakland and Boston having come back against the Seattle Mariners to win, we could be looking disaster right in the face. If we turn a 7–0 blow-out against the Indians, of all people, into an honest-to-goodness loss, it would be potentially disastrous. Far more serious than just giving up one game in the standings, it would get our players spooked and uptight, worried about when the roof was going to fall in again and making them believe that no lead is ever safe.

This now is a serious, aggravating game. What looked like a beautiful oasis has now turned into a nail-biter, typical of the awful month of September in a pennant race.

Henke in the eighth faces five batters and, like in the fourteen-inning Mark Salas game, strikes out every batter he didn't put on base, but in the middle he gives up a double and a walk, allowing a run to score. The strikeouts are more a function of overeager batters. Two of the three are recent call-ups from the minors who go after his sinking split-finger fastball. But his control is off.

Top of the ninth, when we need the Blue Jays to come back with a run or at least some fight, they go down in as much time as it takes me to say, "Duane Ward, I beg you."

There is absolutely no doubt that Ward, who has been warming up, will come in to clean up the ninth. But no. Tenace wants me to suffer. He sends Henke out to start the ninth. Henke has had tendinitis, has not been in a game in a while and, if anything, should have been out there to pitch one easy inning, just to get some work in. Here's Tenace leaving in a guy who already has a sore shoulder to pitch to far more batters than he's used to, even when he's healthy.

Sure enough, that great hitter, Felix Fermin, the ninth hitter in the Cleveland Indians' lineup (the equivalent to being the worst minister in Bob Rae's cabinet), singles for his second hit in two innings. Cole then flies out to Maldonado and I sit back and relax. Even though Henke is in there for too long, I'm still sitting on a three-run lead and we have only two outs to go with Aldrete (remember him) up to bat.

Just as this happens, my two sons arrive with two of their friends, and all Jamie wants to know is how Bo Jackson (playing on WGN, the new super-channel) is doing against Nolan Ryan. The answer is not much better than usual. Bo had struck out in fifteen of eighteen at bats against Ryan coming into tonight's game, whereupon Jamie and I get into a disagreement about whether Bo is any kind of a major leaguer or not. I argue he's a great football player, but only an average ball player — a combination of Rob Deer and Pete Incaviglia as a ball player. Jamie, whose nickname at school is "Bo," disagrees with me, as Henke throws ball two to Aldrete. I'm now being aggravated by Jamie, Tom Henke and Gene Tenace. I'm screaming at Tenace because I don't understand why he would be leaving Henke in. I can't understand it. No other team in baseball, no other manager would leave Henke in in this situation. I take it back; Cito Gaston would. He's got Ward ready. He has two dozen other pitchers. Henke is struggling, tired and has tendinitis.

All you need to do is keep Aldrete off base and you're going to be okay. But no. He leaves Henke in. After I politely invite one of Jamie's friends to move from between me and the TV as Henke goes to three and two on Aldrete, son Robbie arrives to tell me the details of a hockey tournament he has next week. Robbie is now becoming agitated because I am distracted (and honest to God, I really am interested in this tournament), Jamie's friend is walking in front of me with a baseball bat, and Jamie is still arguing about Bo and wants me to flip to channel 45 as I watch Tim McClelland, the home-plate umpire, call a pitch on the inside corner of the plate ball four on Mike Aldrete. I am now mad at Tenace, Henke, the umpire, Jamie, Robbie and Jamie's friend. This brings the "tying run to the plate" with the third, fourth and fifth batters in the lineup coming up. How did this happen to me? Couldn't you give me a break? Couldn't you give me one night off?

BOXSCORE

Blue Jays..................7
Indians.....................4

TORONTO	AB	R	H	BI	CLEVELAND	AB	R	H	BI
White cf	4	1	1	0	Cole cf	4	1	1	1
DBell cf	1	0	0	0	Aldrete 1b	3	1	2	0
RAlmr 2b	4	0	1	0	Baerga 2b	4	0	1	1
Zosky ss	1	0	0	0	Belle lf	4	0	0	0
Carter rf	3	2	2	1	CsMtnz dh	5	0	2	2
Ducey rf	0	0	0	0	Thorne 3b	4	0	0	0
Gruber 3b	4	1	1	1	Tbnsee c	3	0	0	0
CnMldo lf	4	1	2	1	Przchc pr	0	0	0	0
Tabler dh	2	1	1	1	Skinner c	0	0	0	0
MWlsn dh	1	0	0	0	JoGnztz rf	3	1	1	0
Sprgue 1b	3	1	0	0	Fermin ss	4	1	2	0
Olerud 1b	0	0	0	0					
Brders c	3	0	0	1					
MnLee ss	2	0	1	1					
Gnzales ss	2	0	0	0					
Totals	34	7	9	6	Totals	34	4	9	4

Toronto   304 000 000 - 7
Cleveland 000 000 040 - 4

E - Belle (9), Fermin (11). DP - Toronto 2. LOB - Toronto 4, Cleveland 10. 2B - CnMaldonado (12), MnLee (16), CsMartinez (9), JoGonzalez (1). 3B - Carter (3). SB - Gruber (9). SF - Tabler, Borders.

	IP	H	R	ER	BB	SO
Toronto						
JuGzmn (W, 6-2)	7	2	0	0	4	6
Timlin	0	5	4	4	0	0
Henke	1 1/3	2	0	0	2	3
DWard (S, 19)	2/3	0	0	0	1	1
Cleveland						
Otto (L, 1-6)	2 1/3	8	7	7	1	2
Shaw	5 2/3	1	0	0	1	0
Hillegas	1	0	0	0	0	1

Timlin pitched to 5 batters in the 9th. WP - DWard, Shaw. PB - Taubensee.

Someone puts in a wake-up call to Tenace, who finally brings in Duane Ward, and he promptly strikes out Baerga. Then, after I've agreed for a split second to check Bo Jackson on channel 45 to see him strike out against Ryan, I come back to watch Ward walk Albert Belle to bring, would you believe, "the winning run to the plate."

Sheldon calls me so that we can die together on the phone with the last batter. We watch and, God bless him, Carlos Martinez bounces a fielder's choice, Zosky to Sprague, to get us out of a "laugher," 7–4. Thanks boys. Just what I needed.

◇ Coaches

Although the Blue Jays can still hit the Cleveland pitches, the truth is the Blue Jays are now in their second month of a batting slump. It started just after the All-Star break and is continuing more than thirty days later. For most of this time, the talk has been that every player has streaks and every team has streaks. The bats have gone quiet coincidentally, with the pitching cooling off. We hear "we just got to bear down," we just got to keep cool," "we just got to go about our job," "no way Kelly's going to stay in a slump this long." But the bottom line is the entire team has not been hitting in key situations.

It makes me wonder what coaches are all about. Gene Tenace, a lifetime .241 hitter, is our batting coach. What are his credentials? Has he got a different style and unique method à la the legendary Charlie Lau or Walt Hriniak (two seasons: ninety-nine ABs, twenty-five hits)? Does he have proven successes? Has he taken a minor-league team and increased its batting average by ten points?

Lau and Hriniak are, notwithstanding their BAs, the exceptions. There are hardly any major-league batting coaches who are sought after by other teams or who have proven track records. And I don't understand this. In football and even hockey, there are people with clear specialties — goalie coaches, defence coaches, special team coaches, quarterback coaches. And these guys spend all year working on their science, and they seem to get results. But in baseball, it seems that ex–ball players luck into certain niches because they're willing to do a job or accept a low salary.

I really don't understand how Gene Tenace can be said to have been a success as a batting coach when he has not improved Manuel Lee's batting this year or when Pat Borders's batting has dropped so much. One wonders what it would have dropped to if there hadn't been a batting coach at all. When Gruber's average is way down and he refuses even to take coaching to make him more patient at bat. When a natural hitter like John Olerud is not progressing as he should and can't be taught to be more aggressive. When Rance Mulliniks and Mookie Wilson are losing the strokes that carried them through long and excellent careers. When Rob Ducey can't be taught to stop upper-cutting and when our DHs have ridiculously low statistics.

People will say a batting coach can only give advice and instruction; he can't swing the bat up there. But that's like telling me that a quarterback coach can't throw the ball and a goalie coach can't hold a hockey stick. Batting is a tough thing to do, but, like everything, the more you practice it — the more the science behind it can be explained, refined and studied — the better one's chances are of hitting. And in a game like baseball, five hits a year from each of two or three batters can make the difference between first and fourth place.

I was interested to see that the Yankees have a video camera following the team from ground level and taping every batter, every at bat. They're the only team in the American League to do so. The cameraman sets up in front of us and inserts a cassette as each batter comes up. Each cassette has that batter's name on it so that every player, and presumably the Yankees' batting coach, can see every one of his at bats for the entire season.

Teams spend a lot of down time on the road. They sit in hotel rooms and hotel lobbies. They go to bars, restaurants, take bus tours and play golf to kill the time. And they have six months off. It seems to me that in a player's short, seven- to ten-year major-league career, there's no reason why teams should not have expert batting coaches who understand the science of batting, who have read every book written on batting, who have met with people like Ted Williams and Rod Carew, and who are sophisticated analysts and handlers of people.

And the hitters themselves should be absolutely dedicated. They should follow the lead of Tony Gwynn, merely the best hitter in the

National League, who has his own batting cage at his home and works all winter on his stroke. George Will's excellent book *Men at Work* reports that Gwynn puts a Dixie cup on home plate and tries to discipline himself to spit in the cup as the pitch is coming in in order to make sure he keeps his head down, watching the ball as it crosses the plate. Tony's lifetime batting average (.329) is pretty good testimony that this kind of discipline, dedication and effort pays off.

If the Blue Jays have been in a prolonged batting slump, what would they have been in without the batting coach? Would it have been all season? Would their batting averages really be lower? I don't think so, and I don't think this is a Blue Jays problem. I think it's a baseball problem and I think it will change. The science of pitching has changed. Thirty years ago, starting pitchers normally went the whole way. Relievers were failed starting pitchers sent to the bullpen because they had lost something. There was no such thing as "stoppers" who pitched one inning to mop up a game like Eckersley, Henke and Thigpen. But Roger Craig and others introduced new pitches like the split-finger fastball to starters, and Goose Gossage, Kent Tekulve and Dan Quisenberry showed the value of one- or two-inning closers — and the entire game of pitching changed. Dave Duncan of Oakland (maybe with Pat Dobson) has probably become the first world-class pitching coach, and his success with people like Dave Stewart is clear. But this hasn't happened to batting. And I guess I'm critical of the players too.

I can't count the number of times John Olerud has taken a called third strike. I can't count the number of times we've read in the papers about Gaston, Gillick and Tenace all wanting Olerud to be more aggressive at the plate and not take so many pitches. With his "sweet swing" (and it is), if he makes contact on reasonably good pitches, he'll get more than his fair share of hits. But Olerud simply can't or won't take the coaching or make the mental adjustment, and, in my view, this threatens the value of his rookie card, not to mention our franchise and his pension.

Kelly Gruber is struggling. He's had hand injuries that are clearly causing him problems. Right-handed hitters get the power from their right hand, even though it's not the hand that is at the bottom of the bat. Kelly does not have the power he needs or the bat control he would have if he weren't injured. Fair enough. We don't expect the stats from him that we would get in a healthy season. But we can expect smart batting. We can expect him to discipline himself to wait. If Olerud is waiting on too many, it is clear that Gruber just won't stop first-ball hitting. Tonight was an excellent example. The pitcher was clearly struggling, and, instead of making him throw three or four pitches, Kelly swung at the first pitch and grounded out.

Manuel Lee has to know that bright, young Eddie Zosky is waiting in the wings to make a big run at him next year in spring training. Manuel surprised me by doing a pretty good job in the field this year and hitting better than expected till the All-Star break. Although his fielding remains at a high level, he's liable to lose his job because of his weak bat. If I were Manuel Lee and I knew that my fielding was at a major-league level or better but that, because of my hitting, I was liable to end up being platooned or worse next year, I would be spending an enormous amount of time trying to cut down my swing, would stop swinging at pitches in the dirt and would work on becoming a bat-control contact hitter. I would, but he won't.

Pitching is a little more refined. Coaches such as Roger Craig (before he became a manager), Pat Dobson and Dave Duncan have real impact on their pitchers. But this job is too important to be left to the former major leaguers who want to hang around. In fact, it is interesting to note that the players who used to make big dollars, say $1 million plus, often retire with enough money so that they don't need to work for the $50,000 to $100,000 that coaches are paid. Therefore, the front-liners like Jim Palmer, Jim Kaat, Mike Schmidt, Rod Carew, Johnny Bench and Joe Morgan do not retire into the ranks of coaching. They leave that to the players who don't have the financial security because they weren't good enough ball players.

It seems to me that baseball ought to pursue the Palmers and others by recognizing the potential (as opposed to the current) value of top-notch, highly skilled, state-of-the-art coaches. It seems to me that I'd rather have Ted Williams, Stan Musial and Rod Carew teaching hitting than Gene Tenace, Ritchie Hebner and, to use the most bizarre example of all, Mario Mendoza, who is a hitting coach somewhere in the minor leagues and is commemorated in the expression "Mendoza line" because of his .200 lifetime batting average.

The way to do this is to pay these guys what you'd pay a utility infielder at thirty-odd years of age, say $200,000 or $300,000 a year. Give me a coach who can add ten hits a year — that's twenty points — to Greg Myers, or fifteen hits — that's less than one a week — to Manuel Lee to bring his average from .230 to .260, and I say that person is worth a lot of money.

I also believe that if you pay someone $200,000 to $300,000, he might be willing to work at the job twelve months of the year, attending clinics, studying tapes, testing new techniques and travelling from city to city — or country to country to spend a week with Manuel Lee in the Dominican Republic and work on his batting stroke (not to mention his bunting).

All of this applies to pitching coaches. Pitchers' careers disappear overnight when they get rotator cuff injuries, sore arms, sore elbows and the like. They just suddenly lose their control, or their speed or their curve. But there are very few knuckleballers around. Some of these pitchers, if given the time and coaching, could certainly develop a knuckleball pitch. A pitcher who has a really good slider can surely be taught to throw a good curve, and a hardball pitcher, Roger Craig has shown, can be taught to stuff the ball between his index and middle fingers and make that fastball sink (the split-finger fastball).

Skilled pitching coaches with, dare I say it, university degrees in kinesiology could perhaps reduce the number of sore arms on pitchers by studying the causes and the kinds of arm movements that strain muscles. Indeed, Nolan Ryan has become his own best teacher and has developed techniques, pre- and post-game, that include exercise and ice to keep his body and arm at all-star level into his forties. This is not a miracle. It's a simple function of a dedicated, hard-working, smart athlete taking the time, energy and brain power to figure out what makes his arm throw a 95 mph fastball and how to keep it doing that.

He's done it for himself. Is there any chance he will do it for others as a pitching coach when he retires? No.

But a team that can line up four or five great starting pitchers and keep them healthy for a decade will dominate baseball. Teams spend, it is estimated, a million dollars to develop a major-league prospect but only $50,000 a year on a pitching coach to protect the million-dollar investment.

There is often something that is correctable, even in a highly skilled, intelligent and successful pitcher like Tom Candiotti. In almost every outing he's had for the Blue Jays, he's had a rocky first and second inning. It obviously takes him a few innings to get the feel of his knuckleball. Is there not some way to change his warmup routine? Maybe he has to throw more pitches. Should the Blue Jays set up a game-like situation or, as they call it, a "simulated" game under the stands for two complete innings before the game starts? With all the big dollars now coming from television, maybe the teams should throw a piece of it at the coaches instead of just the players.

Before we leave the subject, how about a catching coach? If the Blue Jays had a real catching coach, there is no way on earth that Myers and Borders would be living halfway between the pitcher's mound and home on throws to the plate. There's no way so many balls would be bouncing by them, even when Candiotti is pitching. There's no way so many runners would be stealing. The catcher handles 130 to 150 pitches a game. His skill is vital. This should mean that catchers need double the time with coaches than any other players require, and double the amount of work to do. Carlton Fisk may be in this group, but one doesn't have the feeling that there are too many others.

◇ Post-Game Notes

The next best thing after winning an election is owning a satellite dish. Happily for my bank manager, my clients and my kids' future, we do not have one. But the third best thing is the two new super-channels that arrived just last Sunday, thanks to Ted Rogers and the CRTC (who woke it up?). We now get WTBS out of Atlanta on channel 44 and WGN out of Chicago on 45. Now we can look for hundreds of Chicago Cubs, Chicago White Sox and Atlanta

Braves baseball games. Last night, instead of watching the new female deodorant advertisement, I flipped to channel 44 and found the Braves mauling the Mets. The Mets actually continue to suicide in a certain-to-succeed attempt to (a) embarrass themselves, and (b) get the manager fired. In any event, as I flipped back and forth, I saw four, yes, all four New York Mets infielders, make official or unofficial errors in one inning. But first baseman and great hitter Dave Magadan made the best on a little tapper halfway between the plate and first base. He ran in, gloved the ball and then casually took a couple of steps to tag the runner, only to discover that he had left the ball on the grass.

◆ ◆ ◆

Glenallen Hill, obviously depressed at playing for the Cleveland Indians, pontificated this week that the Blue Jays wouldn't win it because they aren't spirited enough and they don't play tough enough. He is no expert (but then again, neither are the rest of us), and I do think that the Blue Jays will win it, but I agree that they just don't have enough toughness. Give me a Dave Justice, a Robin Ventura, a Pete Rose, a Dave Collins or, for that matter, a George Bell — someone who will demand the base. You've got to want it real bad.

◆ ◆ ◆

Tomorrow will be a great game to watch, even though it better be an automatic "W" for the Blue Jays, with Candiotti going against Swindell, former teammates and buddies. It's a game I'll look forward to watching, but, of course, won't see because the only game shown on Canadian TV will be that game you've been waiting for: the Montreal clowns in their multi-striped uniforms playing the Cincinnati Dead Reds at 7:30 tonight. By the way, who would have thought a year ago the Reds would have been out of the pennant race and the Kremlin this year? Jays four games up. The magic number, folks, is twenty-three. Not low enough for counting yet, but you know I am.

Big Mo and the Triple Play

Tuesday, September 10, 1991   7:35 PM   Toronto SkyDome
Pre-Game Standings

	W	L	Pct.	GB	Ho.	Strk.	P10	Div.
TORONTO	79	60	.568	-	40-30	W-5	7-3	46-32
Boston	73	64	.533	5	38-31	W-6	8-2	30-23
Detroit	72	65	.526	6	43-25	L-2	3-7	27-26

Final Score: Mariners 5, Blue Jays 4   Attendance: 50,196

GOOD NEWS! TIGERS ARE DEAD AND BURIED, having gone three and seven to fall six behind. Goodbye, so long, farewell. On the other hand, the Boston Red Sox have closed within five and now own second place.

It's one of those nights when I'm happy to have a ball game in September: the pennant race, the five-game winning streak, Stottlemyre pitching. It's going to be a fun night at the ballpark. I usually leave home at 7:10 P.M. and, after parking and walking to my seat, arrive just after the national anthems. Tonight I'm so eager to get to the game I head out at 6:50. I just want to sit there and feel this one.

Heading down Simcoe Street, I run into some city employees who apparently can't work nights on highways during the summer but seem to be available at night to tear up part of the King and Simcoe intersection just before game time, when all the traffic is pouring forth. After I patiently wait through two green lights, the worker whose job seems to be to keep me from proceeding on the third green begins to cross in front of me. I wave the flagman out of the way and indicate in no uncertain terms that I am going to disobey the signal and head onwards. He decides to let me through and I blast by. Just miss the national anthems and arrive at the usual time. Little do I know that a few hours hence Devon White will be doing exactly what I just had done — and costing us a key game in the process.

Seattle has just gone in the tank for the Red Sox, getting themselves swept by Boston in Fenway Park and running their losing streak on the road to thirteen. I never like these situations, because the likelihood of any team, let alone a reasonably good one like the Mariners, not producing a win in thirteen road games is pretty small. Their losing streak can't go on much longer. Still, I'm just plain happy to be here to watch the Blue Jays roll home over the next three weeks.

The only worrisome thing is that, on a cool, breezy night, the Dome is unexpectedly open. It will also be interesting to see the effect of the wind. It's a westerly wind that looks like it might cause a home-run derby. But when it gets caught in the roof, we may see it blowing backwards onto the field.

◇ The Game

Stottlemyre begins by offering two of the first three batters opportunities to hit it out of the park. Neither succeeds, with Reynolds and Griffey Jr flying to deep centre and deep left. In fact, although Stottlemyre retires the first nine in order, five of the nine are on pretty solid fly outs to centre left.

In the bottom of the first, the boys decide to let me see just how easy this is going to be. The amazing Devon White starts the game with his daily double. And Carter hits it out of the park after Alomar pops out on a failed bunt attempt. 2–0 at the end of one.

In the third, Alomar singles, Carter doubles, and, after Gruber bounces out, Olerud doubles. 4–0 at the end of three, and the three have been played in a quick forty minutes. This is just about perfect.

Stottlemyre's no-hitter is broken up in the top of the fourth, when Edgar Martinez, a good .300 hitter who's underrated because he plays in Seattle, leads off with a solid single, and then

Harold Reynolds, an overrated but good second baseman, hits a quick homer. 4–2.

After Griffey Jr grounds out, Davis hits a fly ball to Devon White for the second out. White starts to trot in from the field, thinking it's the third out. When he sees no other Blue Jay moving, he tosses the ball in, pretending he knew it all the time. Ironically, when Jay Buhner then grounds out third to first for the third out, Olerud turns to fire the ball around the horn, thinking it's only the second out. Head in the game, boys. As I tell my B'nai Brith team, before every pitch think about how many are out and what you're going to do with the ball if it's hit to you. Still, this game is 4–2, even though 4–0 would be better. We're not sweating. I assure everyone that this is an easy win, and everyone agrees.

Now, we've talked about lots of moments that will be remembered long after the season is done. Jack Clark's grand slam, Alomar's late-inning and extra-inning homers against the White Sox, Mark Whiten clobbering McDowell, Gullickson beaning Carter and Carter grabbing the Fielder home run in Detroit and turning it into a sac fly. Here comes another one.

White leads off the fifth with a single. Alomar follows. Each of them are two for three on the night. So, with runners on first and second, none out and a two-run lead, Carter is due up, with a double and a homer in his first two at bats. We are ready to blow it open. Suddenly, Carter hits a grounder to third; throw to second for one, throw to first, and Rick Reed, another American League umpire, calls Carter out at first. Bad enough, but White has decided to ignore Rich Hacker's hold sign at third base (remember the flagman on King Street?) and head home. Tito Martinez, the September call-up first baseman, fires home to Dave (.179) Valle, and White is out. A tainted but real triple play. First one I've seen in person. It happened in a flash, and it was not fun.

As the Mariners run off the field, they are exuberant.

Before you can blink, the first batter in the top of the sixth, Dave (.179) Valle, gets hit by a pitched ball, and the second batter, Edgar Martinez, hits it out of the park. I didn't time it, but I swear that from the time Carter stepped up to bat through the time he hit into a triple play and Martinez tied the ball game with a two-run homer, it couldn't have been more than three-and-a-half minutes. Damn.

Never mind what the players say, never mind that Carter looked safe, never mind that White ran through the stop sign at third, never mind the fact that it's still a 4–4 game. Make no mistake about it. Big Mo (momentum), having sat in the Blue Jays' dugout for five straight games, is now sitting to my left at the edge of the Seattle dugout, and he isn't about to move. Suddenly, as sure as I was that we were going to win, I know we are going to lose. And we do.

Omar Vizquel, a .229 hitter (it's always that way), leads off the eighth with a double, and, three batters later (good old Harold Reynolds again), another double scores him. 5–4, Seattle. Blue Jays go down quietly in the bottom of the eighth and ninth.

BOXSCORE

Mariners...5
Blue Jays...4

SEATTLE	AB	R	H	BI	TORONTO	AB	R	H	BI
EMrtnz 3b	3	2	2	2	White cf	4	1	2	0
Schefer 3b	1	0	0	0	RAlmr 2b	4	1	2	0
Rynlds 2b	4	1	2	3	Carter rf	4	2	2	2
GrfyJr cf	3	0	0	0	Gruber 3b	4	0	1	0
ADavis dh	4	0	0	0	Olerud 1b	3	0	1	2
Buhner rf	4	0	1	0	CnMldo lf	4	0	0	0
TMrtnz 1b	4	0	0	0	Mllniks dh	3	0	0	0
Briley lf	4	0	0	0	Myers c	3	0	1	0
Vizquel ss	4	1	1	0	MnLee ss	3	0	0	0
Valle c	2	1	0	0					
Totals	33	5	6	5	Totals	32	4	9	4

Seattle   000 202 010 - 5
Toronto   202 000 000 - 4

DP - Seattle 1. TP - Seattle 1. LOB - Seattle 3, Toronto 2. 2B - Reynolds (30), Vizquel (12), White (36), Carter (38), Olerud (24). HR - EMartinez (13), Reynolds (3), Carter (32). SB - Briley (20). CS - Gruber (7).

	IP	H	R	ER	BB	SO
Seattle						
Holman (W, 13-13)	7	9	4	4	1	4
CJones (S, 1)	2	0	0	0	0	3
Toronto						
Stotlmr (L, 13-7)	7 1/3	4	5	5	0	3
Timlin	2/3	2	0	0	1	1
MacDonald	1	0	0	0	0	1

Timlin pitched to 1 batter in the 9th.
HBP - by Stottlemyre (Valle).

After the triple play, only Gruber singled, to lead off the sixth, and he got caught stealing. The last eleven batters went down on six strikeouts, three ground outs and two fly balls. Blue Jays had no gas left after the triple play. They got eight hits in five innings before the triple play, and one hit in four innings *after* the triple play.

This game, as usual, had several turning-points. The obvious ones were the two Seattle home runs and the triple play, but it could have gone either way at several points. Stottlemyre threw seven-and-one-third innings and had runners on base only three times. They all scored. Through nine innings, Seattle got the leadoff batter on four times, and three of them scored. The Blue Jays got the leadoff batter on three times, and one scored. Incredibly, Stottlemyre retired three in a row in each of the seven full innings he pitched, with a leadoff single and home run interrupting him in the fourth and a hit leadoff batsman and a home run in the sixth. A tidy game with only a couple of bad pitches. But they made the difference.

Much will be made of the triple play. Nonetheless, it was White's opinion that the Reynolds home run in the fourth wouldn't have gone out but for the wind. It's also true to say that if Valle hadn't narrowly got hit by a pitch, Martinez's home run would have cashed in one, not two. For that matter, the winning run in the eighth, which was knocked in by Reynolds, was not a terribly hard-hit ball but a ground ball over second, close to a playable ball. The Blue Jays hit Holman all over the park for four runs on eight hits through five innings, but after that they were dead. In fact, Holman and the triple-A call-up reliever, Calvin Jones, together faced the minimum number of batters after the third inning.

◇ Patience and Potential

Tenace, totally unlike Cito, was all over Devon White, saying "the odds of him making it home on a play like that were pretty slim," and "with the number-four batter coming up, you can't take the bat out of his hands." Here's one I would have done the Cito way. The Blue Jays lack spirited, tough ball players like Rickey Henderson, Tim Raines, Don Mattingly, Wade Boggs, Dwight Evans, Dave Parker, Dave Henderson, Will Clark, George Bell. These players don't just fill a uniform. They are, to quote one of the most famous of them all, Reggie Jackson, "the straw that stirs the drink." They don't accept results; they create results. They make a break. They push the other team. They test it. The Blue Jays, meanwhile, have too many players who are unwilling to make things happen.

Since over the long haul most teams will end up within twenty games of each other and the difference between them is only about a game a week or a game every two weeks, the player who forces an error or steals a run can win a pennant for his team.

In my view, White's play wasn't terribly different from the play Alomar made against Cleveland. The Cleveland third baseman got the ground ball and held Alomar at third. As soon as he threw to first, Alomar broke for the plate, beating the well-executed relay throw from first to home just under the tag. Devon White wasn't quite at third when the third baseman got the ball, but the third baseman had to throw to second, and then the ball had to be thrown to first and home. White's was as reasonable a gamble as Alomar's, and the only difference was that Alomar's worked. But if you live by the sword, sometimes you're going to die by it. By now the other teams know that the Blue Jays are going to steal that extra base and play aggressively. That knowledge will cause errors. It didn't work tonight; it may tomorrow night. But you've got to know that the Seattle infielders will be coming up quicker on the ball, will be thinking more about the play, will be tenser knowing that White (or Alomar) is on the bases.

The only one of Tenace's criticisms I agree with is that White clearly had been held up by the third-base coach. Whether the third-base coach and/or Tenace was right or wrong in wanting him held up doesn't matter. What matters is the team decision has to be implemented. It can't be a free-for-all on the base paths. Alomar and White usually have a green light to do what they want on the bases, but, when Hacker has clearly held them up, in my view they have no option. The runner has to hold, and I'd be saying the same thing even if White had scored. But Tenace wouldn't be all over his face if he had ignored the sign (as he did) and successfully scored (which he didn't).

Confidence is what this game is all about. Look at Otis Nixon, a career Mendoza hitter, who didn't look like he belonged even in the Montreal Expos' lineup. He went to Atlanta this year and is hitting .300. Has he suddenly learned to swing the bat differently? Has he suddenly bought a new pair of glasses? Why, he hasn't even changed leagues. What the manager (Bobby Cox) has done is give the guy a chance, take the pressure off of him and let him play. This won't work with many ball players, but it works with some.

Kelly Gruber unbelievably is an example of a great ball player who was almost lost. After Gillick took him from the Cleveland Indians, who left him off their protected list in 1984, the Blue Jays were patient. They stuck with him through several seasons when he struck out too much and was far more "potential" than production. Suddenly, two years ago, he matured.

No one will ever know how many ball players failed to make the major leagues simply because they were with the wrong team at the wrong time with the wrong manager. Once players get to double-A ball, I believe, they are separated more by maturity, coaching and discipline than by talent. A player lucky enough to bump into a good minor-league manager in a good minor-league system has a far greater chance to make the bigs than a more talented but neglected or overmanaged young ball player.

Now, my comments about sticking with players and giving them confidence are inconsistent with how I feel about John Olerud, I hear you say. But they aren't, I protest. Olerud is getting in the big leagues what he needed to get in the minor leagues. In the minor leagues he would have been batting .320 and .330 every year. He would have been under little pressure. He would have learned to be aggressive at the plate without worrying about a pennant race or the media. He could have grown up. I fear that Olerud will always perform below "potential" because he's been rushed and hasn't learned his art.

White is performing to his potential because he's been on the circuit, had the ups and downs. He's now being respected for the mature talent he has become. Before we forget Devon White, a sign of his maturity was his role in the Carter/Gullickson incident in Detroit. Sparky Anderson was right in the middle of it, and White went up and said, "Sparky, what the hell are you doing in the middle of this? Get out of here before you get hurt." When Sparky didn't leave but hung in there to try to keep the peace, White responded by saying, "I'm going to stay right here," meaning he would hang around to make sure no one harmed Sparky. Sparky commented later that White was "a fine young man." This about the man who Doug Rader, now fired (as predicted) as the California Angels' manager, felt was a difficult-to-manage kid.

◇ Post-Game Notes

Tenace has moved Kelly Gruber into the cleanup spot. I felt all along that Kelly Gruber, if he began to hit to his potential, could make September an easy ride for us, and lately he has been producing. Tenace, still playing the confidence game, rewarded that by the move. Paradoxically, that takes pressure off Gruber, who I think was working too hard batting in the sixth and seventh spots. I still think he's vulnerable to the "Otto Velez" disease, but he's responding well to the cleanup spot, and I think his performance has had a lot to do with Carter's resurgence lately. Olerud has been dropped to fifth and, in my view, should be batting seventh or eighth. It is interesting to compare Olerud with Gruber at this point in the season. Olerud is batting .257, Gruber .251, but, in forty-three fewer at bats Gruber has two more home runs and only five fewer RBIs. Gruber belongs ahead of Olerud in the batting order.

◆ ◆ ◆

They regularly have promotions at the Dome. The first 20,000 or 25,000 fans get nice Blue Jays' mugs, hats, bats, scarfs, etcetera. Why do the sponsors get away with providing gifts only to the first 25,000 fans? The sponsors get enormous publicity for these special days. They know there will be 50,000 fans in the stadium. Like most season-ticket holders, I arrive later than earlier, though I rarely miss the first pitch. I have not once this year received any promotional flag, hat, bat or mug. I would guess most of the fans do not come to more than a half-dozen games a year; they come early to look at the park, watch batting practice and get some food. I'd like to see the Blue Jays one year say to these sponsors of special days that they're going to have to give out 50,000 items. Come on guys. Treat us all equally.

◆ ◆ ◆

Final note. Never met a baseball fan I didn't like, and Bob Rae is the real thing. An honest-to-God baseball fan. I like the Premier a lot, but not his politics, and he's had a rough year. Seeing him watch Joe Carter reminds me of the true story of when Babe Ruth was asked in 1927 whether he thought it was fair that he earned more money than the president of the United States. Ruth answered, "Sure, I had a better year." Joe might feel the same way about Bob. Anyway, Bob and his kind wife, Arlene, were sitting on the aisle near us, and, as I stopped to chat on the way up to get a diet Coke after the fifth inning (yes, just after the triple play), I asked Arlene if she was cold since she was wearing a summerish sleeveless dress. She was freezing. As a long-time Exhibition Stadium attendee, I come overprepared for outdoor baseball, even at the SkyDome. At Exhibition Stadium, I would often wear long underwear, a turtleneck, a sweatshirt, a scarf, a winter parka and gloves, as well as two pairs of socks and a pair of boots. At the SkyDome when the roof is open at night in the fall, I wear a t-shirt and a shirt, but I always bring a sweatshirt and a jacket in a bag.

I offered Arlene the sweatshirt (University of Western Ontario). She more than happily accepted.

Aiding and abetting the enemy.

It's more than I would do for Harold Reynolds or Ken Griffey.

We Left Our Hearts in San Francisco

Friday to Sunday, September 20-22, 1991   Oakland Coliseum
Pre-Game Standings

	W	L	Pct.	GB	Ho.	Strk.	P10	Div.
TORONTO	82	65	.558	-	42-33	W-1	5-5	46-32
Boston	79	67	.541	2 1/2	40-32	W-2	7-3	36-26
Detroit	75	70	.517	6	44-26	L-3	3-7	30-31

Final Score (Sunday): Blue Jays 3, Athletics 2

Date line: Oakland. Yes, I have succumbed. I haven't had a holiday from life since last Christmas and from the Blue Jays since March 1. I need to get away from both. So what do I do? I decide to take a five-day break — not somewhere like Antigua in a hotel or resort that can't get even CNN, but in San Francisco, across the Bay from Oakland where the Blue Jays just happen to be for a three-game series.

We've just come off a hideous, nerve-wracking three-game series in Seattle. As you know, I hate these western road swings when the games keep us up till early morning. Two losses, one win. The magic number is still a big fifteen and our lead is down to only two-and-a-half over Boston. Boston's winning almost every night.

We are well into our traumatic twenty-three games against the West to finish the schedule, and so far we are 3–5. Not good enough, considering that five of those eight have been home games.

◇ The Friday Game

Although I knew that the Oakland Alameda Coliseum would have a full out-of-town scoreboard (unlike the SkyDome), I did a final check on the ESPN before we left for the game and found that the Red Sox with Roger Clemens were, of course, beating the Yankees. We took the Bay Area Rapid Transit (BART), a quick, quiet, well-kept, carpeted, clean transit system, out to Oakland. It is cool — Exhibition Stadium time. Foggy, damp and windy.

We end up sitting behind Mrs Turner Ward and Mrs Linda Tenace. I offer Linda far more advice than Gene will need or want for the rest of the season.

Devon White leads off with a home run. In the home of Rickey Henderson, this is wonderful. No one in the park will miss the significance. Quickly, Alomar follows with a single, and we're back in the pennant race. Alomar steals second and looks to be safe. Yet another questionable call. Alomar goes so crazy that both Mike Squires and Gene Tenace have to hustle out there to hold him back. Alomar would not have gone berserk like that if he thought he had been tagged before he got to second.

Carter, still in a slump, strikes out, followed by a Gruber walk. This puts us with two out and a runner on first, instead of one out with a runner on first and third, had the ump made the right call. Olerud goes out easily second to first, and we're out of the inning with just one run. Killers like the Red Sox would have put up three or four, so would the A's, and we all feel that we're going to live to regret this one.

And it doesn't take long.

Every Blue Jays' fan from Tony Kubek to Ernie Whitt knows that you can't put Rickey Henderson on base. The Jays walk him. Rickey, of course, steals second easily. Greg Myers heaves yet another ball into centre field, putting Henderson on third. The patented Rickey Henderson formula — get a walk and end up on third two pitches later. One out later, Canseco comes up and, of course, hits a home run a ton out of the park. 2–1, Oakland. A double and two more walks later and Stottlemyre stumbles out of the inning. Bob Welch suddenly remembers he is a former Cy Young award winner and strikes out the side in the second. In the third,

White, continuing to streak, singles, followed by an Alomar walk and a Carter RBI single. Tie ball game, 2–2.

The teams stick at 2–2 with the only events after the top of the third being another Canseco at bat in the bottom of the third. Canseco grounds a ball over second base, which would be an easy single. Alomar makes an incredible play doing the splits and sliding to stop the ball, jumping up and firing to first. Olerud with his left foot nailed to the base as usual does his awkward crossover routine to backhand the ball and ends up being pulled off the base. Credit Alomar with a sensational play, credit Canseco with a single, discredit Olerud with a technical foul. If Olerud had stretched properly, he would have had the ball and been able to keep his right foot, yes, his right foot, on the base. Canseco immediately steals second on Myers, but goes no further.

On the other hand, in the top of the fourth Dave Parker draws a walk and we are stunned to see him take off for second with one out. I think Greg Myers is equally stunned as there is no way Parker is trying to steal. The hit and run was clearly on, Myers missed the sign, did not swing and Parker was out by a mile. Now we've played four innings and Greg Myers has made an error on Henderson's steal, and allowed Canseco to steal in the third, as well as striking out in the second and missing a hit-and-run signal in the fourth.

In the fifth, it is simple. Stottlemyre and Timlin, who relieved him, give up three unintentional walks plus two intentional walks, two singles and a sacrifice fly to allow three runs on two hits. Oakland 5–2. Looks like another loss. But in the top of the sixth, after an Olerud single and a Maldonado walk and a pitching change, Pat Borders incredibly hits his third homer of the year to knock in three and tie the game. Joy on the Blue Jays' bench. The game stays tied until the eleventh. In the seventh, Alomar leads off with a single (making it two singles and two walks in four at bats) and then, after Carter and Gruber again fail to deliver, Olerud doubles. Now, the other night in Seattle, Rich (Fired-by-the-Last-Place-Cardinals) Hacker sent Olerud home with none out only to have him thrown out by the length of the Golden Gate Bridge. Tonight he is totally spooked, holding up Robbie Alomar in the same situation (trying to score from first on a double) with two out. Alomar could give Olerud a twenty-yard head start, carry Rich Hacker, John McLaren and Cecil Fielder on his back and still beat Olerud in a one-hundred–yard dash. Further, in this case, the odds against scoring a runner held at third are much higher since there are two out versus the other night, when there were none out. But no. Hacker holds Alomar at third and he dies there two batters later.

The rest is history. David Wells, who has been going pretty well lately, gets through the ninth and tenth giving up only a single. Tenace goes to Duane Ward, who hasn't been throwing well lately. Ward leads off the eleventh by putting you-know-who on base for the third time in six at bats. Yes, Rickey leads off the eleventh with a single. He is sacrificed to second. Then Ward strikes out Canseco and intentionally walks Baines. Ernest Riles is brought in to pinch hit for Brook Jacoby. Now, let's be clear. Ernest Riles is hitless in his last seventeen at bats, zero for seventeen. He has pinch hit twenty-one times this year and got one hit — that one against Duane Ward! How many pinch hits has Ernest Riles now got this year? And how many has he now got against Duane Ward? That's right, two. It's midnight in Oakland, 3:00 A.M. in Toronto and even later in the Blue Jays' dressing room. Four losses in the last five games.

◇ Post-Game Notes

This game was lost, or not won, by the Blue Jays in three key plays, all involving Alomar.

1. The umpire's bad call on Alomar's steal of second in the first inning.
2. In the three-run Oakland rally in the fifth, with Henderson on first and Canseco on second, Baines hit a ground ball to Alomar behind second. LaRussa has a hit and run on, so it would be really difficult to get Canseco at second. But Alomar made a mistake. He decided to go for him and missed, leaving all runners safe and the bases loaded. Had Alomar thrown to first, he would certainly have got Baines, putting runners on second and third with two out. Highly unlikely Oakland would have put up three runs if that play was made.

3. Had Hacker not chickened out and held Alomar at third in the seventh, we might well have got the go-ahead run and won.

◆ ◆ ◆

The Blue Jays are statistically the worst drawing attraction on the road. In other words, fewer people go to see the Blue Jays' games than any other team in the majors. I guess this is true. But let's put things in perspective.

The Blue Jays *might* be the worst road attraction in the American League, but something tells me that the Indians, the Brewers and the Orioles, to name just three, are a lot worse. Could the difference possibly be that when we or anyone else goes to Cleveland to play, for example, *they* produce 8000 spectators? Whereas when Cleveland comes to Toronto, we produce 50,000 fans regardless of whether Cleveland is fielding a major-league team, a minor-league team or a sandlot team (all of which they have, recently).

If we had the benefit of playing at the SkyDome as a visiting team, I suspect our "road attraction" figures would be a lot higher.

◆ ◆ ◆

The screen at Oakland is small, but they know how to use it. They show highlights of the Minnesota-Texas game, which finished earlier today. They also show a great catch made last night in the Astros' ball game. This is creative, immediate and interesting use of the board.

◆ ◆ ◆

After an extra-inning loss, the trip back to San Francisco on BART is a lot longer and unhappier.

When we get out and come up onto one of the most famous corners in North America, which is the terminus of the trolley car, we are greeted by sixteen homeless people sleeping on the park benches around the circle. It is depressing and puts two things in perspective. One: my unhappiness over the Blue Jays blowing this pennant; and two: complaining about taxes in Canada, which are used, at least in part, to reduce the occurrence and eliminate the acceptability of the sad scene in Union Square.

◇ The Saturday Game

The Blue Jays seem loose on the field. Happy, talking to fans. I don't know. I guess the Red Sox are doing the same at Fenway, and it's a sign that they're not "tight." But, somehow, I'd just like to see them a little more edgy and focused on the game.

We can deal with this one really quickly — just as did the team. They played uneventfully through seven full, gorgeous, comfortable, enjoyable innings. The Blue Jays get four hits in the first seven and runners on base in every inning except the first. Jimmy Key looks like the Key of several years ago in what I think is his best pitching performance of the year. After giving up the obligatory single to Canseco in the first with two out, he retires twelve in a row and doesn't give up another hit until the seventh. Through seven he gives up no runs on two hits, one walk and strikes out seven, including Canseco and Rickey Henderson twice each. He is wonderful. Meanwhile, the Blue Jays simply can't do anything with their runners, leaving three on second and one on third through seven. In the eighth, disaster strikes, quickly and irrevocably. The eighth goes like this.

McGwire-ground out
Gallego-single (under Lee's glove on a play that looks eminently makable)
Bordick-sacrifice
Rickey Henderson-intentional walk
Willie Wilson-double
Canseco-intentional walk
Baines (pinch hitting for Dave Henderson)-single
Steinbach-single
Jacoby-ground out

Oakland 4, Toronto 0. Why bother talking about the ninth? As soon as LaRussa saw his team up one run, let alone four, he warmed up Eckersley. Need I say more? By this time, Boston was leading the New York Yankees by a converted touch down, and our division lead had gone. One-half game.

◆ A BASEBALL ADDICT'S DIARY

Post-Game Notes

It was simple. Key pitched a great game, and the only one of the first three batters in the eighth who got on base was Gallego, with his little single underneath Lee's glove. It's a play Fernandez and Zosky both would have made. Don't even think of asking about Alomar. But, more importantly, it's a play that Lee has made fifty times this year. He's either got the September disease or his leg injury is making it tough for him to get down. If it is, he shouldn't be in there. It cost us the game.

◆ ◆ ◆

The difference between Tony LaRussa's managing style and the Toronto style, no matter who's managing, is never more evident than in the eighth-inning rally. His team is already up by two runs. His cleanup batter, designated hitter Dave Henderson, batting .280, is coming up. Henderson is without question one of the better players in the league. He is a money player with a history of delivering in the clutch. But when Tenace replaces Key with Acker to pitch to the right-handed–hitting Henderson, LaRussa does not blink, does not pause, does not worry about Henderson's ego. His players know he plays hard and plays to win. He pinch hits Harold Baines. Baines, of course, singles to drive in two runs. That's the difference.

◆ ◆ ◆

I bought one of the fine Oakland programs, in which is inserted good, valuable information. Included are major-league standings as of the day, plus a summary of the A's record over the last nine games and in extra-inning games. Also shown are Toronto's and Oakland's leaders in twelve offensive and three pitching categories. Why don't we find such information in the SkyDome programs?

◆ ◆ ◆

As we walk across the elevated walkway to the BART platform, we see the players' parking lot below us: Porsche (Canseco), Jaguar, Mercedes, Porsche, Mercedes, Mercedes, BMW, BMW, Corvette (Dave Henderson), Mercedes, Mercedes, BMW, Nissan 300 ZX (must belong to a September call-up).

◇ The Sunday Game

Ron Darling gets through four innings facing only thirteen batters. Meanwhile, the Great Guzman — again — performs well. He gets the first six A's, walks McGwire to lead off the third, then Gallego. Two walks to the first two batters. Bordick, the number-nine hitter, is up to sacrifice them to second and third. He bunts the ball right at Guzman. McGwire is a sure and easy out at third — but Borders tells Guzman to play to first, which he does. Further evidence of the Blue Jays' subpar defensive catching is this poor call by Borders. Pennant race pressure — and he plays it too safe.

Runners on second and third, thanks to Borders. Guzman throws high to Rickey Henderson. It bounces off Borders's glove to the backstop. Passed ball, McGwire scores, one run on no hits, one mental error by Borders and one physical error by Borders. Guzman gets Rickey and Dave Henderson easily. End of three. Jays, no runs, one hit, one mental error, one physical error; A's, one run, no hits, no errors.

BOXSCORE

Blue Jays...3
A's..2

TORONTO	AB	R	H	BI	OAKLAND	AB	R	H	BI
White cf	4	0	0	0	RHdsn lf	4	0	0	0
RAlmr 2b	4	0	1	0	DHdsn cf	4	0	0	0
Carter rf	3	0	0	0	Brosius 2b	0	0	0	0
Olerud 1b	4	0	0	0	Cnseco rf	4	0	0	0
CnMldo lf	3	2	1	0	Baines dh	4	0	1	0
Gruber 3b	4	0	1	0	Stnbch c	4	1	2	0
DPrker dh	3	0	1	0	Hemnd pr	0	0	0	0
Tabler dh	0	0	0	0	Jacoby 3b	2	0	0	0
Brders c	3	1	1	2	Riles 3b	1	0	0	0
Gnzales ss	2	0	0	0	Blkshp ph	1	0	0	0
Mllniks ph	0	0	0	1	McGwr 1b	3	1	0	0
Zosky ss	0	0	0	0	Gallego 2b	1	0	0	0
					Bordick ss	1	0	0	0
					WWlsn cf	0	0	0	0
Totals	30	3	5	3	Totals	29	2	3	0

Toronto   000 020 100 - 3
Oakland   001 000 100 - 2

E - RAlomar (15), Gruber (13). DP - Oakland 2. LOB - Toronto 5, Oakland 5. 2B - Gruber (17), Baines (25). HR - Borders (4). SB - CnMaldonado (4). CS - Gallego (9). S - Bordick.

	IP	H	R	ER	BB	SO
Toronto						
JuGzm (W, 8-2)	8	2	2	0	4	7
Wells (S, 1)	1	1	0	0	0	2
Oakland						
Darling (L, 3-5)	8	4	3	3	4	9
Campbell	1/3	1	0	0	0	1
Klink	0	0	0	0	1	0
Chitren	2/3	0	0	0	0	0

Klink pitched to 1 batter in the 9th.
WP - JuGuzman. PB - Borders.

Maldonado singles to lead off the fifth. A stolen base and two outs later, Borders atones with his third homer off Oakland — second in the series and fourth of the year. Jays 2, Oakland 1. Borders accounts for all three runs.

Darling will give us a run in the seventh on a single and three, yes count them, three walks. Bottom of the seventh, 3–1 Jays.

Waiting for disaster. We are tense. Everything is a struggle.

Sure enough, Steinbach singles with one out. Guzman gets Ernest Riles (remember him?) on a fly ball. Two out. Wild pitch gets Steinbach to second.

Guzman, still in control, gets McGwire to hit a tough but playable bouncer between the mound and third base. Gruber fields it, has lots of time, looks comfortably to first and throws it into the dirt! John Olerud, who will not get a job at Baskin-Robbins (no scoop), not only does not dig it out but seems to be looking away from his mitt! The ball goes wild. Another give-away run. Blue Jays 3, Oakland 2.

David Wells is brought in to get us through the ninth, but of course gives up a single to bring the winning run to the plate. Why do they do this every time? Anyway, he gets them out and suddenly the Blue Jays are back to one-and-a-half games ahead. The magic number is twelve.

◇ Cito Bet the Farm

Did they leave their heart in Oakland or in Toronto? Or maybe it's playing left field for the Cubs. No fire. The *San Francisco Chronicle* refers to the Blue Jays as an "uninspiring opponent." Imagine, at this stage of the season!

The Red Sox are 31–10 since August 7. They have won fourteen of their last eighteen. Jack Clark, a revisionist of whom Lenin would be proud, now says, "no player in this clubhouse ever said we were out of it." Sure, Jack.

The Jays meanwhile are trying too hard to be calm. Smiling and casual in batting practice, they look less focused than the A's, who are in third place ten games back. They are trying too hard not to panic. They are trying too hard to stay calm. They *are* Cito. They epitomize "Don't worry, be happy."

But, on the field, the pressure is showing. This weekend alone:

- Hacker fails to send in Alomar.
- Alomar fails to take a sure out at first, all runners safe.

- Olerud fails to scoop Gruber's throw out of the dirt.
- Olerud leans the wrong way on a simple play at first, all runners safe.
- Gruber throws the ball away on an easy play.
- Borders makes a bad call on a bunt and allows a passed ball for a run.
- Lee fails to grab a routine ground ball, costing Key the ball game.
- Tenace fails to pinch hit for Lee (where have I heard that before?).
- Carter is one for twelve; White two for thirteen; Gruber two for thirteen; shortstops one for nine; DHs one for nine; Duane Ward four hits, one run in two-thirds of an inning.

What's going on here?

This team is so busy pretending that "steady but sure" wins it that it's not intense enough to go out and grab the win. In fact, it's so busy working on not being *tense* that it's succeeding in not being "intense."

The trademark of a winning team should be Robbie Alomar or Joe Carter, but on this team it's unflappable John Olerud. It's time to get flapped. Someone has got to get angry. Someone has to say, "I'm not going to let this team lose." This is the time for Carter to wake up and go 7–13. For Gruber to produce — no excuses. There is a spirit and a fire lacking on this team that is present in others.

Cito bet the farm on keeping us calm and confident. It isn't working. We need adrenalin, not Valium.

We are heading down to L.A. to meet the Angels — Finley, Langston and Abbott, three of the best starters in the league and all with seventeen wins. This is the last leg of the extended western road trip. It was as bad as we feared back in April. In Seattle 1–2, in Oakland 1–2; at home Oakland 2–1, Seattle 0–2. And we're still in the West.

I'm tired of hearing the rationalizations; "when we get good pitching, our hitting is not there." "When we get good hitting, our pitchers are letting us down." It's as though what happens is totally beyond their control. Are they spectators, or are they participants?

As we've seen throughout this diary, I'm the first to argue that there is much luck in baseball. But as LaRussa said yesterday, you should find a way to put across three runs any day and every day.

USA Today Baseball Weekly reports that the Blue Jays are getting an incredible 40 percent plus of their team offense from White, Alomar and Carter. They are batting .289 while the rest of the team is batting .249. They've over half the team's home runs and triples, almost half the team's doubles and runs and three-quarters of their stolen bases. This is a depressing stat. This means that if the opposing teams can get by the top three, they are in good shape.

Still, Boston blew, we won, it's one-and-a-half.

◇ Post-Game Notes

Juan Guzman 8–2. Anyone paying attention? He is, without doubt, the AL rookie of the year.

◆ ◆ ◆

What happened to Ed Sprague? How long can this continue? The bottom six in the order are hitting less than .250. Sprague has been batting .270 and better the entire year, and he remains on the bench. Worse, the Jays have stolen a season from him. Only 157 at bats. He needed the three or four hundred he would have got in Syracuse. If they weren't going to use him in the big leagues, he should have been sent to Syracuse to learn to catch so that he can replace Pat Borders, as certainly is the plan, next year. For one thing, he blocks the plate.

◆ ◆ ◆

The Oakland fans were friendly and knowledgeable. They kidded us about the Red Sox, they had fun with their own Canseco and they knew the game. It was atmosphere, it was chatty, it was a shared experience.

Textbook Baseball, Mookie Magic

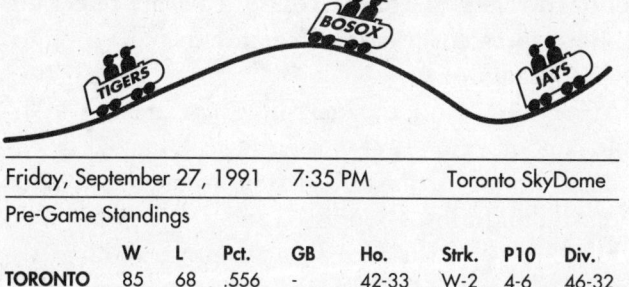

Friday, September 27, 1991			7:35 PM		Toronto SkyDome		
Pre-Game Standings							
	W	L	Pct.	GB	Ho.	Strk.	P10	Div.
TORONTO	85	68	.556	-	42-33	W-2	4-6	46-32
Boston	82	70	.539	2 1/2	42-33	L-1	6-4	39-29
Detroit	78	74	.513	6 1/2	47-30	W-1	3-7	33-34
Final Score: Blue Jays 7, Twins 2					Attendance: 50,326		

WHO WOULD HAVE THUNK IT? A week ago we were down to a half-game lead. It was 1987 revisited, and almost every other year for that matter. Today, we are sitting with a three-and-a-half–game lead. The magic number is four. By the end of last Sunday, we were up to one-and-a-half, thanks to a Pat Borders homer and a Boston loss.

Boston got cocky and the Blue Jays got angry after all.

On Monday, in a memorable game, and unbelievably enough with Tom Candiotti pitching, the Blue Jays gave up seven runs to the Angels in the first inning. Facing Chuck Finley, one of the best pitchers in the league, a depressing loss loomed after the uplifting sudden win on Sunday. Oh yes, they lost, but first they tried hard to come back, and the game ended 10–9 for the Angels. As for "throw-away" runs, the Jays allowed three when it didn't look like they counted in a California blow-out. They ended up costing us the game. What also hurts was another hideous umpiring call. Dave Parker was called out at second base when he had arrived about twenty minutes before the ball and thirty minutes before the tag.

But following the win in Oakland, the Jays did not lie down after they were behind 7–0. They showed fight and determination, and this loss may turn out ironically to have been one of the turning-points in our rollercoaster. The Jays turned a 7–0 Angels lead into a game they felt they would have won but for another bad call.

While the Jays were unsuccessfully fighting back, the Red Sox were successfully losing.

Tuesday night was a gem. I got home late and tired from Oakland and swore not to watch the game. I flipped on the television with the mute button pressed just to watch the first few innings. Yes, I'll just have *one* peanut too!

Hours and extra innings later, the incredible happened. Jim Abbott pitched about as good a game as I've seen all year. He was dominating, impossible to hit with great stuff, great movement and quick innings. Well after midnight I was depressed and figured we had no chance. Meanwhile, Stotts for the Blue Jays was not matching Abbott pitch for pitch but still doing pretty well. Then the impossible. In the tenth inning, Maldonado singled and Tabler was intentionally walked, bringing up Pat Borders. Abbott delivered a good fastball and so did Borders — pow, over the fence. 3–0 Blue Jays, and they held it in the bottom of the inning. Abbott pitched maybe his best game of the year: 112 pitches and 82 strikes. But he made one mistake.

Boston and Baltimore rained out. Lead is two. Magic number is ten.

Wednesday, thankfully, was an afternoon game, which meant no late night, although by the time the game came on on the little TV in my office I felt like it was midnight, I was so tired. An unusual game for the Blue Jays. A blow-out. Easy win, 7–2.

Magic number is nine.

Meanwhile, the Red Sox were rained out *again* in Baltimore.

Thursday was a much-needed day off for the Blue Jays. It was like a holiday. No tension, no late nights, no extra innings, no leaky bullpens, no runners left on base; nothing. Peace and quiet. I love it.

The Red Sox were playing two with Baltimore to make up for one of the rain-outs. We just presumed they would win both, especially with Clemens going in the first. On my way out of the office at 6:00 P.M., someone told me that Clemens had easily won the first game and that it was 5–1 Boston in the second. During dinner, Sheldon called, and, honouring the rule that we don't accept calls during

Textbook Baseball, Mookie Magic

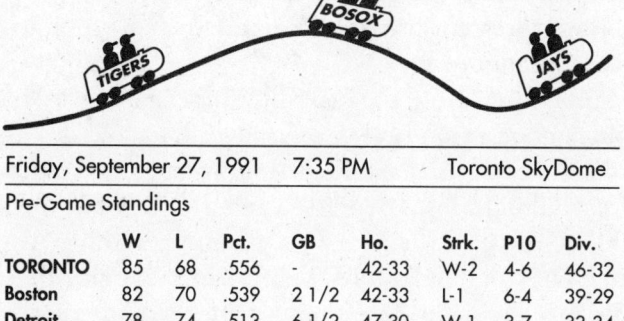

| Friday, September 27, 1991 | 7:35 PM | Toronto SkyDome |

Pre-Game Standings

	W	L	Pct.	GB	Ho.	Strk.	P10	Div.
TORONTO	85	68	.556	-	42-33	W-2	4-6	46-32
Boston	82	70	.539	2 1/2	42-33	L-1	6-4	39-29
Detroit	78	74	.513	6 1/2	47-30	W-1	3-7	33-34

| Final Score: Blue Jays 7, Twins 2 | Attendance: 50,326 |

WHO WOULD HAVE THUNK IT? A week ago we were down to a half-game lead. It was 1987 revisited, and almost every other year for that matter. Today, we are sitting with a three-and-a-half–game lead. The magic number is four. By the end of last Sunday, we were up to one-and-a-half, thanks to a Pat Borders homer and a Boston loss.

Boston got cocky and the Blue Jays got angry after all.

On Monday, in a memorable game, and unbelievably enough with Tom Candiotti pitching, the Blue Jays gave up seven runs to the Angels in the first inning. Facing Chuck Finley, one of the best pitchers in the league, a depressing loss loomed after the uplifting sudden win on Sunday. Oh yes, they lost, but first they tried hard to come back, and the game ended 10–9 for the Angels. As for "throw-away" runs, the Jays allowed three when it didn't look like they counted in a California blow-out. They ended up costing us the game. What also hurts was another hideous umpiring call. Dave Parker was called out at second base when he had arrived about twenty minutes before the ball and thirty minutes before the tag.

But following the win in Oakland, the Jays did not lie down after they were behind 7–0. They showed fight and determination, and this loss may turn out ironically to have been one of the turning-points in our rollercoaster. The Jays turned a 7–0 Angels lead into a game they felt they would have won but for another bad call.

While the Jays were unsuccessfully fighting back, the Red Sox were successfully losing.

Tuesday night was a gem. I got home late and tired from Oakland and swore not to watch the game. I flipped on the television with the mute button pressed just to watch the first few innings. Yes, I'll just have *one* peanut too!

Hours and extra innings later, the incredible happened. Jim Abbott pitched about as good a game as I've seen all year. He was dominating, impossible to hit with great stuff, great movement and quick innings. Well after midnight I was depressed and figured we had no chance. Meanwhile, Stotts for the Blue Jays was not matching Abbott pitch for pitch but still doing pretty well. Then the impossible. In the tenth inning, Maldonado singled and Tabler was intentionally walked, bringing up Pat Borders. Abbott delivered a good fastball and so did Borders — pow, over the fence. 3–0 Blue Jays, and they held it in the bottom of the inning. Abbott pitched maybe his best game of the year: 112 pitches and 82 strikes. But he made one mistake.

Boston and Baltimore rained out. Lead is two. Magic number is ten.

Wednesday, thankfully, was an afternoon game, which meant no late night, although by the time the game came on on the little TV in my office I felt like it was midnight, I was so tired. An unusual game for the Blue Jays. A blow-out. Easy win, 7–2.

Magic number is nine.

Meanwhile, the Red Sox were rained out *again* in Baltimore.

Thursday was a much-needed day off for the Blue Jays. It was like a holiday. No tension, no late nights, no extra innings, no leaky bullpens, no runners left on base; nothing. Peace and quiet. I love it.

The Red Sox were playing two with Baltimore to make up for one of the rain-outs. We just presumed they would win both, especially with Clemens going in the first. On my way out of the office at 6:00 P.M., someone told me that Clemens had easily won the first game and that it was 5–1 Boston in the second. During dinner, Sheldon called, and, honouring the rule that we don't accept calls during dinner, Jamie answered to tell the caller that we'd call back. I listened from the dining-room as Jamie said, "They what? Hold on, wait till I tell my dad. Dad, it's Sheldon. He says Boston lost 6–5."

So, I broke one more dinner rule. I turned on the headline channel 38 news to see the beautiful numbers come up: Baltimore 6, Boston 5. Probably the biggest win of the year, and it was accomplished by Dwight Evans, former Red Sox great, just standing there accepting ball four from Greg Harris with the bases loaded.

The Red Sox are moaning that their great reliever, Jeff Reardon, was injured and unavailable. No sympathy here, folks. Henke's been unavailable for most of the year because of injury, and Stieb's been gone all year and Gruber was gone part of the year.

Our weekend games against Minnesota were all sensational ball games. Textbook baseball, exciting baseball, great pitching, clutch hitting, super defence. Friday night we won 7–2, Saturday we lost 5–0 and Sunday in a squeaker we won 2–1.

But the game I want to talk about is Friday, September 27.

This was a game to remember. It was Mookie Wilson night at the SkyDome. He likely won't have any more great nights in baseball. He's been a wonderful gamer. He almost singlehanded lifted the 1989 club up by its collar when he arrived in August and showed it how to hustle, care, think, play smart baseball and win. He's one of those players who hasn't got a lot of power, has no arm, but radiates electricity, and he's brought that important energy to Toronto.

◇ The Game

It's Kevin Tapani against Juan (Should-Be-Rookie-of-the-Year-but-Won't-Be) Guzman. Tapani has been great the last part of the season and is 16–8, while Guzman is 8–2, having won eight in a row after going 0–2 when he first came up. Tapani, Morris and Erickson will be facing us this weekend. They're a key reason the Twins are about to go from last (last year) to first (this year).

Randy Bush leads off for the Twins with a walk, but then is erased on a failed hit-and-run attempt by a good throw to second (for once) by Borders.

In the bottom of the first, Devon White again leads off with a triple. He's been slumping lately. It looks like he's taking his head off the ball and starting to upper-cut the ball. I think his recent home-run streak has made him believe he's a home-run hitter. In any case, he hits a good solid triple. Alomar, who you'd expect to be hitting to the right side to score White hit the ball to the left side through the drawn-in infield for a single. Two batters, 1–0 Blue Jays.

Alomar does the expected, which is try to steal second. I knew it, Sheldon knew it, Tapani knew it and Minnesota manager Tom Kelly knew it. As a result, a pitch out and Harper, the underrated Minnesota catcher, guns Alomar by a mile. Tapani, who has walked more than three batters in a game only once in his career, walks Carter. Olerud, still being allowed to bat cleanup, hits into a fielder's choice, moving Carter to second. Gruber then singles to leave runners on first and third for Maldonado. Candy strikes out. End of the first, three hits and a walk but only one run. Anyway, 1–0 Jays.

Guzman pitches easily through to the fourth, partly thanks to a sensational — and I mean sensational — play by Manuel Lee. Lee goes far to his right on a ground-ball hit by Harper and throws a long, good, hard fastball to Olerud to get Harper. In the fourth, Chuck (Bound-to-Be-Rookie-of-the-Year-Because-He-Has-Had-Big-Publicity) Knoblauch hits a tough fly ball to short centre field, which Alomar makes a great play on. Then, trouble. Guzman walks Puckett and Hrbek, and then that pesky Harper singles Puckett home from second base. Tie game, two men on and one out. Guzman gets out of the inning with a ground ball and a strikeout.

Bottom of the fourth coming up. Olerud still batting cleanup — with a .260 average, just a few more RBIs than White and only one more than Alomar — grounds out to open the inning. Gruber then singles and steals second. Maldonado walks, bringing up Dave Parker. Parker has been sensational, batting .300 since he joined the Jays. What a great acquisition. Parker then lines a ball down the right-field line, which looks to be foul. Kent Hrbek, the first baseman, goes absolutely berserk while the play is on, jumping in the air and waving his arms at the umpire. Parker ends up on second, Maldonado on third and Gruber scores easily. 2–1 Jays. Two runners in scoring position, one out. On the replay, we see that the ball did hit the foul line, but only just.

Borders with his hot bat comes up, with only a single needed to give us a three-run lead, but he bounces out. Lee is the last batter, and he indeed is the last batter. End of four — Blue Jays two runs on five hits, Twins one run on one hit. Tapani walks three batters in three innings.

Guzman gets through the next two innings easily until Paul Sorrento, a .194 two-home-run call-up, gets a homer to lead off the seventh. This is the kind of game you hate. You outplay, outfield and out-hit the other team, and suddenly it's 2-2 in the seventh. Guzman strikes out the last two batters after the home run.

Now, for the bottom of the seventh. This is an inning we'll remember. This time Dave Parker doubles down the left-field line, giving himself a two-for-two day with two doubles and a walk. When he gets to second, he's clapping his hands high in the air. This is the kind of rah-rah guy I've wanted and the Blue Jays have needed. Some excitement, enthusiasm, passion. If they were Liberals (perish the thought), Johnny Olerud would be Herb Gray, and Dave Parker would be Sheila Copps.

Cito, who must have been watching a lot of aggressive National League baseball on the new cable channels while he was hospitalized with his bad back, does the unexpected by managing as aggressively as Parker is playing. Even though it's "only" the seventh, he sends Mookie Wilson out to pinch run for Parker. Parker, unlike some athletes who sulk when they're taken out, claps his hands high in the air as he waits for Mookie and then runs off with a big smile to huge applause by 50,315 fans, all of whom booed him when he was with the Angels. Borders comes up next and does what he's learned to do this year and couldn't do last year — moves Mookie to third with a sac bunt.

Then, what is this? Pinch hitting for Manuel Lee? In the seventh? Incredible. Yes, it's Rance Mulliniks coming out of the dugout. Mulliniks falls behind in the count and then lifts a fly ball foul down the left-field line. It's not deep, and, in fact, it's in where the stands start to widen beyond third base. Mookie tags up using third base as a starting block. Dan Gladden, the Minnesota left fielder, could have let the ball drop foul. But he decides that since he has a decent angle on the ball and momentum coming in, he has a good chance to get Mookie at the plate. The ball crashes into his glove, and away we go — the race to the plate. Mookie arrives just after the ball. Devon White, the on-deck batter, is behind the plate, signalling madly to Mookie to slide. But Mookie sees the Minnesota catcher, Harper, leaning well into foul territory to take the throw and decides his best chance is to come in full blast standing up so as not to lose speed and touches the edge of the plate on the first-base side. He does it. Executes it perfectly. Avoids the tag and gives us a 3–2 lead on his speed and baseball sense. Guzman follows by getting a three-up, three-down eighth with two strikeouts, including Puckett.

Tom Kelly, the top-notch Minnesota manager, now decides to replace Tapani with Terry Leach. I've never seen him throw a good game, but he has decent stats. Tapani has given up only six hits, and, in fact, after Gruber singled in the fourth, the only two baserunners were Dave Parker with a double in the fourth and one in the seventh. It didn't look to me like a pitcher who needed to be removed. But Kelly overmanaged and brought in Leach. He would pay.

3–2 Jays, bottom of the eighth. Alomar and Carter both ground out. Looks like we're going to have another one-run squeaker. But no. Parker's clapping, Mookie's running and the crowd's cheering must have woken up Johnny O, who strokes a clean double. Tom Kelly decides to give Gruber an intentional walk and pitch to Maldonado instead. Having blown his first decision by removing Tapani, Kelly sits and watches as Leach follows up the intentional walk to Gruber with an unintentional walk to Maldonado to load the bases.

As fate would have it, this brings up Mookie. We experts in the stands feel it's time to bring in Rob Ducey or maybe even Greg Myers instead of letting Mookie bat. But, on balance, I agree with what Cito ultimately does, which is let Mookie bat. Mookie has had a better season than his stats indicate. He's had some key hits and, like Maldonado, has a good RBI–hits ratio of twenty-five RBIs off fifty-six hits. His hits tend to count.

Mookie, in a position to blow this game open with a single, promptly doubles down Dave Parker's right-field line. Suddenly, it's 6–2 Blue Jays. But Mookie's not done. Still with two out, Pat Borders comes up and lines a single. Mookie scores just ahead of an enormous outfield throw by sliding under and beside the tag to bring in the seventh run. Every inning, every out, every run counts for Mookie. Blue Jays end up putting up four runs in the eighth with three hits and two walks and all with two out.

I would have had Guzman start the ninth, particularly sitting on a big lead, but Cito brings in Duane Ward, who wipes out the ninth without making us sweat for once. Blue Jays win 7–2.

Let's be clear, though. This was a night to remember not only because the Blue Jays picked up an important win to reduce the magic number to seven, but also because it was a spectacular night for Mookie Wilson. He ends up with only one at bat and having played not an inning in the field, but he would account directly for the five-run difference between the Blue Jays and the Twins. If Mookie hadn't been the runner at third base on the short foul fly to left field, it's unlikely we would have scored. With the bases loaded in the eighth, we don't know what Parker, Ducey or even Myers or Sprague or anyone else would have done in that spot, but we do know that Mookie produced a bases-loaded double, driving in three more runs, and we do know that on Borders's single, maybe only White, Alomar or Derek Bell would have scored from second for the seventh run.

BOXSCORE

Blue Jays 7
Twins 2

MINNESOTA	AB	R	H	BI	TORONTO	AB	R	H	BI
Bush rf	3	0	0	0	White cf	4	1	1	0
Knblch 2b	4	0	0	0	RAlmr 2b	4	0	1	1
Puckett cf	3	1	1	0	Carter rf	3	0	0	0
Hrbek 1b	3	0	0	0	Olerud 1b	4	1	1	0
Harper c	4	0	1	1	Gruber 3b	3	2	2	0
Srrento dh	4	1	1	1	CnMldo lf	2	1	0	0
Gldden lf	3	0	0	0	DPrker dh	2	0	2	1
Pglrulo 3b	2	0	0	0	MWlsn dh	1	2	1	3
Gagne ss	3	0	0	0	Brders c	3	0	1	1
					MnLee ss	2	0	0	0
					Mllniks ph	0	0	0	1
					Gnzales ss	1	0	0	0
Totals	29	2	3	2	Totals	29	7	9	7

Minnesota 000 100 100 - 2
Toronto   100 100 14x - 7

DP - Minnesota 1. LOB - Minnesota 4, Toronto 5. 2B - Puckett (28), Olerud (29), DParker 2 (25), MWilson (12). 3B - White (10). HR - Sorrento (3). SB - Gruber (11). CS - Bush (2), RAlomar (10). S - Borders. SF - Mullniks.

	IP	H	R	ER	BB	SO
Minnesota						
Tapani (L, 16-9)	7	6	3	3	3	5
Leach	1	3	4	4	2	0
Toronto						
JuGzm (W, 9-2)	8	3	2	2	3	9
DWard	1	0	0	0	0	1

HBP - by JuGuzman (Pagliarulo).

◇ Mookie Magic

Mookie. Well, I guess Mookie won't be remembered long after his career is over, except by those who have seen the Bill Buckner World Series error committed on Mookie's ground ball. But when I think of the Jays I've enjoyed watching, I will always think of Mookie. You already know that on my list are George Bell and Fred McGriff and even Fernandez for a couple of seasons and Dave Stieb, nothwithstanding his temper and temperament, and Dave Collins, notwithstanding his "'tude," and Ernie and this year Dave Parker.

I've been frustrated by Mookie this year, I guess, the way I was frustrated by Lloyd Moseby a couple of years ago. I wasn't really frustrated because of their diminishing talents and skills. I was frustrated by the managers' insistence on using them on a regular basis in the batting order and in field positions that just could not be justified at that stage of their careers. It's painful to say it, but it's true. Moseby had no right to be leadoff emeritus, nor can Mookie with a weak arm be said to have a "claim" on left field. And sad to say, as a DH he just can't, on an everyday basis, match the other designated hitters in the league.

But Mookie's just one of those guys who seem to make themselves or find themselves at the centre of action. Excitement follows him around, and it's always been that way. His persona somehow fits his name. When he appeared on the cover of *Maclean's* magazine in 1989, he looked like a lifelong Blue Jay and a contented and happy and sparkling Canadian.

For those who insist on measuring ball players by their personal lives and by their characters, Mookie is an all-star. He is professional, proud but modest. He doesn't seek the limelight, nor does he avoid it. He attracts attention because of his play and his manner and his style and his intensity.

In his post-game interview tonight, he said matter-of-factly something like: "Well, sometimes experience and age count for something." In the post-gamers, he just exuded the attitude that "I'm a professional." Tonight the hit dropped in and he was lucky enough to have the throw go offline a little bit. But it was clear he knew that his speed and his decision when he reached home were what made the difference. The era when major leaguers hook slide, knock down catchers blocking the plate or make split-second decisions of any sort as they hit home plate is mostly gone. Alomar will keep the skill alive, but it takes a certain intensity, a certain enthusiasm, intelligence and a degree of reflex to make it all work. Mookie's never lost that.

Yup. Mookie has brought to this team for two years a certain élan, professionalism, spirit and intensity that young ball players should emulate. Mookie is one of those guys who have gone much further on their talent than they would have if they hadn't been such intense, dedicated athletes.

You will never see Mookie take a single thing for granted on the baseball field. If the catcher drops a third strike to Mookie, he'll take off for first as quickly as if the ball has been hit in the gap in left centre. If he hits a two hopper to short, he'll try to break the steroid-aided 30-yard sprint record. I'll bet he's never been the first or third out at third base. I'll bet he has never been caught in those once-a-year situations where the lead runner dogs it coming home, allowing a runner going to second to be thrown out for the third out of an inning before the run crosses the plate.

Blue Jays shouldn't let this one get away. Pay him whatever you must to get him to manage or coach in the minors and later in the majors. He knows the game, and his passion for its professionalism is unmatched.

I suspect we will be saying goodbye to you as a Blue Jays player in a couple of weeks, Mookie. So long. It's been real good to know you.

◇ Post-Series Notes

My apologies to the 2/3-tron operator. Someone has suddenly got permission to do as I suggested, which is to use the *entire* tron — not always, but occasionally — for replays! Indeed, it makes the fantastic difference I thought it would. Thank you.

◆ ◆ ◆

We are really delighted to see the continuation of a habit that started with Canseco's grand slam during the Oakland series here. When Sorrento hit his home run in the seventh Friday night, the fans in the bleachers tossed it back on the field. Good stuff.

◆ ◆ ◆

Meanwhile, on Friday night, the Red Sox continue to lose, this time blowing only a two-run lead to put us three-and-a-half up and lower the magic number to six. On Saturday, the Blue Jays are whipped 5–0. Candiotti, who seems star-crossed, hasn't got his usual knuckler working for him but is okay through to the fifth, when he walks the leadoff batter and then gets Harper to hit an easy double-play ball down to Olerud. Olerud boots the double-play ball and ends up lobbing it to Candiotti covering first. But Harper, the only player on the field with spikes, hits first the same time as Candiotti and spikes Candi unintentionally. The rest, as they say, is history. Thanks, John.

On the other hand, this Minnesota team, which didn't seem too impressive to me when I looked at their lineup on Friday, is showing how they got from last to first. Not only do they have three or four hitters hitting over .300, but they also have a great pitching staff and they play fundamental baseball. Some examples:

1. Shane Mack played great left field, charging every ball and not allowing any Blue Jay a chance to grab an extra base.
2. After Olerud blew, and I mean blew, the double-play ball to first base, Mack singled to put runners on first and third. Greg Gagne then hit a ball to left field, which Maldonado played well — but not as well as Shane Mack would have done. Mack hit third base running, and Maldonado sensibly threw to second to hold Gagne at first, presuming that with one out Mack would not risk going home. He was wrong. As soon as Maldonado unloaded to second, the third-base coach, Ron Gardenhire, waved Mack home, and, notwithstanding a good relay, he was safe.
3. The Twins executed three sac bunts perfectly, including one that was a suicide squeeze. It was so well laid down by Al Newman (.201) that it went in for a single.
4. Something you'll never see in Toronto. One of the sac bunts was laid down by ex–Blue Jay Pedro Munoz who was pinch hitting, that's right, pinch hitting, for the cleanup batter Kent Hrbek. In case you were wondering, Hrbek is batting about .283 with seventeen homers and eighty-two RBIs while Olerud, who apparently is not allowed to be pinch hit for, is batting .261 with sixteen homers and sixty-three RBIs. Kelly needed a sac bunt and brought in Munoz, who is a better bunter than Hrbek. I don't know whether Hrbek's feelings were hurt or not, but I do know they won the game.

While we lose 5–0, Boston blows it 4–1, and even Red Sox players are admitting it looks bad for them. We stay at three-and-a-half. Thank you, Brewers.

Sunday is a typical Blue Jays game. We beat the Twins and Scott Erickson 2–1. White leads off the game with a double, scampers to third on an Alomar ground ball and ends up safe with Alomar at first. After a walk to Olerud, Gruber hits a sac fly and Maldonado a single to score the Blue Jays' only two runs of the game. Erickson after the first, in fact, will face only three batters over the minimum, but it will be too late as Stottlemyre, Timlin, Wells and then Ward close out the Twins on only one run.

The Blue Jays give an example of heads-up baseball themselves after their sloppy performance of Saturday. In the seventh inning they catch pinch runner Jarvis Brown, representing the tying run, making a wide turn off third, and Borders fires hard to Gruber to snuff out the rally.

Fans are unusually noisy and excited in the first inning and then become funereal for most of the game. This is one of those games with a single riveting highlight. It occurs after Larkin doubles to lead off the seventh. Larkin will ultimately score, thanks to a single by Sorrento, but Mike Pagliarulo, who bats immediately after Larkin, unloads an enormous bomb to deep centre field that looks like it is going to go over the wall. Devon White quickly, but confidently, runs back towards the outfield fence and at the last moment leaps high, extending his body full length, and scoops the ball inches from the top of the wall. If he doesn't make that play, Pagliarulo has a double, maybe a triple. Two singles follow in the inning and would have tied or have won the game. White wins this one, make no mistake about it. And don't forget his leadoff double to start the game.

◆ ◆ ◆

The Boston Red Sox were beating the Brewers 4–0 when we left the park and 4–0 half an hour later, when I was listening to Pat Gillick on "Jays Talk." An hour later, I tuned in to the 6 o'clock news to hear that Milwaukee came back with five to beat the staggering Sox 5–4. Perfect choke.

We are an incredible four-and-a-half up with six to go (in our schedule), and the magic number is not five, not four, but three.

Dare I say it?

I Was Never Worried!

Wednesday, October 2, 1991 7:35 PM					Toronto SkyDome		
Pre-Game Standings							
	W	L	Pct.	GB	Ho.	Strk.	P10	Div.
TORONTO	88	70	.557	-	45-35	W-1	6-4	46-32
Boston	83	74	.529	4 1/2	42-34	L-1	3-7	40-33
Detroit	81	76	.516	6 1/2	49-32	W-2	6-4	36-36
Final Score: Blue Jays 6, Angels 5					Attendance: 50,324		

WAS I WORRIED WHEN HENKE WENT ON THE DL? Was I worried when Stieb went on the DL? Was I worried when we blew four to Boston? Was I worried when Detroit tied us? Was I worried when Boston was a half back? Was I worried when they left Olerud at cleanup? Was I worried when we couldn't beat Seattle? Was I worried tonight when we fell behind 3–0? Was I worried when, after four walks and a single, Carter hit the first pitch for an inning-ending double play? Was I worried when Gruber popped up on the first pitch after a leadoff walk in the sixth? Was I worried when White struck out with the bases loaded later in the sixth to end the inning? Was I worried when Winfield hit a homer to tie the game in the eighth? Was I worried when Timlin gave up the go-ahead run in the ninth? Was I worried when Ruben Amaro Jr hit a single that would have given California a two-run lead in the ninth (only to have Carter gun down Gallagher at the plate)? Was I worried when California brought in Brian Harvey, the best relief pitcher in the league, to pitch the ninth inning against us?

Worry? Who me? I was never worried.

I WAS NEVER WORRIED! ◆

◇ The Game

Blue Jays, six runs on eight hits; California, five runs on ten hits — but two important errors. It was a night to remember. Losing 5–4 in the bottom of the ninth. White leads off with a clutch first-pitch single into right field. Hard and well hit.

Robbie Alomar, who has been smart enough to take two walks in four at bats, comes up in the ninth and hits a hard drive to rookie second baseman Kevin Flores. Flores makes a decent play to dive and knock it down, but then he tries to throw out the speedy White at second from his knees. He whips it right past Dick Schofield, the shortstop covering second, and the ball goes into no-man's land between third and left field. White runs like Mr Ismail and scores easily, with Alomar ending on second. Tie game, none out, runner on second and Joe Carter, the last of the big three, coming up. Carter's had a terrible time recently, and tonight he has struck out, hit a routine ball to third that went for an error, hit into a terrible double play in the fifth and struck out in the seventh. About as bad as you can get. But he played an important game in the field. He went into the stands, in the seventh inning, with a runner on and two out, to snag a ball from the hands of an idiot fan. Carter ended up in the stands, but with the ball.

BOXSCORE

Blue Jays..6
Angels...5

CALIFORNIA	AB	R	H	BI	TORONTO	AB	R	H	BI
Polonia lf	4	0	1	0	White cf	5	1	2	1
Vnable rf	2	0	1	1	RAlomar 2b	3	1	0	1
Gllgher cf	2	0	1	1	Carter rf	5	0	1	1
Felix cf	2	0	0	0	Olerud 1b	3	1	1	0
Amaro rf	2	0	1	0	Gruber 3b	4	0	0	0
Parrish c	0	0	0	0	CnMldo lf	4	1	1	2
Wnfield dh	4	2	2	1	DPrker dh	2	1	1	0
Stevens 1b	4	1	1	0	MWlsn dh	1	0	0	0
Gaetti 3b	4	0	2	2	Brders c	3	1	1	0
Schfield ss	4	0	1	0	DBell pr	0	0	0	0
Orton c	3	0	0	0	Myers c	0	0	0	0
Abner cf	0	1	0	0	MnLee ss	2	0	1	0
Flora 2b	2	1	0	0	Mllniks ph	0	0	0	0
					Tabler ph	1	0	0	0
					Gnzales ss	0	0	0	0
Totals	33	5	10	5	Totals	33	6	8	5

California   001 200 011 — 5
Toronto   000 022 002 — 6

No outs when winning run scored.
E - Gaetti (17), Flora (2). DP - California 1. LOB - California 7, Toronto 9. 2B - Stevens (6), Gaetti (22), Schofield (9), Olerud (30), DParker (26). 3B - Venable (2). HR - Winfield (28), CnMaldonado (12). SB - Felix (7), Gaetti (5), Flora (1), RAlomar (53). S - Flora. SF - Venable.

	IP	H	R	ER	BB	SO
California						
Grahe	4 1/3	1	2	2	5	4
SLewis	2/3	0	0	0	0	0
Bailes	1/3	2	2	2	1	0
Eichhom	2 1/3	3	0	0	0	5
ClYoung	1/3	0	0	0	0	0
Harvey (L, 2-4)	0	2	2	0	0	0
Toronto						
Candiotti	6 1/3	7	3	3	2	2
Wells	2 1/3	1	2	2	2	1
Timlin (W, 11-6)	1/3	2	0	0	0	0

Harvey pitched to 3 batters in the 9th.

Then, with two out in the ninth and the Blue Jays losing 5–4, he gunned down Gallagher at the plate with a perfect clutch throw. So, here he is, up in the ninth with Robbie on second. In September, when we needed him, Joe wasn't there. In September, he batted .236, and in the last half of September only .200.

Harvey winds to deliver the first pitch to Carter, not paying attention to the incredible Alomar, who in this clutch situation swipes third so easily that the Angels don't even bother to make a play. Runner on third with none out and the Eastern Division championship sitting there waiting for us. All we need is a fly ball.

Carter gets the fastball he was looking for and drives a looping single to short centre field. Carter throws himself in the air right in front of us at first, Alomar scores, we win it. I was never worried.

There were plenty of great plays in this game, including the fielding by Carter. And, incredibly, both Borders and Myers block the plate on close plays.

But my favourite play of the night was unquestionably the Alomar steal of third. It was the winning run. The difference between second and third was everything, and, if he had been thrown out, it would have been a real killer. But, as Robbie told us earlier in the year, he takes third only when he *knows* he's got it, like *knows* he's got it. And he had it by a mile. Beautiful, gutsy, heads-up play. He was thinking about it from the time he got on second; no one else was. Beautiful play.

I was never worried.

◇ Post-Game Notes

The way we won tonight was typical of the team. Never overpowering, hardly ever putting up a big inning. We've spent most of the year with my friends Olerud and Gruber relatively unproductive. We and, I believe, the opposing teams really felt there was little threat after they got by Carter. There was no Canseco or even Winfield. No Thomas or Fielder or Clark to worry about.

Instead, the hallmark of this team has been great pitching — and I mean *great* pitching — great base running and great fielding, and an ability to scratch for runs. Not many runs, but an ability to scratch for just enough of them to win.

Four and two, but they really had to scratch for their four wins. Mookie's base-running, errors by the other teams, one and only one clutch hit and usually only a single at that, and Robbie stealing bases like tonight.

The fielding — Carter and Maldonado both gunning guys at the plate and Alomar and White making great plays twice tonight, with Robbie making some plays never before seen in this city ... no make it this country ... no make it this continent.

Frustrating, yes. Frustrating because they do not capitalize often. 2–1 seems to be quite enough for them. Once they have a lead they tend not to be able to score any more runs. They strand a lot of runners, they're overeager and they first-pitch hit far too often. And the manager? Well, he just won't pinch hit often enough and go for broke when he has the chance.

But all season long they seemed to have good chemistry, and they seemed to believe they had the talent to win, even when the Sox and the Tigers pulled close. And believing you have the talent means a lot. Somehow in the ninth inning, the fans felt that we were going to come back. And it seemed to me that it was over in a flash. White, Alomar and Carter just went to work and did it, and they did it fast the way they've been doing it all year.

There are those who think chemistry doesn't mean much. But it's there. You could see it in the dugout all season. You could see it tonight. You could hear it on the post-game interviews. But what came through clearest during the victory celebrations was a refrain echoed by every single young player interviewed. Randy Knorr, Eddie Zosky, Derek Bell, Ed Sprague all said the same thing, something like: "When you join the club, all the guys make you feel comfortable. They don't make you feel like you should be hiding in the corner, or that you're not part of the team. They all try to help.

◆ ◆ ◆

A week from today, I'll be tight, tense and nervous again, sweating through the ALCS. But tonight, like the Blue Jays and like all the other fans, I will be sitting back just enjoying what has been a tense, exciting, nerve-wracking rollercoaster. Don't know what next week brings, but these guys are champions. Tonight.

Outmanaged, Outcoached, Outpitched, Outlucked

I'M PICKING THE BLUE JAYS TO WIN IT IN FIVE — AT THE MOST. Like the other entries in this diary, these words stay no matter what happens. The reason I think the Blue Jays will do it is because Alomar, White, Carter, Mookie, Guzman and Ward bring a certain intensity and desire to win every game. This team knows that its job is only one-third done. This team was hungry in the ninth inning of the clinching game. You can match Minnesota and Toronto position by position (except for Alomar) and, depending on who's doing the matching, end up with a draw or either team ahead. The intangibles — the hunger, the desire, the emotion, the intensity, the need to win and the ability to play every inning full out in a heads-up fashion — are what will make the difference.

All year when I had counted them out, having been let down by different folks in the same uniforms in previous years, the Blue Jays rallied back. Somehow they refused to lose — when Detroit tied us, when Boston was a half-game back in Oakland. Minnesota's season is a huge success, having gone from worst to first, and they want to keep going, but somehow it's not life and death for them. The Blue Jays have the emotional edge. It has been instilled in them by Robbie and Devo and Joe, not by the manager. But I will say that the manager set the table. He made it easy for them to lead, couldn't even remotely be said to have got in anyone's way and kept his players comfy. Not a style I like, but to the extent his leaders were able to lead, it worked. But now you're going to have to manage, Cito.

Cito has chosen to go with a four-man rotation. Must be the first time in the modern era that a team with three dominating starters like Candiotti, Key and Guzman went to a four-man rotation. It's particularly risky since Henke is not at his best. The Blue Jays never put up many runs, and you've got to figure that every game will be close. You have to know that you've got a setup man to come in and close down the Twins in the seventh and the eighth and a stopper to set them down one, two, three in the ninth. Henke doesn't seem ready to be the stopper again. Ward is probably more capable than anyone else right now. This leaves Wells as the setup man. He has been effective over the last few weeks, but not overwhelmingly so. Stottlemyre is the perfect setup man. Instead of the fourth starter, he should be the nightly setup threat out of the pen. He's tough, he's smart, he throws a mean ball and he can keep the Twins off balance. Knowing that the right-handed setup man is Stottlemyre instead of Mike Timlin would be a great difference. Mistake, Cito, win or lose.

And Cito is giving Candiotti the extra start by having a starting rotation of Candiotti, Guzman and Key. It ought to be Guzman, Key and Candiotti; or Key, Guzman and Candiotti. Candiotti just missed the earned run average title and has been impossible to hit in some games. But his last three outings have been poor, and he admits to having been nervous in a couple of games, including last week's title-clincher. If he was nervous then, what about tonight?

Reading between the lines in the newspaper stories, it is also clear that the players are upset with the choice. Key unquestionably is upset, and his teammates certainly seem to feel that he should have got the start. In the papers too, the Minnesota scouts are anonymously quoted as saying Guzman is the pitcher that they find hardest to hit.

Sorry, Cito. This rotation should be Guzman, Key and Candiotti, with Stottlemyre in the pen.

I still think we'll win in five, maybe even four, but this rotation could kill us.

◆ The Game

Lots of reasons why we lost this one. This was a game that we should have won and could have own. There were several contributing factors, but most of all we were:

◆ Outmanaged

I said, as did most of the media and most of the scouts around the league, that the only way the Blue Jays could lose this series was by having a stupid pitching rotation. Sure enough, as everyone predicted, starting Candiotti was a mistake. We'll get to Candiotti in a moment, but because Cito started Candiotti, who was terrible, he ended up having to use David Wells for three innings and Timlin for three. This is going to hurt him if he needs relievers the next few games.

But most of all, Candiotti is still slumping. No way he should have been the starting pitcher.

That single decision cost us the game.

The next way in which we were outmanaged is that Cito did nothing to adapt his team to the circumstances, the stadium, the pressure or the Minnesota pitching. On the other hand, Tom Kelly clearly drilled his team on how to handle Candiotti. He had them all staying back, flat-footed, with minimum body movement, not trying to kill the ball, but waiting till the last moment and then simply trying to make contact. This worked. Candiotti gave up seven hits in two-and-one-third innings. When the Blue Jays went to the hard-throwing Wells and Timlin, Kelly had his batters make the appropriate adaptation. As well, with Candiotti on the mound, Kelly had his team run, since the knuckler is easy to steal on. As a result, Candiotti gave up nine baserunners of whom four, yes four, stole a base on him.

Kelly had a strategy to deal with the game situation. Cito did not.

The throw-away run did it again. As usual, Cito waited too long before pulling his pitcher. If he had pulled Candiotti after the first or second, or maybe even after he walked the second batter in the third, we would have won this game. But no. He waited too long. On the other hand, Morris was pulled by Kelly while he still had a lead. If he hadn't been, we might have won this game.

◇ Outcoached

The Blue Jays, down 5–0 after three innings, had their key players, Alomar and Carter, start off the fourth with hits. Alomar singled with none out and Carter doubled. Down five runs needing baserunners and a rally, Rich Hacker did something not even John McLaren would do. He sent Alomar home with none out. Alomar was out easily at the plate. Instead of having runners on second and third with none out and Olerud, Gruber and Maldonado coming up, the Blue Jays had one out with a runner on second. This was a game they would lose by one run. Conceivably, the Alomar out at the plate was the one run. Minnesota rookie third-base coach Ron Gardenhire made no such stupid mistakes.

◇ Outpitched

Candiotti was true to form — he was nervous in a big game and had a terrible first inning. Going into tonight his earned run average in the first inning was over four runs per game. The first two batters tonight would single and subsequently score. All in all, Candiotti faced sixteen batters. Nine got on base, four stole second and five scored. Not the stuff of pennant winners. Of the six pitchers from the two teams who would throw tonight, only one would be ineffective: Candiotti. While Morris would end giving up four runs total and three in the sixth on five consecutive singles, he was generally effective.

◇ Outlucked

For all the above, Cito's poor managing would not have cost us the game if we hadn't run into an unbelievable run of bad luck. In the second inning, after Shane Mack led off with a single and stole second, Pagliarulo hit a fly ball to Carter. Mack tagged up and went to third base; Carter unloaded a perfect throw that would have nailed him at third base, but the ball hit him as he slid into third. If the ball doesn't hit Mack, he's out.

Blue Jays hit a bunch of balls to the warning track, including Maldonado's long fly with two on and one out in the sixth inning. A few more feet and the Blue Jays take a 6–5 lead.

For that matter, the hits that Gladden and Knoblauch got to lead off the game both ended in runs — but both were seeing-eye singles between short and third. Mack's leadoff single in the second (he would also score after the play with Mack at third base) was a grounder off Candiotti's leg. It rolled towards the statue at first, whose foot was nailed to the bag — thus allowing Mack an infield single. Yes, we were outlucked.

Any combination of better pitching, better managing, better coaching or a little more luck would have won this game for us. Still, I think we'll win tomorrow.

BOXSCORE

Twins.....................5
Blue Jays.................4

MINNESOTA	AB	R	H	BI
Gladden lf	5	1	2	0
Knblauch 2b	3	1	2	1
Puckett cf	4	0	0	0
Hrbek 1b	4	0	1	0
CDavis dh	2	1	1	2
Harper c	4	0	2	0
Ortiz c	0	0	0	0
Mack rf	3	1	2	1
Pgliarulo 3b	2	0	0	0
Leius ph-3b	1	0	0	0
Larkin ph	1	0	0	0
Newman 3b	0	0	0	0
Gagne ss	4	1	1	1
Totals	33	5	11	5

TORONTO	AB	R	H	BI
White cf	4	1	1	0
RAlomar 2b	4	1	2	0
Carter rf	4	2	2	0
Olerud 1b	4	0	2	2
Gnzls pr-1b	0	0	0	0
Gruber 3b	4	0	2	2
CnMldo lf	4	0	0	0
Mllniks dh	4	0	0	0
Brders c	4	0	0	0
MnLee ss	3	0	0	0
Totals	35	4	9	4

Minnesota 221 000 00x - 5
Toronto   000 103 000 - 4

E - Gruber 2(2), Borders (1). DP - Toronto 1 (RAlomar and Olerud). LOB - Toronto 4, Minnesota 8. 2B - Carter (1), Harper (1), Mack (1). SB - Gruber (1), Knoblauch 2 (2), CDavis (1), Mack (1). CS - Knoblauch (1), Mack (1).

	IP	H	R	ER	BB	SO
Minnesota						
Morris (W, 1-0)	5 1/3	8	4	4	0	4
Willis	2 1/3	0	0	0	0	2
Aguilera (S, 1)	1 1/3	1	0	0	0	2
Toronto						
Candiotti (L, 0-1)	2 2/3	8	5	5	1	2
Wells	3	2	0	0	2	2
Timlin	2 1/3	1	0	0	1	2

◇ Post-Game Notes

Managers. Cito's pre-game managing (the pitching rotation) and lack of game plan cost us this game as did his game-time managing (leaving Candiotti in too long). This is ironic. Today, the tenth manager this year was fired. Stump Merrill was fired by the Yankees today, and, surprisingly, Joe Morgan was fired by the Red Sox, to be replaced by Butch Hobson. Here's Joe Morgan, an eccentric and a guy I don't want managing my team. But he took a team with only one pitcher that was decimated by dissension and injuries, and he brought it really close to the Blue Jays. For all that, he's fired. Interesting interview on TV, where he says that if you sit down "Bruno or Clark" for one day, their egos can't take it. No problem here in Toronto. Cito wouldn't think of doing something like that.

Cito says after the game that he was mad at Candiotti for not throwing his knuckler enough. What is this? Was Cito watching the game on television? Was he back in a hospital bed two thousand miles away? Was he tied to his chair in the dugout? If he was mad at Candiotti for not throwing the knuckler, why didn't he march out to the mound and offer that mild observation to his star pitcher that he selected to pitch the first game against all expert advice?

◆ ◆ ◆

I do not want to ruin my enjoyment of this series by getting aggravated over the CBS coverage. But just so it's on the record, let's talk about some of the CBS (Columbia Blooper System) gaffs this evening. A list will do. Dick Stockton and Jim Kaat commit the following:

- Say that Maldonado started the season with the Indians, then moved over to Milwaukee before coming to the Blue Jays. Wrong.
- With Devo on first base in the sixth inning trying to distract the pitcher, Jack (or, as they would have it, Joe) Morris, Devo fakes the steal of second as the pitch goes to the plate. Stockton announces, "the runner goes."
- After Olerud hits the fourth consecutive single in the sixth, he overruns first base. Hrbek gets the ball from the outfield and dives at Olerud, who gets back cleanly and clearly safe. Stockton says "Olerud is out." Silence. Then, "I guess he's safe."

Enough. In my view, even one of these errors is too many.

Camera work in the bottom of the first. Knoblauch's single was missed by the camera. We saw it only on a replay from a camera other than the one the director put on the screen as the hit was occurring. Further, the camera was late getting to every foul ball.

The NBC playoff and World Series broadcasts used to rate a nine out of ten. Give this broadcast a four.

Strangely Calm

WELL, THIS IS ALMOST A HOLIDAY. The game starts at 3:00 P.M., and you can count on the city closing down at about 2:45. I worked till 2:50 P.M., then grabbed a cab and headed home to settle in for a more enjoyable afternoon than dealing with client's mortgages, law suits, bankruptcies and bank managers, as well as students, bills, faxes, mail, phone calls and editing this diary. More enjoyable, that is, if the Blue Jays win.

Despite yesterday's loss, I go into today's game still feeling confident about my prediction that the Blue Jays would win it in five. I feel that the comeback in yesterday's loss, from 5–0 to 5–4, perhaps had the same effect on the Blue Jays as their 10–9 loss in Anaheim a few weeks ago, when they came back from 7–0. They continued to look like a team, in control, hot and confident.

So Shaker and I settle down in front of the TV to watch the game, and I'm strangely confident and calm. I'll remain this way until the Blue Jays fall behind or until Jamie and Robbie arrive home from school to give me an audience for my agitation.

◇ The Game

Devo and Robbie come out to win it right off the top. They seemed determined to do this the way they did it yesterday, before they ran out of time.

Kevin Tapani is pitching for the Twins. He is such a good pitcher I picked him in the office pool. But he has not beaten the Jays this year and has looked hittable, not overwhelming.

Devon White leads off the top of the first with a good, hard, solid single to centre. Then, to this fan who has been hungry for years for a home-team Rickey Henderson– or Maury Wills–type of I-know-I'm-stealing, you-know-I'm-stealing, we-all-know-I'm-stealing kind of ball player, it is a joy to see Devo steal second. In the first, one wouldn't expect a sacrifice. But Alomar, knowing the importance of us getting the first run in this game at all costs, lays down a textbook sac bunt to move Devo to third.

This makes it easy for Carter to score the run by just hitting to the outfield. Joe, whose bat is coming alive when the chips are down in the playoffs, decides instead to single to right centre. 1–0 Blue Jays.

Carter, trying to keep the rally going and the pressure on, tries to steal second but gets a late start and is out.

Johnny O grounds out (this is not news), but we have that 1–0 lead.

It won't be till the third that Devo, Robbie and Joe are up again, so there won't be any runs for a few minutes. Don't even ask about Guzman. He has a rough patch in the first inning, issuing a couple of walks. But he always seems in command and roars through the Twins as he has all year. 1–0 going into the third when the boys come up again.

Devo doesn't want to have to steal second this time, so he leads off with a double. Alomar hits an infield single to put the speedsters on first and third. Carter pops out to the shortstop. Shaker now looks over to me as Olerud comes up, and the look in his eyes indicates that he knows Robbie Alomar is going to steal second on the first or second pitch. Shaker is right, and it is not even contested.

Olerud, having popped up in the first, strikes out with Alomar in scoring position. Wonderful. They have Hrbek as a cleanup hitter, and we have Olerud.

In any case, it looks like we're not going to do anything with two men on when Kelly Gruber hits a broken-bat single to right field. White and Alomar both score. Jays 3, Twins 0. Maldonado lines out to second.

Twins kind of get to Guzman in the bottom of the third with three singles and one passed ball (which, of course, is called a wild pitch), all resulting in one run. If it weren't for the passed ball/wild pitch, there would have been no runs. Blue Jays 3, Twins 1. Twins put up another run on a hit and a walk in the sixth. Then, in something we haven't seen in years, Tom Henke is brought in in the sixth with two out and two on. One pitch is all it takes, and Henke is out of the inning and it's 3–2 Jays.

We've talked during the year about how important it is to snap back with a run after the other team scores. Bottom of the order coming up, so it doesn't look like we're going to do it. Lee walks with one out and then, after Bedrosian replaces Tapani, good old Devo walks. First and second and Robbie Alomar coming up. It's showtime. Alomar singles to right. Shane Mack, a first-class outfielder, bobbles the ball, allowing Lee to score and White to go to third. Carter follows with a sac fly. Blue Jays 5, Twins 2. Henke will pitch the seventh, getting three up and three down and striking out two of them. He will be followed by the new Tom Henke — Duane Ward — and when Ward storms to start the bottom of the eighth, we're feeling totally confident. It is no contest. Ward gives up a hit and works through the eighth and ninth, striking out four of the six. The Twins never looked like they were in it.

Guzman, of course, continues to be sensational in his rookie year. Five-and-two-thirds innings, four hits, two runs, four walks and two strikeouts. He seems consistently calm, cool and in control. He simply believes he can do it. What does Guzman say? "No pressure. I pitched against them five times. I know what I can do. I know what they can do."

The umpire was squeezing the strike zone on him. Guzman's response: "I had to fight that and stay calm." He's not giving me the outside corner, so I have to throw it down the middle. Okay, I throw it down the middle."

But he threw it down the middle so fast — 93 mph, 94 mph, 95 mph — that the Twins couldn't catch up.

The secret to the Blue Jays' club is no secret. It's good pitching and Devo, Robbie and Joe. In two games, White is three for eight, with four runs scored. Alomar is four for seven, with two runs scored. Carter is three for seven, with two scored and two RBIs.

White and Alomar have each stolen a base. They are doing what Rickey did to us in 1989. Everyone knows keeping them off the bases is the key to beating us. Everyone is thinking about it, and they can't keep them off the bases. And when they get on the bases, they make it happen. They steal, they run, they bunt, they upset the other team's rhythm and concentration. And they get the Jays' adrenalin going.

On top of all that, the boys have been greatly aided in the two games by the same Kelly Gruber I said could have ensured an easy AL East championship had he been hot in September. Gruber is four for eight, with four RBIs. If Gruber provides this kind of support throughout the series, we win in spite of Cito's pitching shenanigans.

BOXSCORE

Blue Jays...5
Twins..2

TORONTO	AB	R	H	BI	MINNESOTA	AB	R	H	BI
White cf	4	3	2	0	Gldden lf	3	0	0	0
RAlomar 2b	3	1	2	0	Knblch 2b	3	2	2	0
Carter rf	3	0	1	2	Puckett cf	3	0	1	1
Olerud 1b	4	0	0	0	Hrbek 1b	4	0	0	0
Gruber 3b	4	0	2	2	CDavis dh	3	0	0	0
CnMldo lf	4	0	0	0	Harper c	4	0	1	1
Mllniks dh	2	0	1	0	Mack rf	3	0	0	0
Tabler dh	1	0	0	0	Larkin ph	1	0	0	0
Brders c	4	0	1	0	Pgliarulo 3b	4	0	0	0
MnLee ss	3	1	0	0	Gagne ss	3	0	1	0
Totals	32	5	9	4	Totals	31	2	5	2

Toronto   102 000 200 - 5
Minnesota   001 001 000 - 2

E - Mack (1). DP - Toronto 1, Minnesota 1. LOB - Toronto 5, Minnesota 6. 2B - White (1). SB - White (1), RAlomar (1), Gladden (1). CS - Carter (1). S - RAlomar. SF - Carter.

	IP	H	R	ER	BB	SO
Toronto						
JuGzmn (W, 1-0)	5 2/3	4	2	2	4	2
Henke	1 1/3	0	0	0	0	2
DWard (S, 1)	2	1	0	0	0	4
Minnesota						
Tapani (L 0-1)	6 1/3	8	4	4	2	5
Bedrosian	1/3	1	1	0	1	0
Guthrie	2 1/3	0	0	0	0	0

WP - JuGuzman.

◊ Post-Game Notes

In the radio and TV interviews, Henke, Gruber and others are all speaking very matter-of-factly. They have a piece of business to do, and they're out to do it. And that business is not simply to win the AL East, which they've done, but to win the World Series. They know there's lots more work to do in the series.

◆ ◆ ◆

I am really tired of hearing all the talk about the noise in the Metrodome and what an impact it has on the players. These players are professionals who are paid a lot of money to produce in these kinds of situations. I believe that it helps energize the players on both teams, not just the Twins. And I believe that it is as effective a weapon for the Blue Jays when they do well as it is for the Twins. For example, when the crowd gets all excited waving those irritating hankies and then Guzman strikes out Kent Hrbek in a clutch situation, the decibel levels switch from the Indianapolis 500 on Memorial Day to Cleveland Municipal Stadium in October, and that's got to feel good for the Blue Jays.

◆ ◆ ◆

I have my complaints about Toronto fans, but give me a good team with quiet fans over a mediocre one with noisy fans. We aren't a great team, but we're a damn good one. We aren't great fans, but we're good and loyal.

◆ ◆ ◆

When Alomar scores, he does so sliding way around Harper and reaching back with his hand to touch home plate. As he says in the paper the next day, "You don't practise that slide, it's just instinct." And that's the difference between Alomar and the rest of the world.

Canada's Funniest Home Videos: Cito Uses Timlin in the Tenth

TORONTONIANS HAVE THE SERIES WON. Nobody thinks it's even going to go six or seven games. Everyone is talking about it, including my daughter's friend who asked as they watched the game how many innings a regulation game is. Yesterday, I was in the bank with the lawyer for my father's estate, and, as we sat with the bank manager, she answered the phone not with a "Hi, how are you?" or a "How's the family." She simply said, "One down, three to go."

The players on both teams somehow seem to have this thing won for the Blue Jays. The Twins are down and think they blew their chance to win it already. The Blue Jays are confident and sure they're going to do it. Of all the members of both teams, only Tom Kelly, the Minnesota manager, seems unaffected and calm.

Cito is calm too, but the difference is that Cito seems calm because he's just calm, whereas one has the impression Kelly seems calm because he's got a game plan. Cito looks like he's finished thinking and is just going to lie back and watch what happens next.

◆ 215 ◆

◇ The Game

It's Jimmy Key against Scott Erickson. I'm not worried about this match-up. Blue Jays can hit Erickson, who's had a relatively weak second half of the season after being Cy Young for the first half. He'll win the Cy Young anyway, but we can hit him. Key, although he likes working on only four days' rest, insisted on missing his last regular season start in Minnesota to keep the Twins from going to school on him. Key was disappointed he wasn't picked to start the first game, and he hinted so. He pitched a simulated game five days ago in order to work his arm into a state of readiness. He should be ready to go.

And he is. He retires the first eleven batters cleanly, quickly and easily.

The scoring in this game is simple. In the bottom of the first with two out, Joe Carter, who clearly is "seeing the ball well again," slams a home run straight over centre field to give us a 1–0 lead. Olerud then accepts a walk from Erickson, Gruber (still hot) singles and Maldonado doubles for his first hit of the series and an RBI. 2–1, Blue Jays. Rance Mulliniks ends the inning with runners on second and third by flying deep to centre field. That's it for the Blue Jays' offence. Say good night.

They don't get another hit until White singles in the seventh, and their only hit after that comes when Alomar singles in the ninth. They are gifted with seven walks, enough to win the game, but they don't know what to do with them.

The scoring for the Twins is not so simple. Shane Mack leads off the fifth with a long fly to right. In one of those plays we'll remember, Joe Carter climbs the fence in right field and, in fact, has the ball hit his glove. But it bounces out and away from the fence. To the horror of every fan this side of the juvenile noise dome in Minneapolis, Carter crashes down, hobbling on his ankle; and, before he can lurch to the ball and dribble it back to second base, Mack is on third. Kent Hrbek grounds into a fielder's choice. 2–1, Blue Jays.

Next inning. Pesky, irritating Chuck Knoblauch, who can really get under my skin, doubles, and Kirby Puckett, having been hitless in his first two games, follows his fourth-inning double with a single, scoring Knoblauch.

But hold on. It isn't that simple. Knoblauch, a good runner, is on second all right, and Kirby's single is a solid one to right field. But Carter, though hobbling, comes in on the ball and fires what looks to us to be a fairly hard straight throw to the plate. It seems to be a bit up the line, but it's clearly going to be a play at the plate. Suddenly and incredibly, John (Sluggish) Olerud cuts the ball off! Worse. He doesn't only cut the ball off to hold the runner on first, but he also wheels and throws to Borders, who was in line to get the ball *before* Olerud's interception. Borders, seeing the interception, eases up and comes off the plate. By the time the speedy [sic] Olerud turns and relays, Borders is (a) up the line, (b) surprised and (c) too late to get Knoblauch.

What in the world is going on here? The throw comes in from the outfielder. It is supposed to be low enough so the cutoff man can intervene and make a play to hold the baserunner, but the cutoff man does this only if the catcher tells him to. It is the catcher's call. It is obvious from the game situation and Borders's positioning that he wants the ball to come through. Why does Johnny O snag the ball? Only he knows. If Olerud thinks there's a play at the plate, why would he slow up the ball's trip to home — probably by a full second — by catching and relaying it? Should have been trained at Syracuse.

Key finishes the sixth, Wells comes in to pitch a sterling one-and-one-third innings, striking out two. Then with Knoblauch again (damn him) on second and two out in the eighth, Henke comes in to retire Puckett on one pitch and to strike out three batters in the ninth. With two out in the bottom of the ninth and a tie game, Alomar singles. But now Ducey, in the game replacing Carter because of his injury, grounds out meekly to first. Why not pinch hit Sprague for Ducey? Sparky would. LaRussa would. Cox would. Kelly would.

Extra innings and we're in trouble.

Tenth inning 2–2. Game 3.

Mark this down as a key moment in the entire history of the Blue Jays. Key has produced a quality start through six. Wells gave us a pretty good one-and-a-third innings and Henke was just short of spectacular through the ninth. What to do next? No choice, no option. Sir John A. Macdonald, Patti Starr, John Olerud, Bishop Tutu, Ted Kennedy, Margaret Thatcher, Bill Vander Zalm and even Jimy Williams would have known what to do. Bring in

Duane Ward. He is dominant, unhittable most nights and well rested. The game is on the line. A must-win game for the Blue Jays. A win here and our momentum is locked up, and, with Guzman going (finally) tomorrow, we can be up 3–1 if only we can put this game away.

As the Blue Jays take the field in the top of the tenth, we look to the bullpen. No, it can't be. It's not possible. Sheldon says, "I swear it is." Melissa says, "Dad, I can't believe it. What is he doing?" Les stands up one section over and throws his hands in the air. I realize my eyes are not lying. It is not Duane Ward. It isn't even Todd Stottlemyre who, if he were not foolishly in the starting rotation, could come in and carry us through a couple of innings. No. Do you remember the Blue Jays' pitcher who has let ten of his last eleven inherited runners score? That's right — it's the one, the only, the tired, the slumping Mike Timlin.

BOXSCORE

Twins...3
Blue Jays..2

MINNESOTA	AB	R	H	BI	TORONTO	AB	R	H	BI
Gladden lf	5	0	0	0	White cf	5	0	1	0
Knblauch 2b	5	1	2	0	RAlomar 2b	3	0	1	0
Puckett cf	5	0	2	1	Carter rf	3	1	1	1
CDavis dh	4	0	1	0	Ducey pr rf	1	0	0	0
Mack rf	4	1	1	0	Olerud 1b	2	1	0	0
Hrbek 1b	3	0	0	1	Gruber 3b	5	0	1	0
Gagne ss	2	0	0	0	CnMldo lf	4	0	1	1
Sorrento ph	1	0	0	0	Mllniks dh	1	0	0	0
Newman ss	0	0	0	0	Tabler ph	0	0	0	0
Ortiz c	3	0	0	0	MWlsn pr-dh	1	0	0	0
Larkin ph	1	0	0	0	Borders c	3	0	0	0
Harper c	0	0	0	0	MnLee ss	4	0	0	0
Leius 3b	3	0	0	0					
Pgrulo ph 3b	1	1	1	1					
Totals	37	3	7	3	Totals	32	2	5	2

Minnesota   000 011 000 1 - 3
Toronto   200 000 000 0 - 2

E - Timlin (1). DP - Minnesota 1, Toronto 2. LOB - Minnesota 6, Toronto 10. 2B - Knoblauch (1), Puckett (1), CnMaldonado (1). 3B - Mack (1). HR - Carter (1) (off Erickson), Pagliarulo (1) (off Timlin).S - RAlomar, Borders.

	IP	H	R	ER	BB	SO
Minnesota						
Erickson	4	3	2	2	5	2
West	2 2/3	1	0	0	3	3
Willis	2	1	0	0	0	1
Guthrie (W, 1-0)	1/3	0	0	0	0	0
Aguilera (S, 2)	1	0	0	0	0	0
Toronto						
Key	6	5	2	2	1	1
Wells	1 2/3	1	0	0	0	2
Henke	1 1/3	0	0	0	1	3
Timlin (L, 0-1)	1	1	1	1	0	1

Erickson pitched to 1 batter in the 5th.

Timlin is brought in to start the tenth. Let's make it simple. With one out, Kelly brings in Mike Pagliarulo to pinch hit for Scott Leius. Pagliarulo smacks it over the right-field fence. Twins 3, Blue Jays 2. Say good night.

◇ You Can't Be Serious, Cito

If the Blue Jays' win on Wednesday afternoon was a prototype of the wins they've had this season, tonight was equally a prototype of the games they've lost.

This is a team whose hitting has been poor, truth to tell, all year.

In the entire league, only the Orioles, the Indians, the Tigers, Seattle and, surprisingly, Oakland had lower batting averages. The Blue Jays were second after the Tigers in strikeouts, and only the Indians and the Yankees — this is really embarrassing — had fewer RBIs. And only the cellar-dweller Indians, Yankees and Angels scored fewer runs. The Blue Jays won on their pitching, which was the best, and their fielding and base running. Once again we were outmanaged.

I said in April that Cito wasn't up to it. I said it in June. I said it in August. And he proved it again tonight. Some examples:

1. Maldonado and Mulliniks walked to lead off the fourth. Sitting on a 2–1 lead, two on, none out, ready to bust it open. Borders and Lee are up next. Lee couldn't hit a ball off a batting tee into right field under pressure; Borders has had a good last half of the season. So what does Cito have him do? Sacrifice the runners to second and third to put them in scoring position for Manuel the clutch. In case you were wondering, Manuel had 29 RBIs in 445 at bats this year. That's right — 29. Ed Sprague had 20 in 160 at bats. Tabler had 21 in 185 at bats, while even Cory Snyder had 17 RBIs in 166 at bats and Mookie 28 RBIs in 241 at bats. In fact, Manuel Lee has the lowest percentage of hitting balls out of the infield. I could go on, but you get the picture. Cito has Borders sacrifice the runners to second and third. Now, what is the point in this? There's only a point in having runners at second and third with one out if the *next* batter is likely to be able to score the runner at third. Everyone from Lady Di to the cameramen in front of me to Tom Kelly knew that this wasn't about to happen. Lee drove the ball all the way to the pitcher for an easy pitcher-to-first out, holding the runner at third. (For the record, White drove one to centre field for the third out.)

2. Fast forward two innings later to the sixth. Tabler leads off with another walk. It's now a 2–2 game. Gaston sensibly pinch runs

Mookie Wilson. If you are using up one of your baserunners, you've got to have him in there to do more than be fodder. There are three ways to get him to second base. One is to have him steal, the second is to have Borders bunt and the third is to have Borders hit away. If Cito thought that sacrificing to bring up Lee was a good idea two innings ago, he now flips a coin and it comes up the other side and he has him hit away. When you look at the options, statistically the best chance of getting Mookie to second base (even with a left-handed pitcher) is to steal. Borders hits into a double play. Wrong move, Cito. If you put in the speed, use it.

3. Ninth inning, tie ball game. Lee, White and Alomar scheduled up. White and Alomar, playing terrifically, are the keys to our offence. Why send up Manuel Lee to lead off the ninth? We need a baserunner. Ed Sprague was second on the team in on-base average. He should have been brought in to pinch hit for Lee, and, if the Blue Jays didn't score, he could have been left in the game in the tenth to play right field or put at third and Gruber moved to right field; or Gonzales could have been brought in to play short and Sprague taken out. At this point, one of your best hitters, Carter, is out of the game, and your one and two DHs, Mulliniks and Tabler, are out of the game as well. You have to get some power back into the lineup. But, no. Cito sticks with Manuel Lee, and Lee continues his "zero for the ALCS" streak by taking a *called* third strike. (We call this an "Olerud.")

4. When Key left the game after six good innings, Cito went to Wells, who took us through to one out in the eighth with Puckett coming to bat. Puckett bats right, so Cito wanted a right-handed pitcher in the eighth in a tie game. Now, Henke has shown in this series he can pitch and get batters out, but he has shown us this season that he can pitch to only three to five batters at most and certainly can't give you more than one inning. Ward, on the other hand, has been devastating and can give you two or three innings, not just one. It's a tie game, our big RBI man is out of the game and we've got to pull out all the stops to keep Minnesota off the board. The logical thing to do here would be to bring in Ward to throw the last out in the eighth and take us through the ninth and tenth and maybe even the eleventh. But, no. Cito brings in Henke, who can give us only the one inning and does

so very well. This strangles him for later on, but we are sure that after Henke's tour of duty he'll go to Ward. But, no.
5. When we go to the tenth inning, Cito brings in not Duane Ward to take us through ten, eleven and twelve, if necessary, but Timlin. Now, think about this. Timlin has been terrible lately, whereas Ward is rested and has the Twins baffled and intimidated. I can't think of any conceivable reason why Cito wouldn't bring in Ward except that he's always playing it safe in case the game goes to twenty innings. He's always saving his best for later.
6. After the game, there was some suggestion made on "Jays Talk" that Cito was doing the right thing by saving Ward for his classic "save" situation because he's his closer. Excuse me? Last time I checked, there is no save situation in extra innings when you're the home team. Yup, I've checked it again. I've looked over all extra-inning games over the last ten years and I've found an amazing statistic. When the home team scores in extra innings, the game is over immediately. There is no final at bat for the visiting team. In fact, immediately after the home team scores the winning run in extra innings, everyone goes directly to the clubhouse to celebrate. Will someone please explain to me why you save Ward. Were you saving him for the twelfth to fifteenth? Statistics show that most extra-inning games are over by the eleventh or twelfth. Why wouldn't you go with your best — Duane Ward — and let him go to the tenth, eleventh and twelfth? Chances are if you haven't put up a run by then with your best bats out of the lineup, you're in big trouble anyway. Was Cito saving him for the sixteenth to nineteenth or the post-season junket to Japan? There is no conceivable excuse. Ward is overpowering, and the Twins don't want to see him. Trust me. There were smiles right next to us in the Twins' dugout when they saw Timlin coming in. Timlin has been terrible; Ward has been great. What was he saving Ward for? Cito says, amazingly, "for the save situation." Enough reason to fire him right there.
7. What has been forgotten in all this is the silly, four-man starting rotation that Cito insisted upon. Had Cito done what every manager has done from the time Ty Cobb placed his first wager on a sporting event, he would have had a three-man rotation and put Stottlemyre in the bullpen. Had Stottlemyre been in the bullpen

where he belonged, Cito, you could have gone to Stottlemyre instead of Timlin if you were going to insist on saving Ward till the fifteenth. Or, for that matter, you could have gone to Ward in the tenth, knowing you could always fall back on Stottlemyre if the game went longer.

8. Seventh inning, tie game. Devon White leads off with a single. Alomar is coming up, with Carter and his sore ankle next. Alomar is our hottest hitter. Lots of things to do here, one of which is to have White steal second, another to have Alomar bunt him to second, and another to have Alomar hit away. I would have had Alomar hit away because Alomar is one of the few players we have who is likely to get a hit. Carter tonight is a double-play threat because he can hardly run. Also, if you bunt White to second base, you not only lose an out but you also risk taking the bat out of Carter's hands. You're opening up first base, and Tom Kelly, who's a gutsy, aggressive manager, could walk Carter rather than face his hot bat. Needless to say, Alomar sacrifices and Kelly walks Carter intentionally. I don't have to tell you what Olerud did next. The only surprise was it wasn't a called third strike.

Sorry, folks. Sorry, Cito. We lost two games by one run. Proper pitching rotation and aggressive managing would have had us up 3–0 now, not down 2–1. Let me put it another way: Tom Kelly, in our dugout, would have had us up 3–0.

◇ Post-Game Notes

Do you think I've been too hard on John Olerud this year? Do you think that I've been wrong in saying that the opposition pitchers do not worry about who's batting after Joe Carter? How often have you seen a team walk the number-three hitter to pitch to the number-four or cleanup hitter? Well, you'll recall that that's exactly what happened in the seventh inning. Tie game, Alomar on second and Joe Carter up, batting with a bad ankle. Tom Kelly walks Joe Carter. Kelly puts a potential fourth run on first with one out in order to get to our intimidating cleanup batter who, so far tonight, has walked three times. Sure enough, on the first pitch Olerud flys out. That tells you more about Olerud than everything else I've written so far this year.

◆ ◆ ◆

Got home at 1:00 A.M. Melissa asked me how I could have been so wrong. She knows my track record of sensing how the game will go is pretty good. And, in spite of the goofs I've talked about, I was confident throughout that we were going to win. I find it inconceivable, notwithstanding Cito's weak managing, Olerud's weak fielding and the absence of Manuel Lee, that we are going to lose this series. It's our series. We're the better team. The season will not be a success if we don't get to the World Series, and the team knows it. It wants it. It's hungry for it. It needs it. I assured Melissa throughout the game that we would win it. Even when Pags went over the fence in the tenth, I could not believe we were going to go quietly in the bottom of the tenth. We did, and the fans went quietly out of the Dome. Couldn't get to sleep till 2:30 A.M. I wonder if Cito had the same problem.

Anatomy of a Blow-out

THE EXCITEMENT IS GONE. No one, but no one, thinks we're still in this, and the media for the first time this year is actually openly taking on Cito and his love affair with Manuel Lee and his refusal to use his best pitchers. Yup. It's getting ugly.

As always, I'll faithfully write it here at the risk, once again, of being embarrassed when you read this, but I refuse to count these guys out just yet, in spite of their manager. The odds are heavy against it, but I've seen this before.

Still, as jubilant as this town was twenty-four hours ago, it is quiet, sombre, depressed and fatalistic today. Yesterday we were in the World Series. Today we are wondering what trades will be made over the winter. I bumped into a friend of mine as I headed in for a haircut this afternoon near my office on St Clair. He said to me, "I was just downtown and I can't believe how quiet it is." I think the city is already sitting *shiva*.

Maybe premature, but talk about rollercoaster! Yesterday, everyone was sure we were a lockup. Today, we are equally sure we are a lockout. Well not me, not yet. We'll see in a few hours, since we're now in a "must win" game and, thanks to Cito's bizarre pitching rotation, we have our fourth-best pitcher against Minnesota's best pitcher.

In the afternoon, I switched between the Clarence Thomas confirmation hearings and the Atlanta-Pittsburgh NLCS. One clear conclusion? Cito should not manage in the National League. With Atlanta up 6–2, they had one of the best pitchers in the National

League, John Smoltz, steal second. A pitcher stealing second? Innovative. Exciting. Not in the manager's handbook of predictable plays. Designed to keep the other team off balance.

Somehow, I don't think you will see Cito making moves like that.

◇ The Game

A disaster. A flat-out, top-to-bottom, length-to-breadth disaster.

Blue Jays score a lucky run in the second on two singles, one in the sixth on two doubles and one in the ninth with forty-two staff, six executives and ten fans left in the Dome. Minnesota blows it open in the fourth after Stottlemyre had looked overwhelming in the first three. It went like this:

Puckett-homer
Hrbek-fly out
Davis-double
Harper-ground out
Mack-walk
Pagliarulo (you remember him)-single
Gagne-hit by pitch
Gladden-single
Knoblauch-strikeout

Three runners score after two were out. Twins add two in the sixth, one in the seventh, one in the eighth and one in the ninth.

This is too painful to describe. A series that we expected to win 4-0 or 4-1 and close out this afternoon in our favour is about to go down the drain.

The fourth game in the series is almost always the key game. This was it. The gory details don't matter, but here is an anatomy of a blow-out:

1. *Blue Jays fail to score runners.* Jays left one on in the second, two in the third, one in the fourth, one in the fifth, one in the sixth, one in the seventh, one in the eighth, two in the ninth. Baserunners in every inning, except the first.
2. *Joe Carter's injury.* Carter, who was having a great series, ends up zero for five with three strikeouts. He left six men on base.

3. *Failure to execute the basics of station-to-station baseball.* As was the case the previous night, Blue Jays couldn't score when they had runners on second and third. In the third, White and Alomar did their usual routine, getting back-to-back singles and then executing a perfect double steal. Runners on second and third. Carter struck out. Olerud grounded out. Inning over. Ball game over right there. Blue Jays fail to execute and build on a 1–0 lead, and, moments later in the top of the fourth, the Twins put up four runs.
4. *No cleanup hitter.* Olerud is one for five on the night.
5. *Unreliable fielding.* Twice Olerud fails to scoop up scoopable one hoppers thrown by his infielders. One is scored an error to Lee, one a hit. Olerud should have scooped them both. Gruber commits his third error of the series lobbing an easy toss into right field, turning a double play into a run.
6. *Manuel Lee.* What to say? Lee is hitless in the series. On Friday night he left at least a dozen runners on base, and on Saturday night he had three at bats, all of which ended innings. He grounded out to end the third with a runner on first. He struck out to end the fourth with a runner on first. He grounded out to end the sixth with a runner on second. As one National League scout is anonymously quoted in Sunday's paper: "If the Blue Jays meet Atlanta in the World Series, the Atlanta pitchers will out-hit Lee." Ain't it the truth.
7. *Cito Gaston.* Knowing Lee is cold, he does the following:

- Carter has to DH because of his ankle, thereby bringing Mookie Wilson into the lineup. So Cito has Manuel Lee bat eighth, and puts up Wilson ninth. No one this side of Doug Rader is unaware of the fact that Mookie is a better ball player and better hitter, even at his age, than Lee. Why move Lee up in the order and put Wilson ninth? Had Cito not made this gross error, it would have been Wilson batting with two out and one on in the second, fourth and sixth; and Mookie ended the day two for three.
- Given Cito's incredible reluctance to pinch hit for the worst hitter this side of Cory Snyder, someone explain this to me. The game is a tough one to win, but not impossible in the bottom of the sixth. It is 6–2 for Minnesota, and Lee is up with a runner,

Pat Borders, on second. A single makes it 6–3 with three innings to go and changes the complexion of the game. Does Cito pinch hit for Lee in this situation? No.

In the ninth inning, when the game is 9–2 and Manuel Lee is leading off the inning (that means, Cito, there was no one in scoring position), does he then pinch hit for Lee? Yes. Someone explain *this* to me. If he isn't good enough to hit leading off the ninth inning in a 9–2 ball game, why is he good enough to hit with a man in scoring position in the sixth inning, in a 6–2 ball game?

Maybe he didn't want to "use up" Gonzales and was saving him like Duane Ward last night for the twelfth or thirteenth inning in case he needed a pinch runner

♦ We are now down 3–1. We have faced Minnesota's best pitcher, Jack Morris, twice in four games. He has beaten us twice. We have used our best pitcher, Juan Guzman, only once, and he won that game. What does this tell you about the starting rotation that Cito selected? The series would look entirely different if our best had been going against their best.

And what about Duane Ward? Guzman and Ward are the two Blue Jays' pitchers the Twins fear the most. Haven't seen Ward since last Wednesday afternoon. In this series where the Blue Jays face a superior hitting club and where they know they have to rely on pitching and fielding, Ward has appeared once. Exactly once. And

BOXSCORE

Twins..9
Blue Jays..3

MINNESOTA	AB	R	H	BI	TORONTO	AB	R	H	BI
Gladden lf	5	1	3	3	White cf	5	0	2	0
Knblauch 2b	5	0	0	0	RAlomar 2b	5	0	2	1
Puckett cf	4	2	3	2	Carter dh	5	0	0	0
Hrbek 1b	5	0	0	0	Olerud 1b	5	0	1	0
CDavis dh	4	1	2	0	Gruber 3b	4	1	1	0
JBrown dh	0	1	0	0	CnMldo rf	4	1	1	0
Harper c	5	1	1	0	Borders c	4	0	3	2
Mack rf	3	1	1	1	MnLee ss	3	0	0	0
Pgliarulo 3b	4	2	2	2	Mllniks ph	0	1	0	0
Leius 3b	0	0	0	0	MWilson lf	3	0	1	0
Gagne ss	4	0	1	0					
Totals	39	9	13	8	Totals	38	3	11	3

Minnesota   000 402 111 - 9
Toronto   010 001 001 - 3

E - Gagne (1), Gruber (3), MnLee (1). LOB - Minnesota 9, Toronto 10. 2B - CDavis 2 (2), Harper (2), Pagliarulo (1), Gruber (1), Borders (1). HR - Puckett (1). SB - Gladden (2), White (2), RAlomar (2). CS - Gagne (1). SF - Puckett, Mack.

	IP	H	R	ER	BB	SO
Minnesota						
Morris (W, 2-0)	8	9	2	2	1	3
Bedrosian	1	2	1	0	1	2
Toronto						
Stottlemyre (L, 0-1)	3 2/3	7	4	4	1	3
Wells	1 2/3	2	2	2	0	3
Acker	2/3	1	0	0	0	1
Timlin	2	2	2	0	1	2
MacDonald	1	1	1	1	1	0

HBP - by Stottlemyre (Gagne). WP - Morris 2.

that was in guess what game? That's right, the game we won. He pitched two innings and struck out four. Cito has managed to use Wells *three* times, Timlin *three* times, Henke *twice* and Duane Ward *once*.

There's No Tomorrow — Someone Tell Cito

IT WAS UGLY. IT WAS SAD. IT WAS ALSO UNNECESSARY. Rumours had floated around after last night's loss that Cito might actually play to win and start Guzman instead of Candiotti. But when we arrived an hour early at 3:00 P.M., it was Candiotti, all right. The mood was sombre. Restrained. Genuine nervousness.

Yet, both Tommy Lasorda of the Dodgers and Bobby Cox of the wonderful Braves had pointed out that, if we could get by today, we were going into Game Six with our best pitcher and Game Seven with our second-best pitcher, and that it was still doable. It just didn't feel that way.

◇ The Game

Kirby Puckett slapped it to us early with a home run with two out in the first. In the second, two singles sandwiched a passed-ball third strike, allowing Brian Harper to get to first base and produce a run. 2–0, Minnesota. Finally, in the bottom of the third, someone named Manuel Lee singled after Mookie struck out, White and Alomar singled and Joe Carter doubled to give us a 3–2 lead.

In the fourth, Lee and Wilson singled, White walked and Robbie knocked in two with another single. Blue Jays 5, Twins 2.

They had sucked me in again. I was now sure that we were going to hold this lead and go back in good shape to Minnesota. Sheldon warned me about this, I fought it off and now I had succumbed. I was back on the rollercoaster, riding up.

But while the Blue Jays were taking a 5–2 lead, Candiotti had given up two hits in the second, a baserunner in the third, two singles in the fourth, two singles and a walk to load the bases in the fifth. It was clear that he was struggling. He had no three-up, three-down innings, and he had given up seven hits and ten baserunners in five innings.

Now, I've watched hundreds of playoff and World Series games over the years. When a team's back is against the wall, when there is no tomorrow, you pull out all the stops. It was clear after the third inning that Candi was struggling. Cito had Wells, Ward and Henke in the bullpen and in the circumstance you would even consider using Key and maybe even Stottlemyre. You use whoever is necessary for whatever length of time, be it one batter or ten, to keep us in the game. If you don't win today, it doesn't matter how well your pitchers are rested for tomorrow. Tomorrow is, in fact, a day of rest before the next game.

But no. Cito, true to form, lets his starter carry on until he gives up two singles to start the sixth. By the time Candiotti was taken out, five of the last six batters had got on base — and seven of the last twelve. In a "back-against-the-wall" game, you move a lot quicker than this.

Key had been warming up in the bullpen. Had Stottlemyre not been used as a starter (which he shouldn't have been), he would have been ready to come in in this situation. Ward was well rested, as was Henke.

But who does Cito bring in? You guessed it: the man with 99 of 100 inherited runners scoring — Mike (Tired) Timlin. Not wanting to rest on his Friday night laurels, he arrives with two on and none out in the sixth. Timlin gets Greg Gagne, the number-nine hitter, to pop out.

Then Dan Gladden. It's a ground ball to Gruber at third base. Now, with a three-run lead and one out, you play to first to get the second out and concede the single run. If you're *sure* you can make the play at the plate, you might come home. Gruber was charging the ball, was not far from home plate, and he decided to go home. Not necessarily a bad decision, but he threw it wide and high and Borders was only too willing to get out there and get it since you wouldn't expect him to be blocking the plate. In a move that might make the CNN play-of-the-day, Borders catches the ball in his glove and tags the runner, Shane Mack, with his empty bare hand!!! Error to Borders, but it could just as easily have been to Gruber.

Still 5–3, one out. Runners on first and third. A double play gets us out of this. But that irritating Chuck Knoblauch is up. And Mike Timlin is still pitching for us, though Duane Ward is now working in the bullpen. There is no way against a hot-hitting Chuck Knoblauch that you don't bring in Duane Ward. Cito doesn't. Instead, Timlin gives up a double to Knoblauch to tie the game.

BOXSCORE

Twins...8
Blue Jays..5

MINNESOTA	AB	R	H	BI	TORONTO	AB	R	H	BI
Gladden lf	5	2	1	0	White cf	4	1	2	0
Knblauch 2b	4	1	1	2	RAlomar 2b	4	1	2	3
Puckett cf	5	2	3	2	Carter dh	4	0	1	1
Hrbek 1b	5	0	2	2	Olerud 1b	4	0	0	1
CDavis dh	4	1	1	0	Gruber 3b	4	0	0	0
Harper c	5	0	1	0	CnMldo rf	4	0	0	0
Ortiz c	0	0	0	0	Brders c	4	0	1	0
Mack rf	5	1	2	1	MnLee ss	3	2	2	0
Pgliarulo 3b	4	1	2	0	Mllniks ph	1	0	0	0
Gagne ss	4	0	1	0	Gonzales ss	0	0	0	0
					MWilson lf	4	1	1	0
Totals	41	8	14	7	Totals	36	5	9	5

Minnesota   110 003 030 - 8
Toronto   003 200 000 - 5

E - Harper (1), Gagne (2), Borders (2). DP - Minnesota 1, Toronto 1. LOB - Minnesota 9, Toronto 6. 2B - Knoblauch (2), Carter (2). HR - Puckett (2) (off Candiotti). SB - Gladden (3), Mack (2), White (3), MWilson (1). CS - Gagne (2). S - Pagliarulo.

	IP	H	R	ER	BB	SO
Minnesota						
Tapani	4	8	5	5	1	4
West (W, 1-0)	3	0	0	0	1	1
Willis	1	1	0	0	0	0
Aguilera (S, 3)	1	0	0	0	0	1
Toronto						
Candiotti	5	9	4	2	1	3
Timlin	1/3	1	1	1	0	0
DWard (L, 0-1)	2 1/3	3	3	3	1	2
Wells	1 1/3	1	0	0	0	2

Candiotti pitched to 2 batters in the 6th. WP - Candiotti. PB - Borders 2.

Only then does Cito have Gene Tenace remove Timlin, and, of course, as soon as Ward comes in, he strikes out the toughest batter in the lineup, Kirby Puckett, and gets Hrbek, the cleanup batter, to pop out. One batter earlier, two batters earlier, we might have won this game too.

We play the Twins even through the next couple of innings — we were three up, three down, in the sixth, and they were three up, three down, in the seventh. In the eighth, however, with Ward now working his third inning, he gives up a Gladden single, an irritating

Knoblauch walk and a Puckett single. He's relieved by Wells. By the end of the inning, it's all over folks. 8–5 in a game we were leading 5–2.

The rest is boring and is also history. After the Blue Jays' two-hit rally in the fourth, they got *one* hit. After the Blue Jays' rally in the fourth, the Twins got six runs on nine hits.

Just for the record, Cito did in his 167th game of the year something he didn't do in the first 166 games. He finally stood up for his ball players against bad umpiring after Maldonado was called out on a marginal third-strike call in the second inning. Cito got tossed out of the game, but of course made all the inadequate decisions noted above from the runway or the dressing room.

What can I say? The game ended with the Minnesota celebration, which I observed while I stood next to the Ford Taurus in the right-field stands. I couldn't bear to be next to the Minnesota dugout while the celebration went on. As I stood to leave with one out in the ninth, I wished Jack Morris good luck. He smiled, threw Melissa a baseball and waved goodbye.

Cito, there is no tomorrow. Honest.

Epilogue and Eulogy

◇ A Clinic in Mismanaging

Some Blue Jays are saying "the better team won." I don't buy it. The better *managed* team won. We were outmanaged. I have been watching baseball for some forty years. I have never seen a series in which one team lost it almost exclusively on the basis of poor managing decisions.

Here is the case, your honour:

1. The Twins won four games, two of which were won by their best pitcher, Jack Morris, who pitched the first and fourth games. Our best pitcher was allowed to pitch only one game; he won it.
2. Other than Jim Acker, Mike Timlin has been our worst and most unreliable relief pitcher in the past several weeks. Mike Timlin got into four of the games, giving up five hits and two walks in five-and-two-thirds innings. And, of course, he gave up the back-breaking Pagliarulo home run in the tenth inning on Friday night.
3. Tom Henke, who even with his arm problems was effective, got into only two games. He pitched two-and-two-thirds innings or, in other words, got eight batters out, five by strikeouts, while walking only one.
4. On Friday night Borders was required to sacrifice runners to second and third with none out to bring up Manuel Lee. Lee failed

to produce. In the ninth inning of that same game, with Lee leading off the ninth inning, he was pinch hit for.
5. When Carter went down, he became the DH and Mookie Wilson was inserted. Wilson was inserted in the ninth spot in the lineup and Lee was moved to eighth. On Saturday, Lee came up in the second, fourth and sixth, with two out and Borders on base and produced nothing. Mookie was two for three. If Mookie had been batting eighth instead of ninth, where any sensible observer would have had him batting, we might have won that game even though it turned into a blow-out. In any case, can you tell me anyone, anywhere, anytime who wouldn't bat his worst hitter ninth?
6. Cito managed all year with the shortest bench in baseball. A team that batted .249 in the playoffs, had only one home run and left thirty-five runners on base did not use Ed Sprague, one of the better hitters in the club. It had Rob Ducey and Pat Tabler bat only once, Greg Myers not at all, and Gonzales not at all. As was the case all year, Cito went with nine guys and not even his best pitchers.
7. Henke's tendinitis put pressure on the bullpen. Stottlemyre would have relieved that pressure and made it possible to avoid using a too-tired Timlin. Timlin (and Cito) cost us the series.

Overall, Cito managed in the playoffs the way he managed all year. No changes, nothing innovative, didn't pinch hit, didn't use his complete roster. Cito always believed in saving for later, in waiting for tomorrow. We saw him lose some games during the year because he went to the bullpen too late (the night he left Candiotti in instead of bringing in Henke). He was always reluctant to pinch hit in the event he might have to make a defensive change. He wouldn't use his best relievers till he had a save situation. As a result he sometimes never got a save situation. Friday night was the perfect example. I will never know how he could have gone with anyone other than Ward on Friday night. He was unwilling to go with his hot players while they were hot. When Sprague was hot and Gruber returned to the lineup, he sent Sprague to the bench. After Gruber returned to the lineup in June, Sprague got twenty-six at bats in July, seventeen in August and a pitiful nine in September and October. He still ended up batting .275.

He refused to go with his hot pitchers — Juan Guzman was maybe the hottest pitcher in baseball — and refused to back off players when they were going bad — Candiotti had cooled off at playoff time.

He continued to tolerate Borders's and Myers's refusing to block the plate, and he paid for that on more than one occasion.

With decent bats in the dugout and unused (Sprague .275, Myers .262), he stuck with Manuel Lee and even moved him up to eighth spot. And he batted John Olerud, the least-feared cleanup hitter in the league, at cleanup through the playoffs.

It was not pretty. It was avoidable. You could hear it in the players' voices, and read it in their words in the papers. They questioned the field leadership they were getting, but wouldn't say so. They were mystified by the pitching rotation. They were depressed by the failure to pinch hit, and they were rattled by seeing Timlin, not Ward.

There is no tomorrow, Cito. Guzman is well rested and will be ready to pitch Tuesday. The only problem is there's no game Tuesday. Timlin, on the other hand, *can't* pitch Tuesday, not only because there's no game, but because he couldn't pitch yesterday, or the day before or the day before. You used your worst and saved your best. The best are ready, rested, primed to go and the envy of every team in baseball. They've got their best clothes on, but they have no place to go.

Mark this one down to Cito.

◇ Nice Wedding, but Bridesmaids Again

And so it's over. The rollercoaster has ended the way it began — a loss at the SkyDome. I am unhappy and frustrated, a little angry, but, at last, relieved. Our ride for now is over. No matter how many times we warned ourselves against it, Sheldon and I got sucked in again. We got swept up by the great streak around the All-Star break, we got panicky when Detroit tied us and Boston came close. We were sure we'd win the World Series when we won the division title. Then we got left at the altar again.

Sheldon is even threatening to sell some of his tickets for next year. He won't, but it ain't fun here at the altar alone.

Was it a good year? Yes, some great baseball. Was it a successful year? No. Jimmy Key had it right: "This was not a successful season by any means ... This team was put together to win it all. Pat Gillick did his best to bring in the best ball players ... He did his job, we didn't do ours ... we should have gone to the World Series this year." Key is a pro. He knows that Pat pulled out all the stops. Indeed, Pat admitted as much when he said that the price he paid to get Candiotti was not only high, it was in fact too high. But they were going for it all. When the silly acquisition of Cory Snyder didn't work out, Gillick (unlike Gaston) moved again and got Maldonado. When Mulliniks and Tabler were clearly providing the worst DHing in the league, he went out and got Dave Parker (albeit too late).

No, it wasn't a successful year, but it was a fun year. I enjoyed it a lot, despite the agonizing moments. It was a happy team and it made us happy to see them playing so comfortably with one another.

For the first time in a long time, a Toronto sports franchise can boast one of the very best players in the game, Robbie Alomar. It makes me smile just to see him play. Stealing second when the pitcher and the catcher both know he's going, and they still can't get the ball there as he makes a perfect head-first slide out of the way of the tag and grasping the base with his hand. Won't forget the plays he made diving in the hole, or leaping in the air to catch and throw at the same time and the clutch-hitting (one hit shy of .500 in the playoffs — .474).

Devon White, an artist practising his craft daily. He led all major-league outfielders with a fielding percentage of .997. Moving with grace and panache, flicking the glove, tucking the ball away beside his left ear, at his chest or twelve feet above the ground. Majestic, perfect, joyful.

Juan Guzman. A friend of mine who knows an AL umpire says the umpire told him that Guzman has the best stuff he's ever seen. Blue Jays haven't had many rookies coming out of nowhere to become front-liners. The Blue Jays feel they are going to win every time he's out there — and they just about did.

Maldonado, a good, classy, solid, hard-hitting outfielder. Not spectacular numbers, but a good arm and a pro. Nice to see him in our uniform.

Joe Carter, a gamer. Had about as hot a streak as you'll ever see. Made some great plays in the outfield (remember that snatch of a home run off Cecil Fielder in Detroit and the dive into the stands against the Angels to keep us in the clinching game just before his hit won it?). Large, infectious, genuine smile.

Candiotti, whose wonderful pitching has left him just a touch short of the earned run average title, should not be forgotten because of his late-season problems. He is one of the best pitchers in baseball.

Jimmy Key, still one of the best pitchers in baseball. Todd Stottlemyre, who matured into a front-line pitcher, and Duane Ward, who didn't shake the Jekyll and Hyde virus completely but this year for the first time made us beg for him when the game was on the line. Henke, who has clearly lost something of his fastball but still put up a lot of Ks.

Obviously, we need some changes. Let's look at the offence.

What do you think of this lineup? Would you like to go into the ALCS with this team? With Cito managing?

	HR	RBI	AVE
Larry Walker	16	64	.290
Carlos Baerga	11	69	.288
Fred McGriff	31	106	.278
Gary Gaetti	18	66	.246
Dan Pasqua	18	68	.259
Sid Bream	11	45	.253
Hector Espinoza	5	33	.256
Bob Melvin	2	24	.250
Dick Schofield	0	31	.225

Not much, eh? My pal Siskind researched the numbers, and, as you can see, the above lineup has the same offensive stats as the Jays.

Devon White	17	60	.282
Roberto Alomar	9	69	.295
Joe Carter	33	108	.273
Kelly Gruber	20	65	.252

John Olerud	17	68	.256
Candy Maldonado	12	48	.250
Pat Borders	5	36	.244
Rance Mulliniks	2	24	.250
Manuel Lee	0	29	.234

DH should be the easiest position to fill because you just need a one-dimensional long ball–hitting ball player in his thirties who can give you twenty home runs and eighty or so RBIs. Pedro Guerrero, Dave Winfield, Danny Tartabull maybe and, miracle of miracles, maybe even Bobby Bonilla. Our DHs — basically Mulliniks (.250) and Tabler (.216) — produced a grand total of *three* home runs and forty-five RBIs. (To be fair, Mookie did some DHing and added some RBIs, but only two more home runs.) To compare, Chili Davis, picked up as a free agent by Minnesota, hit .277 with twenty-nine homers and ninety-three RBIs. Jack Clark — .249, twenty-eight and eighty-seven. Dave Winfield — .262, twenty-eight and eighty-six. I could go on, but you get the idea. This one was easy, though; all they had to do was keep George Bell — .285, twenty-five and eighty-six RBIs.

At the very least, Blue Jays can play Derek Bell in left field and have Maldonado DH. This would be a great improvement, but I think we need more home runs.

First base, Blue Jays cannot continue with Olerud. He's got to improve or be sent to the minors or made a part-time player. No more waiting for the "sweet swing." Seventeen homers and sixty-eight RBIs are not good enough for a first baseman — particularly a first baseman whose fielding skills are well below average. Consider Joyner, Mattingly, Thomas, Hrbek, McGwire, Davis, Quintana, Palmiero, Molitor/Stubbs, Fielder, Aldrete and Benzinger. Only Aldrete and Benzinger are worse choices. Olerud may turn out to be what everyone thinks he will, maybe even next year. But I don't think he'll grow into being a front-line fielder, and, until he shows he can hit for power and/or average, he can't be a regular first baseman or even a DH. Not for a pennant winner.

At shortstop I predicted Lee would be gone by June, and I admitted in June or July that I was wrong and he had performed better than I had expected. I take it back. I was right after all. He's not up to it. He's an easy out, and his fielding has waned. Look for Zosky next year, or look for Dick Schofield of the Angels or maybe even Ozzie Smith for a couple of years till Zosky's ready.

Third base. Gruber was a disappointment, but he's still one of the better third basemen in baseball. Don't know what the problem is, but the Blue Jays should be thinking a lot and talking a lot with Gruber in the off season. We simply can't rely only on the top three next year for 40 percent of our output. I think if the Blue Jays get the right offer, they would trade Gruber. How about Gruber and Stottlemyre (provided they take Acker too) for McGriff or Canseco?

Catching. I think one or both catchers are going to be gone. Ed Sprague has got to be a starter next year, platooning at first, DHing or catching. We haven't seen him catch; we have seen him perform erratically at third and as a non-gold glover at first. He should spend the winter learning to catch and catch fifty to seventy-five games next year. Catchers are hard to come by in baseball these days, but, whatever the Blue Jays do, the prerequisite for catching next year has got to be a willingness to block the plate.

On the mound. Pray for Stieb, please sign Candiotti, thank God for Guzman, so long Acker, fix Timlin's arm and Ken Dayley's vertigo.

Overall, count on Gillick not to stand pat. I'm confident he's going to add a hundred RBIs to this club.

Rich Hacker? Might as well rehire McLaren. Make a change.

Oh yes, and one other thing. Did I mention the manager? I like Cito, everyone likes Cito. He was the perfect manager for the irascible, unfriendly, non–team oriented gang he was hired to manage in 1989. But Gillick replaced that team with a pitch, run and field team that had to have the management and strategy to scratch out runs, to hit and run, to steal, to sacrifice, to pinch hit, to change pitchers — to grab every run available, protect every lead and guard against every opposition run.

Cito's strength was perfect for the 1989 team, but not for the 1991 team. This is a team that needs an aggressive, knowledgeable field manager. To have Cito back would be the same as starting Candiotti in the playoffs because he's a nice man. Cito can help the club, and I wouldn't want to lose him from the organization, but he's not up to the job. If he's rehired as manager, it's a mistake.

Pat Gillick did his job, as Jimmy Key said. He had every right to expect that Gruber and Olerud together would give him 160 RBIs when he traded McGriff and Bell. They gave him 133. He had every right to expect that Borders would give him 50 RBIs. He gave him 36. And he had every right to expect that Pat Tabler would give him more than one home run.

We'll miss Mookie and Rance. Sorry — hope you stay in the organization.

Yup, I'm exhausted. But at the end of it, what's baseball all about? Entertainment, enjoyment, stimulation and lots of controversy. I got all that this year. We've been spoiled. With the Mets finishing below .500 this year, we are now the only team in baseball to play better than .500 since 1983. In that time we've won between eighty-six and ninety-nine games every year. We have won more games than *any* team in baseball over the last ten years. We expect to win and are disappointed when we lose. The train may not have reached the station, but the trip this year and every year — well, maybe not every year, but certainly this year — was sure worthwhile. It was fun, it was exciting, it was hard on the nerves. I'm glad I was there.

As disappointed as I am, remember there are twenty-two other teams that are far more disappointed and twenty-five other teams that haven't had it this good for this long.

By opening day next year, the Expos may be in Florida or Buffalo. Lee may be in the National League. Acker in triple-A. Stieb we hope will be on the mound. Winfield with the Jays. Sheldon still with his tickets. Olerud still practising his "sweet swing." And Cito in the front office (I wish).

The one thing I know for sure, Guzman will be well rested.